A HISTORICAL TOUR OF

Walt Disney World

A HISTORICAL TOUR OF

Walt Disney World

ANDREW KISTE

FALL
RIVER
PRESS

New York

To my parents and brother, with whom I have
traveled many times to Walt Disney World, where
I have some of my fondest memories, and to my
wife, Andrea, who puts up with my love of Disney
World and my unrelenting conversations about it.

FALL RIVER PRESS

New York

An Imprint of Sterling Publishing Co., Inc.
1166 Avenue of the Americas
New York, NY 10036

ISBN 978-1-4351-6550-2

For information about custom editions, special sales, and premium
and corporate purchases, please contact Sterling Special Sales at
800-805-5489 or specialsales@sterlingpublishing.com.

Manufactured in the United States of America

2 4 6 8 10 9 7 5 3 1

www.sterlingpublishing.com

Cover design by David Ter-Avanesyan
Interior design by Lorie Pagnozzi

Contents

INTRODUCTION

*I*n 1993, I took my first trip to Walt Disney World. As a five year old, I was convinced that I was really floating through a town being ransacked by pirates or touring a house haunted by ghosts and ghouls. I remember standing in line for what seemed endless minutes waiting to get an autograph from and my picture taken with Roger Rabbit, or eating Mickey Waffles while being visited by Pluto and Mickey himself.

As a teenager who struggled with hormones and attitude, I found myself getting lost in the story of the four Walt Disney World parks; as I once wrote in my journal:

> *I feel like I can forget about all my problems and the problems of the world while I'm here. The issues of high school and the drama of my friends seem to melt away while I'm exploring the Magic Kingdom; it's almost like you are in a sheltered world where everything is always happy and crafted to immerse you in the world of the story being told, to the point where nothing else matters.*

Already, as a high schooler, I was noticing the intricacy of the immersive environment that was crafted by the builders and Imagineers who created many of the rides and attractions that I fell in love with as a child.

My wife and I took a trip to Walt Disney World to celebrate our two-year wedding anniversary in June 2012; it was the first time she had been to Disney World in almost ten years, and a lot had changed over the decade since her last trip. Unfortunately, during the course of our vacation, we ended up spending a lot of time with Tropical Storm Irene, which meant that we rushed from ride to ride to try to stay out of the rain and wind.

We made a return trip in 2013 while visiting the parks with my parents and brother in Orlando over Thanksgiving weekend. Unfortunately, because my wife and I only got a few days off from our jobs teaching, we were not able to spend as much time as I would have liked in the parks, and because of the typical Thanksgiving crowds, even while we were in the parks we weren't able to do much more than slog from one long line to another.

As a result, I decided to slow down and try to absorb the detail and story of the parks, to truly pay attention to the things that make Disney famous for immersive guest experiences. It is this attention to detail that makes me appreciate the Disney theme park experience the way that I do.

As a history teacher, much of my day is spent attempting to coax interest from students about historical world events, and more important, trying to make those events interesting enough, and relevant enough, that my students will perk up in their seats, pay attention, and remember. I stress that quite a lot of what happens in the world today is the consequence of events that happened decades or centuries in the past, and that's one reason why history is so important.

In a similar manner, Disney Imagineers use historical details when creating lands or attractions at Disney parks. These details often go unnoticed by park visitors, but for those who understand the historical implications of their favorite ride or show or even restaurant, the illusion of the immersive environment becomes even more complete.

As you read this book, I hope that you will discover and appreciate some of the historical details that the Imagineers considered as they created some of the most popular Magic Kingdom attractions and lands, and that this knowledge will make your next visit to Walt Disney World all the more enjoyable—and, dare I say it, educational, too.

Andrew Kiste
Greensboro, North Carolina
December 2014

Part One

MAIN STREET, U.S.A.

The entrance to Walt Disney World's Magic Kingdom is the Disney Imagineers' attempt at a "grand reveal." After passing through the turnstiles of the park, visitors must pass through one of two tunnels into Town Square, above which is a railroad station. Every five to ten minutes, a steam-powered locomotive stops at the station to pick up guests for a grand tour of the Magic Kingdom. Park patrons emerge out of the tunnels into the sunlight, where they are greeted by a turn-of-the-twentieth-century town. In the center of the courtyard is a flag pole, and on the outside of the courtyard are such buildings as City Hall, the Fire Station, and the Harmony Barbershop. As visitors gaze toward the castle in the distance, numerous stores and businesses line either side of the street, and horse-drawn trolleys and carriages pass up and down the avenue. For nine months out of the year, the street is decorated with red, white, and blue bunting and flags, which evoke a patriotic feel. The stars-and-stripes are absent during the Halloween and Christmas seasons, when they are replaced with holiday-themed decorations.

At the end of Main Street, U.S.A. looms Cinderella Castle, which seems both oddly out of place and perfectly fitting. Most people would not expect to wander through a re-creation of a vintage small American town only to find a large, European castle at the end of the street. However, Walt Disney and the Imagineers who created the Magic Kingdom after his death decided to tap into Americans' love of nostalgia when introducing them to the park.

Many guests don't realize the deliberateness of Main Street, U.S.A. being the first land they experience upon entering the Magic Kingdom. When Walt Disney built Disneyland in 1955, he opened his park with a smaller version of Main Street, drawing on a nostalgic view of small-town America that many park guests remembered from their childhood. Each subsequent "Disneyland-style" park that opened around the world would also feature a Main Street right up front, even if the park were far from America, as in the case of Disneyland Paris, Tokyo Disneyland, Hong Kong Disneyland, and Shanghai Disneyland. Disney himself grew up in the small Midwestern town of Marceline, Missouri, during a formative period of his childhood. Pride in American history was important to him, but little did Walt know that he was establishing what would become an important part of Americana: himself.

This American nostalgia is what the Imagineers tapped into when planning and building the Magic Kingdom in the late 1960s and early 1970s. Many people of Walt's generation had grown up in small towns, and they were still strongly influenced by what they perceived were the values they took with them from those towns as they left to raise families of their own, often after serving their country in World War II, another powerful common experience. The early 1900s were "simpler times," when men gathered around soda fountains or lunch counters in the local pharmacy or department store to exchange gossip, when horses provided transportation of goods and people in the absence of automobiles, and when most shops were small, specialized proprietorships, rather than impersonal one-stop shopping centers.

While this childhood nostalgia for small-town living appealed to adults in the 1970s, many young people and children were not as easily able to associate with this earlier era's culture and architecture. As a result, throughout the second half of the twentieth century the Disney studio released a number of films that took place in small towns, including *Pollyanna*, *Follow Me, Boys!*, and *Pete's Dragon*. Youngsters who went to see these movies, which were set in small towns around the turn of the century, were better able to understand and appreciate the theming of Main Street, U.S.A.

However, as stated previously, Cinderella Castle, while out of place in a small American town, still oddly fits into this section of the park. The castle's placement at the end of Main Street serves two purposes: it tempts guests deeper into the park (famously referred to by Walt as a "weenie," drawing on a metaphor of luring a dog to wherever you want it to go with a frankfurter) and it brings to mind the fairy tales many of them read during their childhoods, creating in them a desire to experience those fairy tales once again. While the castle is modeled after the one seen in the 1950 Disney animated feature *Cinderella*, two other "Disney princess" films had been released by the time the Magic Kingdom opened in 1971: *Snow White and the Seven Dwarfs* in 1937 and *Sleeping Beauty* in 1959. These three classic Disney animated films collectively help to define "Disney magic"; thus, by using Cinderella Castle as the centerpiece, or icon, of the Magic Kingdom, Imagineers were once again hoping to draw on the nostalgia of all park guests to create a greater sense of buy-in to the Magic Kingdom experience.

In order to create the illusion that guests had traveled back in time to a turn-of-the-century town, Imagineers had to re-imagine the history of small-town America from that historical period, as well as generalize the architecture and the types of shops that were characteristic of small towns and cities across the United States during the early 1900s.

CHAPTER ONE

THE VICTORIAN MAIN STREET

A BYGONE ERA

The Magic Kingdom's Main Street, U.S.A., while set during the late 1800s and early 1900s, actually has its roots decades before. During the middle part of the nineteenth century, the railroad industry in America experienced a boom, as companies began to innovate. The weight of heavy goods transported in carts along dirt roads by horses or oxen made the roads rutted and difficult to traverse. Different inventors experimented with the addition of steam engines to the carts to do away with the necessity for draft animals. These steam-powered carts permitted quicker, cheaper transportation of heavy goods, but the roads were still rutted and posed obstacles to the carts. To solve this problem, industrialists experimented with steel beams, which enabled steam engines to leave the roads altogether.

In the 1860s, railroad industrialists began a project to connect the industrial northeast with the west; as small frontier towns sprang up in the west, and as cities began to boom on the Pacific coast due to the discovery of gold and other precious metals, there was a need for supplies and products to be provided by producers from New England and the Atlantic Seaboard. The Transcontinental Railroad was completed on May 10, 1869, joining the Union Pacific and Central Pacific Railroads at Promontory, Utah. Because of the ease with which goods and people could now be transported across the American continent, new, smaller railroad lines began to be built across the United States, and they soon became the main transportation system through which products and ideas were moved.

Small towns often sprouted along these railroad lines, providing goods and services to workers on the line, and eventually, services to travelers who used the railroads as transportation across the countryside. Because it was so vital to the economy of America, many men moved their families to these small towns along the railroads, finding jobs there and building homes. One of these families was named Disney; Walt's father, Elias Disney, moved his family from Chicago to Marceline, Missouri, to work on a farm near a railroad. Small towns such as Marceline often had a strong community feeling, with residents who shared the same religious denomination, culture, and ethnicity. European immigrants to the United States often found jobs working for the railroads, and as a result, started settling west from their entry points in New York City and other East Coast port cities.

Because railroads drew visitors to these small towns on a regular basis, the inhabitants often decided to profit from this thoroughfare by providing goods and services to travelers along the railroad, as well as those working on the railroads. New types of businesses began to develop, benefiting not only those from the railroad, but also the ever-growing numbers of citizens. Many of these shops were proprietorships, owned by an individual or a family. These shops usually sold a specific type of item or items, catering to a specific need based at times on the particular skill of the owner or his family. For example, a family might operate a butcher's shop, drug store, general store, or tobacco shop. These families usually rented out the spaces above the shops, which caused the central business districts of these small towns to also become residential in nature. Owners were usually able to advertise their businesses through either a sign or marquee over the door, but more often their business type and the name of the proprietor was etched or painted on the window so patrons knew what each business offered.

During the latter part of the nineteenth century, however, large department stores emerged that often put these smaller, family-owned companies out of business. Rather than a consumer going to a number of different shops in an afternoon for the supplies they needed, these corporate or chain department stores became a one-stop shopping destination for people to purchase various items. In the 1890s, an economic depression forced department stores to lower their prices, creating competition between small business and the larger stores, eventually closing down the proprietorships. These larger stores were able to purchase consumer goods directly from the manufacturers (Singer Sewing, Remington Typewriter, etc.), allowing them to sell products at lower prices, something that the small family-owned businesses could not afford to do.

Department stores such as F.W. Woolworth and the Great Atlantic and Pacific Tea Company (A&P) also offered services for shoppers, who were usually women, in order to make the experience easier and more enjoyable. For instance, some stores offered child care services for women who brought their children with them. Others provided package delivery, which made shopping easier for women with small children; rather than having to carry their purchases home from town, they were simply delivered to the family home. During the late 1800s, mail order companies like Sears & Roebuck became popular, saving busy mothers and wives time by allowing them to order products by mail.

During this period, suburbs did not exist, and people either lived in town or on the outskirts of town, sometimes quite a distance (by horse-drawn wagon) from the business district. For these people, a trip to town meant a day of shopping and entertainment, and if they didn't bring their own lunch, they needed somewhere to eat it. Department stores often had lunch counters, making them even more of a day-long destination, but family-owned eateries, bakeries, and ice cream parlors also survived, more so than mercantile stores.

In the late 1800s, many buildings were designed by architects in the Victorian Italianate style. This form of architecture was characterized by heavy, fired brick facades on buildings that were usually two to three stories tall, utilizing long wooden, iron, or steel beams. The sturdiness provided by these new building materials allowed for more or larger windows across the front of the structure, as well as larger interior rooms or more open floor plans. In order to save space, there were rarely alleyways between the buildings, so businesses usually shared walls with each other. Even though they shared walls, however, not all buildings were the same size; for example, one building might have been two stories tall, while its neighbor stretched up to three floors. As a result, the elevations of the skyline was variable as one looked down the street. The roof lines of buildings were often flat and undecorated (though this tended to change over time, with renovations). Some buildings had arched windows or windows that were inset from the exterior façade. Doors occasionally had concave hoods or even an overhanging porch or awning. The plainness and utilitarianism of these buildings were mainly because they were designed and built for the working and middle classes and store owners, rather than the upper classes and big businesses.

Over the course of the final years of the nineteenth century and the beginning of the twentieth, as department stores and chain stores began to put proprietors and families out of business, the landscape of small-town America began to change. Because the business districts were already built up for the most part, there was no more room for the chain and department stores to establish themselves, and so they began to buy out the "mom-and-pop" proprietorships. Once a few of these small stores had been purchased, the department stores would begin "warfare" against the remaining shops until they went out of business and the empty buildings put up for sale. These department stores would hire construction companies to go into these buildings and knock down the walls separating them to create one large store that spanned the area where four or five establishments previously were located. On rare occasions, department stores would even expand to build over top of short streets or cul-de-sacs of stores, absorbing the land and buildings in order to sell more products.

The 1880s and 1890s were also an important period in American cultural history. This was a time of high patriotic fervor; America celebrated its one hundredth birthday in July 1876, commemorating victory against Britain and subsequent independence as a result of the American Revolution. New innovations began to be introduced during this so-called "Second Industrial Revolution." Henry Ford began producing automobiles for the middle-class consumer in the early 1900s, revolutionizing the transportation industry. Horses, the main form of transportation of both goods and people in the 1800s, began to disappear from cities as automobiles and motorized vehicles became more common. In the late 1870s and 1880s, electric street lamps began to be utilized in cities and towns across America, replacing gas lights. Sometimes new lamps were installed, while at other times existing gas lamps were modified and fitted out with the wiring and bulbs to allow for electric light. Similar conversions to electric light occurred in wealthy homes and businesses. Also, during the first few decades of the twentieth century, as electric lights became increasingly popular, many businesses began to attach electric light bulbs to the roof lines, awnings, and marquees of the buildings, allowing for the town to be illuminated at night.

Throughout the first half of the twentieth century, technology further hastened the demise of the small town as the center of Americans' daily lives. The popularization and commonality of Ford's automobile allowed for the creation of suburbs; people no longer had to live within walking distance to their jobs, but could now commute from longer distances due to personal and mass transportation. Roads were expanded in these towns to facilitate more motorized traffic. The development and popularization of steel and elevators allowed for the building of taller structures, and many of the buildings in small towns were torn down or built up to accommodate more businesses in a smaller area. Small, independently-owned businesses disappeared for the most part, as the likes of Montgomery Ward, Macy's, Woolworths, Sears and Roebuck, and J.C. Penney took their places, selling bigger selections of similar goods for less.

Because of these innovations, the town increased in size, annexing the land around it and expanding due to the inclusion of new businesses and services. Cities and towns became hubs for shopping, dining, business, and entertainment. During the first few decades of the 1900s, theaters and movie palaces started to become prevalent, showing silent films accompanied by ragtime piano and later by soundtracks and dialogue. Penny arcades also became popular, where young people could watch hand-cranked films using a mutoscope, play a non-electric form of pinball, or even billiards. However, morality usually dictated that places like billiard halls, arcades, and in the 1920s illegal bars called speakeasies, were not appropriate places for young people to patronize and would eventually lead to violence and drunkenness. As a result, people who spent too much time in the cities or even lived within their limits were often seen by "proper" citizens as corrupted, and a period of social segregation began.

Thus, the "golden age" of small town America came to a close.

* * *

The Magic Kingdom's representation of Main Street, U.S.A. is a pretty accurate depiction of what a turn-of-the-century small town might have looked like, albeit with the "Disney touch." Because Walt Disney spent his childhood years in the small town of Marceline, Missouri, he was nostalgic for the charm that these small communities held. Disney believed that his parks should "be a world of Americans, past and present, seen through the eyes of my imagination—a place of warmth and nostalgia, of illusion and color and delight." The re-creation of a small town decorated with red, white, and blue bunting makes guests feel not only nostalgic but also patriotic; the assumption is that the town is celebrating Independence Day. Main Street, U.S.A. is meant to be a prototypical example of Americana frozen in an era which Disney perceived as our golden age. Independence Day is also typically celebrated with parades and fireworks; even though the Magic Kingdom's parades and fireworks shows are not patriotic in nature, they do still fit the theme of Main Street as a celebration of Americana and American patriotism.

Because he grew up in a railroad town, Disney loved trains; his love for locomotives was so great, he had a 1/8th scale railroad built in the backyard of his home in Holmby Hills, California, in the late 1940s. It was important to him that his parks include a steam engine locomotive to transport guests around the park. The railroad sits on one end of Main Street, U.S.A., rather than the middle of town. Near the railroad station is City Hall and the main shopping center, the Emporium. This would allow for city officials to be aware of who was entering town, as well as make the purchasing of goods by travelers or the delivery of goods being shipped by the train easier, due to the shop's proximity to the station.

When my family and I visit the Magic Kingdom, the first thing we do is ride the train completely around the park, getting on at the Main Street station and riding the circumference of the park to disembark at the same place. The station itself is a good representation of those of the late nineteenth and early twentieth centuries. After reaching the top of the stairs to the level of the train station, guests can pass through a set of doors, between which is a ticket booth where riders would be able to purchase tickets in the "real world" version of a railroad. Entering the train station, guests find brass chandeliers complete with gas fixtures (gas light fixtures have the glass bowls pointed upward rather than downward; downward-facing fixtures would cause the liquefied gas to drip out). The floor of the station is made of marble and features an intricate design with a compass rose in the middle of the floor indicating the cardinal directions. Wooden benches line the walls, with large picture windows facing down Main Street and either end of the train station. This allows riders to be aware of when the train is coming as they sit on the wooden benches. The station also features mutoscopes—iron machines with viewfinders on them; guests can pay a penny and turn a crank to watch images on individual cards move quickly to create a moving image. When the train arrives, guests exit through the back doors of the station and onto the train platform where they load onto a train, with a steam-powered locomotive pulling four passenger cars along a one-and-a-half mile narrow-gauge track around the Magic Kingdom.

Upon returning to the Main Street train terminal after the grand circle tour, guests walk back down the staircases into the part of Main Street known as Town Square. At the center of Town Square is an area that many small towns had, both those of the 1900s and those of the modern day: a patriotic memorial plaza. In small towns, this area was often used to commemorate members of the community who had fought and/or fallen while protecting our nation. At the Magic Kingdom, it's home to the park's flagpole, upon which flies an American flag that is raised every morning and lowered every evening as part of the Flag Retreat ceremony. Surrounding the flagpole is a series of planters and fenced-off flower gardens. This area of the Town Square serves as a meeting place for families, but also is often used for character meet-and-greets, where guests can line up to have their pictures taken by Disney's PhotoPass photographers.

On the outskirts of this small plaza sit some of the town's more important buildings: City Hall, the Fire Station, the Main Street Theater, and Tony's Town Square Restaurant. Because City Hall and buildings like it were used for the day-to-day administration operation of small towns, they were often located at the center of town and near the railroad, as news, information, and economic resources typically pass through City Hall before reaching the rest of the town. It was also essential that the fire station be near the railroad, as accidents often happened, and firemen had to be ready at a moment's notice.

While City Hall was the center of government and infrastructure for small towns around the turn of the century, the City Hall of the Magic Kingdom, housed in a large Victorian-style building, is also a first stop for guests entering the park. It's the home of Guest Services, which provides visitors with park maps; complementary buttons for birthdays, weddings, and first visits; and other important services.

Next door to the City Hall is Engine Company 71 fire station. The name of the engine company is a nod to the year 1971, when the Magic Kingdom opened. Guests can enter Engine Company 71 through the open double doors to find one of the headquarters for the Sorcerers of the Magic Kingdom card game. Upon entering the room, guests find a series of horse stables that are roped off. Large bales of straw lay against the partitions of the stables, while horse collars hang on the back walls of each stall and firemen helmets and axes line the walls as decorations. Interestingly, the horse collars are not just merely decoration for completing the immersion that you are in a turn-of-the-century fire station, but also transform into screens to facilitate gameplay for Sorcerers of the Magic Kingdom.

On the other side of Town Square, opposite from City Hall and the fire station, is a grand building, the Main Street Theater. This building is not reminiscent of a cinema, but rather a stage theater. In many small towns and cities around the late 1800s and early 1900s, theaters were used for stage shows, often vaudeville shows, similar to Frontierland's Country Bear Jamboree. These shows featured traveling performers who put on slapstick comedy routines, musical shows, acts of daring, and the controversial blackface, which depicted white men dressed and acting as African Americans.

The function of the Main Street Theater in the Magic Kingdom is a meet-and-greet with Mickey Mouse. Upon entering the theater, guests are ushered down a hallway into a dressing room for Mickey Mouse who is preparing to put on a magic show, which would have been typical for vaudevillian theaters around the turn of the century.

After leaving the Town Square, guests head down Main Street, U.S.A. toward the area ending at Cinderella Castle, which cast members and park enthusiasts call the Hub, as it is the central location from which guests can navigate to the different lands of the park. Bookending Town Square are two large buildings: the Confectionery on the right side of the street, as you're heading into the park, and the Emporium on the left.

While the buildings of Main Street, U.S.A. are designed to look like multiple storefront facades, many of the stores that line Main Street are interconnected. The Main Street Confectionery, a store which would have been popular in any town or city during the early 1900s, is modeled in Victorian fashion, with awnings over the second and third story windows and ornate trim along the roof line. A lighted marquee hangs off the side of the building to let guests know what the store sells. Upon entering the store, patrons find a quaint candy kitchen, selling pre-packaged candy from Goofy's Candy Company, as well as fresh fudge and candied apples being made behind glass windows.

Another of the shops along the right side of Main Street is the Main Street Cinema. Cinemas were extremely popular in the late decades of the nineteenth and early decades of the twentieth centuries. Dubbed "nickelodeons," patrons could visit a theater and pay a nickel to enjoy an afternoon of watching "moving pictures" flicker across a screen while the images were accompanied by ragtime piano music either played live or a player piano.

In the 1970s, when the park opened, the Main Street Cinema showed silent films and classic Disney shorts on loop throughout the day. However, in 1998, the cinema was transformed into a shop offering various Disney-themed merchandise and artwork. In keeping with the theme, Disney shorts continue to be played on movie theater style screens on the walls of the shops.

When the park opened in 1971, a short street—Center Street—intersected Main Street, U.S.A. This street ended in cul-de-sacs approximately fifty yards on either side of Main Street and featured various smaller shops, such as a barber shop, a livery stable for the horses that pulled vehicles up and down Main Street, and a Hallmark card shop.

In 1984 and again in 2001, Main Street went through extensive refurbishments, effectively eliminating West Center Street by expanding the largest shop in the Magic Kingdom, the Emporium. The Emporium announces on a marquee lined by light bulbs that it has been in business "since 1863"; the store itself stretches from Town Square to about halfway to the Hub, down the west (or left) side of Main Street. However, as guests continue their journey down Main Street toward the Hub, they are also journeying through time; while the portion of the Emporium that is located in Town Square was indeed founded in 1863, observant guests will notice that different entrances to the Emporium were added later in the nineteenth and early twentieth centuries, showing how the proprietor of the department store expanded his business over the years.

Although both sides of Main Street look similar, insofar as storefront facades line each side, the reality is deceptive, as the Emporium is a single, interconnected unit that starts adjacent to the Fire Station and ends with Casey's Corner, an eatery near the Hub that is named after an early twentieth-century poem, "Casey at Bat." The Emporium sells everything from clothing to plush characters to Christmas ornaments and other generic park and character merchandise.

Similar to department stores taking over small proprietorships and expanding into multiple buildings in small town America during the Victorian era, the Emporium also expanded, putting other shops out of business as they became less popular. As a result, guests paying attention to their surroundings as they move from room to room of the Emporium may notice changes in the fixtures and decorations of the store as they head toward the Hub; different rooms feature different styles of wallpaper, different types of lighting fixtures, different colored paint on the walls, and even differently themed photographs or decorations. The area that once used to be West Center Street, which was enclosed and made interior store space in 2001, even still has the gas lamppost that was in the exterior courtyard for the first thirty years of the park.

A number of other stores also line Main Street, including a jewelry shop; a glassware shop, where patrons can watch a glassblowing artisan at work; and a bakery, which has recently been converted to house an in-park Starbucks Coffee franchise location.

* * *

Imagineers, the designers of the Disney theme parks, did not stop with the buildings when creating the illusion that guests are walking through a small American town of the early 1900s. Several other details were included to further immerse park visitors. For example, all along Main Street observant guests will notice four-foot tall black posts made of metal capped with a horse's head holding a ring in its mouth. While these posts have no function in the Magic Kingdom, they were prevalent along the curbs of many small towns during the early 1900s. The decorative poles are called hitching posts, and were used to "park" one's horse, looping the reigns of the horse through the ring on the post to prevent the horse from wandering away while the rider patronized the many shops of the town. Small details like these, which the majority of park guests do not notice, help to create the immersive illusion of Main Street, U.S.A.

Because of the limited space within the Magic Kingdom, Imagineers designed the upper floors of the building facades using "forced perspective," which means that the second and third floors of the building are not full size. For example, the first floors of the shops and restaurants along Main Street are about twelve feet tall, the second floors are approximately ten feet tall, and the third floors are about eight feet tall. This is done to create the illusion that the buildings are taller than they actually are.

Another detail that Imagineers have included and added over the past four decades of the Magic Kingdom's history are what are known as the "Windows of Main Street." Most of the windows in question are situated along the second and third stories of the building facades in Town Square and along either side of Main Street, and serve as the "credits" for those who helped develop and build Walt Disney World or who were integral parts of the history of the Walt Disney Company. These windows are well themed to a specific trade, and are similar to the types of windows one would see in a town or city around the late 1890s or 1900s, advertising the proprietor of certain businesses or companies. Prospective patrons were able to determine what shops sold or what services businesses offered by reading the painted or etched explanation and name of the proprietor on the window. The practice of dedicating windows on Main Street began in the 1950s in Disneyland, when Walt Disney dedicated a window on Main Street to his father, Elias Disney; the window reads, "Elias Disney: Contractor, Est. 1895." While Disney publicly recognized his father as a tough man, dedicating a window to him in his theme park was Walt's way of saying thank you to the father that instilled in him a strict work ethic. Elias Disney held multiple jobs throughout Walt's early life, moving his family around the country as opportunities arose; for example, in the 1890s, Elias moved the family to Chicago to take a job constructing buildings for the World's Columbian Exposition of 1893. Elias also has a window in the Magic Kingdom on East Center Street, moved there after the expansion of the Emporium in the early 2000s.

The Main Street at Disney World also has a series of dedicated windows that Disney enthusiasts look for during unofficial park scavenger hunts. Many of these windows pay homage to those who helped design the park. An example can be found above the Crystal Arts store on East Center Street, reading "M.T. Lott Real Estate Investments; A Friend in Deeds is a Friend Indeed; Donn Tatum, President; Subsidiaries: Tomahawk Properties, Latin American Development, Ayefour Corporation, Bay Lake Properties, Reedy Creek Ranch Lands, Compass East Corporation." This window references the various "skeleton companies" that Walt Disney used to purchase property in central Florida in the early 1960s; Walt knew that if the owners of the land realized that the Walt Disney Company was purchasing acreage on which to build another Disneyland, the prices of the land would go through the roof. To stop this from happening, he created a series of false companies to purchase the land secretively. Donn Tatum was the first non-Disney to be the president of the Walt Disney Company.

Another significant window on Main Street is located above the Confectionery and reads, "General Joe's Building Permits; Licensed in Florida; Gen. Joe Potter, Raconteur." This window references General Joe Potter, who helped construct Walt Disney World and the Magic Kingdom in the late 1960s and early 1970s. Potter, an ex-serviceman who served in the Army Corps of Engineers, was known to Walt through his participation in the construction of the New York World's Fair. Walt hired Potter to construct the Florida property, and as a result, he organized the moving of thousands of tons of dirt to carve out the Seven Seas Lagoon, which lies between the Transportation and Ticket Center, the Polynesian Village Resort, the Grand Floridian, and the Magic Kingdom. The dirt that was removed to create the large man-made lake was piled on the site of the Magic Kingdom, raising the park to approximately twenty feet higher than the surrounding landscape, and allowing Cinderella Castle to be seen from far away. Interestingly, the window on Main Street is not the only reference to General Joe Potter; one of the large ferries that transports guests across the Seven Seas Lagoon to the Magic Kingdom is also named after him.

Finally, while many park guests don't even notice, one detail completes the illusion that park patrons really have been transported to a small Midwestern town around the turn of the twentieth century: the background music playing throughout the area. Because of the ambient noises of the park, many guests don't realize that music seems to float around them, seemingly with no source. In fact, hidden speakers embedded in the lampposts and in the upper floors of the building facades emit instrumental music that would have been common in the 1890s and early 1900s. The background music loop lasts approximately fifty-five minutes and plays a series of ragtime and period tunes, including some from popular films and stage musicals set in the late Victorian Era such as *Hello, Dolly!*, *The Music Man*, and *The Happiest Millionaire*. This music is not over the top, emanating above all other noises, but set at a level that is only really noticeable if you pay attention to it. Otherwise, subconsciously, like much of the other instrumental music playing in the themed areas of the park, it completes the immersive experience.

* * *

Main Street, U.S.A. is meant to be the opening experience for guests at the Magic Kingdom. Some have compared entering the Magic Kingdom to the beginning of a film. Guests enter through the turnstiles and are greeted by a large face of Mickey Mouse made of flowers, which some believe is the "title card" of a film. The color of the concrete once guests enter the park is a shade of red, evoking the red carpet of a movie premiere. As guests enter the park through the tunnels, posters line the walls showing many of the attractions they will find in the park, similar to the "Coming Attractions" that play before a film. Main Street, U.S.A. sets the exposition scene of the park, giving guests the background of Walt's origins in Marceline, Missouri, as well as comparing the Americana of Walt Disney World to that of what many believe was a "golden age" in American history. Finally, the windows along the upper floors of Main Street serve as the opening credits to the park, giving recognition to those who made the experience possible, and which, unfortunately, many visitors don't notice. Whether the metaphor comparing the Magic Kingdom to a film was intended by the Imagineers or not, frequent visitors to the park cannot imagine going there without Main Street, U.S.A. as part of the first few minutes of the experience. Maybe this is why every Disneyland-style park in the world has its own version of Main Street.

CHAPTER TWO

THE CRYSTAL PALACE

VICTORIAN DINING AT ITS FINEST

*A*fter reaching the "Hub" of the Magic Kingdom, my family has a tendency to turn left into Adventureland, rather than right into Tomorrowland. Upon park opening, most park guests rush to get into line on Space Mountain, Splash Mountain, Peter Pan's Flight, or the Seven Dwarfs Mine Train. This often leaves the attractions of Adventureland with shorter lines. To avoid the crowds that gather in the Hub, we skirt around the corner of Casey's Corner and along the sidewalk in front of a large, glass structure, the Crystal Palace.

The Crystal Palace, while set back from Main Street, U.S.A., fits perfectly into the theming of the era. However, while Main Street, focuses on small town early America, the Crystal Palace derives from Victorian England of the 1850s. As I did my research about the Crystal Palace, I already had some background knowledge regarding the Great Exhibition of 1851 and the Hyde Park Crystal Palace. I had assumed that the Disney restaurant was simply a re-creation of the exhibition hall used in the London World's Fair. However, after extensive research, I realized that this was not the case. Rather than Disney's Crystal Palace being a re-creation of a historical British icon, the Imagineers took different aspects of the Victorian era and combined them into the Magic Kingdom restaurant. The designers of the Crystal Palace drew from a number of

Joseph Paxton's blueprints to create the glasshouse architecture, and the Imagineers even drew upon furniture and fixtures from the second half of the nineteenth century to create the illusion of one of the golden eras of recent world history. Although these details are usually missed by most guests, the restaurant has been adding to the wonderful theming of Main Street, U.S.A. and feeding thousands of happy guests for the past forty years.

* * *

The origination of the Crystal Palace of Great Britain began in the 1830s. When King George IV of England died in 1830, a new election was required to choose members of the House of Commons, the legislative branch of Britain's government that represents the "common people." As a result of this election, a new political party, the Whigs, replaced the Tories as the majority party in Parliament. Since the Whigs represented liberal interests, they attempted to pass the Reform Act of 1832, which provided more votes to the "rotten boroughs" of England, where the poorest lived under the power of the aristocracy. This reform act would favor the interests of the poor, rather than the aristocratic lords who ran these towns and who generally favored the conservative politics of the Tories. Unfortunately, the political fracture of Parliament between the Tories and the Whigs caused the Reform Act to not be passed by the House of Lords, which meant that the common people did not have as much representation in the government or rights in their daily lives. Instead, the aristocracy was able to keep their power in electing the representatives in Parliament, rather than giving those rights to the people.

The common folk rose up in violent demonstrations known as the Reform Riots. The new monarch, King William IV, was encouraged to add seats to Parliament to secure the passage of the Reform Bill, but refused to do so. As a result, the legislators resigned from office in rebellion against the king, and encouraged their constituents to revolt. In an effort to hold his kingdom together, William threatened the Tories to allow the passage of the Reform Act or he would add new seats to Parliament to allow for its passage without their support. Not wanting to lose their majority, the Tories abstained during the final vote, allowing the Reform Act to pass. More important, however, was that the people began to realize the power they held against the monarch.

Shortly after the controversy of the Reform Act, King William IV died in 1837. The reign of the monarchy was passed to his niece, Victoria, who married her first cousin, Albert, in 1840 (for whom Grand Floridian's restaurant, Victoria and Albert's, is named). Unfortunately for Albert, the public viewed him with suspicion, believing him to be German, as he was from a large extended family related to many of the monarchs of Europe, including Germany.

Throughout the 1840s, liberal revolutions swept much of Europe, enveloping Germany, Italy, Greece, and neighboring France. These revolutions sought to improve the living and working conditions of the middle and working classes, as well as challenges by the upper classes to the absolute power of the monarchs. For example, in France the middle classes challenged the power of Louis-Phillipe and in doing so created the Second Republic of France. Other revolutions focused on the unification of regional kingdoms into centralized nation-states, such as Italy and Germany.

The Reform Act demonstrations of the 1830s coupled with the threat of the revolutions of the late 1840s prompted Prince Albert to act. With the burgeoning of the British Empire, as well as growing trade relations between Europe and the Americas, technology began to flourish. Albert came up with the idea of creating a "Great Exhibition" to display new technologies, as well as giving various European nations and the young United States the opportunity to showcase their culture and promote international peace and free trade. Prince Albert decided to hold this Exhibition in Britain so that his citizens would feel proud of their nation, as well as invite the public, including the commoners, to participate in viewing and learning about the innovations of the new industrial society.

The Great Exhibition was set to be open from May 1 through October 11, 1851. The monarch solicited bids for the design of the building that would house the exhibition, and selected as the winning bid that of architect Joseph Paxton, well known at the time for his glasshouses, which were early ideas for the horticultural greenhouse. Paxton's vision for these glasshouses was "to facilitate the cultivation of an increasing variety of foreign plants in the temperate climate of Northern Europe ... [and he] intended to grant the urban population of London access to clean air, daylight, and a comfortable climate." Because London in the 1840s and 1850s had extensive air pollution due to the growing industrial presence, and often dipped into low temperatures during the winter months, Paxton had envisioned an enclosed park for visitors to enjoy the pleasures of grassy promenades, arboretums, and carriage rides throughout the year, regardless of the weather. Paxton's design was adopted and made a reality by engineer Sir William Cubitt, as evidence of British industrial superiority.

The location chosen for the Great Exhibition was Hyde Park and the building designed by Paxton was dubbed the "Crystal Palace" by the famous British magazine, *Punch*. The building was built out of iron, glass, and wood, with a modular design, as the organizers of the Exhibition were not sure what nations and companies would show up; this would allow the struck to be expanded or shrunk depending on the number of presenters. It also allowed the building to be built and demolished quickly, as the structure was meant to be temporary and taken apart at the end of the exhibition in October. As a result, Parliament prohibited Paxton and his builders from removing trees from the site in Hyde Park, and thus mature elms (and resident sparrows) were enclosed inside the building. Many of the affluent residents of the Hyde Park area were indignant by its selection as the site for the exposition, afraid it would draw "a ceaseless procession of unruly vagabonds" and foreigners. However, the British government and Paxton decided that Hyde Park was the best location for the fair: an open field adjacent to a body of water known as the Serpentine, which allowed for the Crystal Palace to be reflected and enhanced by the water. There would also be a wide open space behind the exhibition hall, allowing for a sort of parking lot for the various carriages that brought patrons to the fair.

Queen Victoria herself officiated the opening ceremonies; the public arrived to be greeted by the queen sitting on a throne in the foyer of the Crystal Palace, while pipe organs played Handel's "Hallelujah" chorus. The exhibition ran for five months and was open initially to the wealthy, with five shillings the cost of admission. After the first twenty-five days, beginning on May 26, admission changed to one shilling on Mondays through Thursdays to allow for middle- and working-class visitors.

Once inside the Crystal Palace, visitors were able to view over one hundred thousand exhibits of new and innovative technologies or national displays exhibiting various European, Asian, and American cultures, as well as the culture of the British Empire. While similar exhibitions had been held by other European nations prior to 1851, the Crystal Palace would be the first to host a collection of exhibits from international groups and nations; Albert believed this would be a chance for England to prove its superiority, as well as help create a more peaceful dialogue between rival and enemy nations. The Great Exhibition of 1851 also gave visitors the opportunity to see, for the first time, inventions such as the Siemens telegraph, the Colt revolver, public toilets, the first voting machine, the first iron frame for a piano, and other revolutionary innovations. Londoners were amazed by "unpickable pockets," a new type of fashion designed to prevent street urchins in European cities from making a living. The exhibition also displayed international and cultural artifacts, such as the world's biggest known diamond, the Koh-i-Noor, as well as silver and gold gilded items from Sindh (part of British India in 1851, but currently in Pakistan). Queen Victoria's ivory throne was on display from India, proving to the world Britain's superiority in colonial ventures. Because the use of steam as a power source was novel in the mid-1800s, many machines were present to display industrial might. For example, the state of Wisconsin sent a stave-dressing machine, which bound wooden slats, called staves, together with a metal ring to produce barrels or kegs which would hold whiskey or flour. James Watt & Company, begun by the inventor of the steam engine, was present to show off ways the steam engine could be implemented on water. A large steam-powered printing press amazed visitors as it printed off five thousand copies of the *Illustrated London News* every hour.

The building itself was also revolutionary in style and function. Because the Great Exhibition took place during the summer months, Paxton had to come up with solutions to the summer heat and the greenhouse effect that would inevitably occur as a result of a building made of glass housing tropical plants, full-grown elms, and up to 80,000 visitors a day. Paxton partnered with the Chance Brothers, a glass supplier from the city of Birmingham, to install glazed glass and thin, translucent sheets of calico to temper the intensity of the direct sun. He also designed the roof of the structure as ridge and furrow, rather than flat pieces of glass, so that there were no direct sun rays coming shining straight in, but rather on an angle.

However, the ridge and furrow shape of the roof and the translucent glaze of the glass ceiling still did not fix the problem of heat during the summer months when temperatures occasionally got as high as ninety-seven degrees. A number of thermometers were placed throughout the

Crystal Palace with measurements taken throughout the day; temperatures were published daily in the local newspapers, including the *Daily News* and the *Morning Chronicle*. Paxton devised two possible solutions.

The first solution was ventilation, so that hot air could exit the building and cooler air from the outside could flow into the large glasshouse. Large fan blades connected to a mechanism drew cooler air into the building, while a system of drains and gutters along the ceiling allowed for condensation to be drained, lowering the humidity inside the structure.

Paxton also developed a system of air cooling in a time when air conditioning and refrigeration still had not been invented. On days when the temperature was hottest, he added wet sheets of calico between the ventilation fans and the interior of the Crystal Palace. As the fans turned and drew air from outside into the building, the air flowed over the moist cloth, cooling the internal air up to seven degrees. He had also proposed the use of a large, ceiling-mounted fan that was kept in motion through the use of a crank operated by Indian servants, but this never came to fruition.

The interior of the Crystal Palace resembled a cross-section of a step pyramid, and had three levels. The ground floor was widest, and had wooden panels on the walls. There was a balcony that hung over each side of the promenade over the first floor, as well as an overhanging balcony that was narrower for the third level, each of which held various exhibitions. The center aisle was completely exposed from the first floor all the way to the ceiling; because electric lights had yet to be invented, the sunlight filtering through the roof allowed for natural light to illuminate all three levels of the building.

The Great Exhibition closed on October 11, 1851. The agreement had been for the building to be torn down at the end of the exhibition. However, because the Crystal Palace was so popular and because the Great Exhibition had been such a grand success, the decision was made to move the Crystal Palace. In 1852, preparation of a new site began on Sydenham Hill, approximately seven-and-a-half miles from the original site in Hyde Park. Joseph Paxton was again called upon, this time to design the gardens and grounds that surrounded the Crystal Palace, complete with terraces and fountains, some of which sprayed up to two-hundred-and-fifty feet into the air. Sculptor Benjamin Waterhouse Hawkins created thirty-three models of life-size dinosaurs, which would become a great draw to the new Crystal Palace Park.

Queen Victoria once again officiated the opening of the new Crystal Palace in 1854. Over the next seven decades, it served as an art gallery for classical and ancient art, Shakespearian dramas, concerts, and even conventions held by the Boy Scouts.

The move of the Crystal Palace from Hyde Park to Sydenham Hill put the exhibition hall into debt, which could not be absorbed by ticket sales. As a result, over the course of the next fifty years, attendance to the Crystal Palace and the Crystal Palace Park declined dramatically, and the building fell into disrepair. A developer bought the land in the 1920s to try to restore the Palace to its former glory. However, on November 30, 1936, disaster struck when a small explosion occurred in the ladies' coat room of the Crystal Palace, starting a fire. Over 400 firefighters arrived to try to save the national landmark, and the glare of the fire could be seen from miles away. Unfortunately, the fire could not be stopped, and the building burnt to the ground, ending one chapter of Victorian culture.

Meanwhile, the United States had built its own version of the Crystal Palace in New York City. Shortly after the Great Exhibition of 1851 came to a close, the Exhibition of the Industry of All Nations began on July 14, 1853. New York's Bryant Park played host to this world's fair, which lasted until November 14, 1854. The building itself was a close similarity to the one built in London, with the main difference between the two Crystal Palaces a large glass dome that caps the center of the New York version.

One of the most notable exhibits of the Exhibition of the Industry of All Nations was Otis' elevator, complete with a safety that caught the elevator if the rope broke. Countries that attended the fair and showcased their culture included France, Switzerland, Italy, Australia, the British possessions and colonies, Russia, and Germany. Various artistic works were displayed at the fair, as well as steam engines, mining implements, textile manufacturing processes, musical instruments, and fine furniture. Unfortunately, just like the British Crystal Palace, the Crystal Palace in New York burnt to the ground, on October 5, 1858.

* * *

The Crystal Palace Restaurant was an original restaurant for the Magic Kingdom, opening on October 1, 1971. It is not a replica of either the British or American Crystal Palaces, but rather a combination of both. It is designed to evoke the exhibition halls and similar types of glasshouses that would have been designed by Joseph Paxton. As guests approach the Crystal Palace, they are greeted by a white building with a grand veranda that stretches around either side. Three glass domes rise from the roof: one on each side of the building and one in the middle. The building itself is decorated with intricate wooden latticework and curved trim. Similar to the buildings on Main Street, the roof line of the Crystal Palace is lined with clear electric bulbs, characteristic of the late Victorian Era; this would have been more accurate to the British version, as the Bryant Park Crystal Palace burnt down before electric lights were invented. The restaurant is shaped like a Greek cross, similar to both the American and British versions of the exhibition hall.

Over the entrance is an arched glass overhang held up by columns and decked out with curvy, decorative trim woodwork. The roof of the overhang is made of glass panels, allowing for light to filter through. A large blue sign (which looks like it is made of crystal) hangs from the overhang and spells out "The Crystal Palace, A Buffet with Character." The arched entrance is inspired by the large glass-arched entrance of the British Crystal Palace, but with obvious differences; the Disney restaurant's glass awning hangs about twenty-five feet over the entrance and is made of wood and glass, whereas the British version extended about five feet past the entrance and was more of a design flourish, made of iron and glass.

Upon entering the restaurant, guests find themselves inside a large, open room with a soaring ceiling decorated with criss-cross molding and both clear and colored glass windows. Metal structures stretch between the columns of the restaurant, allowing for the support of the roof. These metal supports were also used in the British and American Crystal Palaces to ensure the suspension of the glass ceilings.

Across from the entrance is a large planter filled with tropical plants like palms and ferns. Large hanging baskets hang from hooks on pillars and the iron supports, also filled with ferns, harkening back to Paxton's idea for a winter park. While the plants inside the Disney restaurant are not mature elms, they still have the feeling of a greenhouse due to the tropical plants near the entrance.

Hanging between the pillars that surround the planter is a large banner that reads "Welcome to our Friendship Day Celebrashun." Below the banner are topiaries of Piglet, Tigger, Pooh, and Eeyore from the *Winnie the Pooh* films. The Crystal Palace is a character dining experience, where walk-around characters of the *Winnie the Pooh* films visit guests at tables, pose for pictures, and sign autographs. While these characters may seem out of place here, they really are not: the Pooh characters originated in a book series by A.A. Milne, a British author who wrote children's stories in the late 1920s. The use of Pooh and Tigger as walk-around characters *are* historically inaccurate, as the Victorian era ended around 1900, not the 1920s. The only reason that the Milne characters *may* fit at the Crystal Palace is the British connection to the Grand Exhibition.

On the other side of the planter and Winnie the Pooh topiary display is the self-serve buffet. The buffet sits below an arched ceiling lined with windows, allowing for natural light to filter into the restaurant. A large bronze dome rises above the buffet; this dome is a smaller representation of the larger glass dome that caps the center of the building.

Bronze light fixtures hang as chandeliers and are attached to the pillars throughout the restaurant. Similar to the lights on Main Street, U.S.A., half of the fixtures point upward, while the other half hang down. Because the restaurant is reminiscent of a Victorian-era building, the fixtures are reproductions of gas lamps that have been fitted with wires and light bulbs. In order to prevent gas from condensing and dripping onto passersby, gas lamps would point upwards. However, because the periodization of the building is around the turn of the twentieth century, the building has both refitted gas lamps and electric chandeliers.

The Crystal Palace and the Great Exhibition of 1851 were geared toward the public of Britain; Prince Albert used the exhibition to quell the disenchantment of the middle and working classes. But since admission to the fair was so expensive (five shillings, or approximately twenty dollars per person in today's money), many of the people living in and around London during the time of the fair were unable to afford visiting the Crystal Palace. As a result, a day at the Great Exhibition of 1851 was a day spent mainly with the upper-class aristocracy of Britain. This "fancy" experience has been replicated at the Disney World restaurant; guests sit at tables with faux marble tops. The legs of the tables and chair backs resemble decorative wrought iron. The tables and chairs, along with the classical violin music seeming to come from nowhere and the fancily dressed waiters and waitresses, evokes an upper-class dining experience, complete with Mickey waffles, macaroni and cheese, spice-boiled shrimp, and a delicious selection of meats.

Part Two
ADVENTURELAND

One of my favorite lands in the Magic Kingdom, especially at night, is Adventureland. While many fans of Walt Disney World explain that they didn't learn to appreciate the land until they were older, I have always liked it, even through its complexities and amalgam of themes.

Whenever my family visits the Magic Kingdom, we always visit the park in a clockwise fashion, as most people tend to walking to the right, not the left. Because of this, we have found that Adventureland is generally less busy in the morning than other areas of the park, allowing us to quickly get on some of our favorite attractions, including the Jungle Cruise, Pirates of the Caribbean, and my dad's favorite, The Swiss Family Treehouse.

The atmosphere of Adventureland is some of the most immersive in the park. The inspiration for the land, which was imagined initially for Disneyland in 1955, was based on Disney's True-Life Adventures film series, which began with the Academy Award-winning *Seal Island* in 1949. The series was popular to film goers and lasted until 1960, when clips of the films started to be shown on the *Disneyland* and *Wonderful World of Color* television shows. Other popular films from the series include *The Living Desert, The Vanishing Prairie,* and *The African Lion.* The former two films later inspired their own attractions in Disneyland's Frontierland when the park opened in 1955, but it was *The African Lion* that inspired the adventure spirit that was capitalized on for Disneyland's Adventureland, and later the land of the same name in Walt Disney World's Magic Kingdom.

* * *

Florida's Adventureland is very overgrown, utilizing the more mature vegetation that had been planted for the park's opening day in 1971. The land has two defined areas that make up the theme of Adventureland: the Arabian Village and the Caribbean Plaza, neither of which were present on the park's opening day. The Caribbean Plaza was added to the Magic Kingdom to allow for theming the back corner of Adventureland when the Florida version of Pirates of the Caribbean opened in 1973. The Arabian Village opened when The Magic Carpets of Aladdin, a spinner similar to Dumbo the Flying Elephant, was added in 2001. The rest of the land, which is not defined as a sub-area within Adventureland, maintains the similar Polynesian and Caribbean motifs that were present when the park opened in October, 1971.

Adventureland is home to five different attractions: the Swiss Family Treehouse, based on the novel, *Swiss Family Robinson* by Johann David Wyss; The Jungle Cruise, which evokes the adventures of European imperialists during the late nineteenth and early twentieth centuries; The Magic Carpets of Aladdin, a Dumbo-like spinner based on the 1992 Disney film, *Aladdin*; The Enchanted Tiki Room, an attraction originally developed for Disneyland and one of the first to utilize Audio-Animatronics technology; and Pirates of the Caribbean, based on the relationship between the European colonial colonies and pirates in the Caribbean during the 1600s and 1700s.

Adventureland is themed to immerse guests in the spirit of expedi-
tionaries, explorers, and adventurers. There is no one time period for
the land, as the attractions range from approximately the 400s BC (Magic
Carpets of Aladdin), to the 1600s (Pirates of the Caribbean), early 1800s
(Swiss Family Treehouse), and the 1930s (Jungle Cruise), through the
1960s and 1970s (Walt Disney's Enchanted Tiki Room). However, the
theming of Adventureland encompasses the areas of the world that are
considered by many Americans as exotic and mysterious, such as the
South Pacific, the Caribbean, the Middle East, Asia, and Africa.

Adventureland's story begins before guests even officially enter the
land from the Hub. The only way to enter Adventureland from the park's
center is across a wooden bridge. The bridge was arched until the 2000s,
which allowed for a grand reveal of the land for guests. However, due to
accessibility issues and the number of strollers in use in the park, the
bridge was flattened after a refurbishment in 2011. The bridge has a distinctly tropical feel, with a series of bamboo scaffolds that stretch a piece
of canvas with the land's name across it. On either side of the canvas sign
is a multitude of spears surrounding a tribal mask. The mask has the skull
of a horned cow surrounded by a mane of grass. Human skulls and Tiki
masks surround the sign and are attached from the bamboo scaffolding.
On either side of the bridge are light posts framed by Tiki masks and tribal
shields; ropes hang from the poles suspending lanterns, evoking hanging lights on a ship or in a tropical port. The theming of the bridge is even
more complete at night, as the lanterns look as though lit by an internal
flame and large torches flicker on either side of the bridge. During both
night and day, the sound of beating tribal drums draws guests across the
bridge and into the mysterious, adventurous land.

Once guests have crossed the bridge, they find themselves transported
to a different part of the world, surrounded by tropical ferns, palms, and
other exotic plants. The air in the area seems to grow thicker and more

humid due to all the plants that have become overgrown. Buildings line the right side of the walkway; on the lower levels of the buildings are shops and counter service restaurants, while businesses and apartments seem to be located on the upper levels. The buildings have heavy shutters over their windows to protect them from hurricane-force winds. Many of the upper levels also have balconies and red clay tile shingles on the roofs.

The first attraction guests encounter upon entering Adventureland from the Hub is tucked away from the main path of the land, and many guests walk past it without even knowing it is there. Based on the book by Johann David Wyss in 1812 and the Disney film of the same name in 1960, the Swiss Family Treehouse is only evident by its sign, which is planted near a wooden bridge that crosses a tropical stream and takes guests to the large tree that hosts the attraction. The sign not only announces the presence of the treehouse, but also begins the story of the attraction by explaining that in 1805 the Robinson family, composed of a husband, wife, and their three sons, became shipwrecked along an unknown shore and built themselves a home in a giant tree in the woods. Guests are invited to cross the bridge and climb steps around the side of the tree to observe the home which the Robinsons fashioned for themselves. Guests climbing the tree will observe the various rooms of the treehouse, including the master bedroom, the boys' bedroom, and the kitchen via suspended bridges and steps. Careful observation of the treehouse reveals that the Robinson family utilized parts from their wrecked ship to build the home, including spindles from the ship's railing, nautical rope, the masts, as well as natural resources such as the tree itself (which was made of concrete by the Imagineers) and coconuts.

The architecture in Adventureland changes as guests move through the land. While the buildings near the bridge from the Hub have a modern Caribbean feel (such as the Aloha Isle snack stand), the motif of the architecture changes based on the various parts of the land. For example, the buildings around the Magic Carpets of Aladdin seem to be made of clay and look thick and heavy. The main shop of this part of Adventureland, the Agrabah Bazaar, is draped with blue- and gold-striped cloth as though the shop is located inside a large tent. The round, pointed arch that was characteristic of Iranian and Persian architecture decorates the sign of the shop. Set in approximately the 400s BC, the fictional town of Agrabah in the Arabian Peninsula would likely have been a trading town centered around an oasis. As a result, the town would have been fitted with both permanent structures made of mud clay and temporary structures such as tents. These trading towns allowed for merchant activity to occur between the various caravan traders and nomadic peoples of the region.

Another shop in the land is Zanzibar Trading Company, which has wrought-iron balconies and looks similar to French colonial architecture. The architecture of the area surrounding Caribbean Plaza, including the Tortuga Tavern restaurant and the Pirates of the Caribbean building, evoke a Spanish colonial architecture, complete with mud brick walls and red clay tiles that were typically used in the tropical island colonies. Interestingly, the Spanish architecture of Caribbean Plaza creates a smooth transition to the land adjacent to Adventureland, Frontierland, as part of the American West included Spanish possessions in Texas and Mexico.

However, it is the architecture of Walt Disney's Enchanted Tiki Room that seems to define the feel of Adventureland, which may be due to the fact that it towers over everything else; a nine-tiered tower made of thatched straw acts as the "weenie" drawing guests deeper into the land, and is topped with busts of gazelle and water buffalo. The use of the gazelle and water buffalo on top of the Tiki Room building was intentional; because the animal busts could be spotted from Frontierland, the animal outlines could appear to be horned cattle to fit with Western theming. Near the Tiki Room is the Sunshine Seasons Terrace, which draws inspiration from a thatched-roof drink stand that one may find on a Polynesian or Caribbean island.

The buildings and foliage of Adventureland not only create an immersive environment for guests, but also influence the other senses. Steel drum music plays throughout the land, providing a Caribbean feel. The restaurants and snack stands also provide a tasteful immersion for visitors. For example, one fan favorite is the counter service snack location Aloha Isle, which sells the ever-popular Dole Whip ice cream treat and Dole Whip Float. Another snack location is The Sunshine Tree Terrace, serving desserts, fruity beverages, and orange ice cream floats.

At night, the immersion of Adventureland becomes even more complete, as torches lit by real tongues of fire illuminate the land. The sound of the tribal drumming seems to become louder, and the dense foliage even thicker, in an almost claustrophobic manner. A foggy mist seems to hang about the area, making it more mysterious. Cannons in the clock tower of the Pirates of the Caribbean building go off, defending against the threat of pirates in a nearby port. A favorite tradition for my family is climbing the Swiss Family Treehouse at night, lit only by the lanterns suspended by nautical rope, and looking out over the Magic Kingdom, enjoying the color changing lights shining on Cinderella Castle and the neon of Tomorrowland. A tip from prior experience, however: if you decide to enjoy Adventureland at night, be aware that you will be trapped in the corner of the park during the evening parade, unable to exit Disney World until the show is over; the parade route begins in Frontierland near Splash Mountain, crawls into the Hub, down Main Street, U.S.A., and exits the park near the Fire Station, effectively closing off Adventureland for the duration.

CHAPTER THREE

WALT DISNEY'S ENCHANTED TIKI ROOM

WELCOME TO OUR TROPICAL HIDEAWAY

*T*he Tiki culture of the South Pacific and Polynesia permeates the theming of Adventureland. Gargoyle-like statues of Tiki gods hang off the edges of the roof of the Sunshine Seasons Terrace holding torches that become illuminated at night. The inside of the peaks of the thatched roofs of the Enchanted Tiki Room have colorful designs of faces and ocean creatures that are characteristic of the South Pacific island cultures of the Maori in New Zealand and the native Hawaiians. Another popular, but often overlooked section of Adventureland is a small circular nook near the Jungle Cruise that is lined by a series of six wooden Tiki god statues of varying heights and gaits, known as the Liki Tikis. When guests stand before the various statues, each plays its own distinctive tribal drum rhythm, and occasionally squirt water at the unsuspecting guests.

Although the Tiki culture that is seen throughout Adventureland has significance to the culture of the United States around the mid-twentieth century, the South Pacific Tiki religion stretches back thousands of years. According to Polynesian creation myths, the first man was named Tiki. Polynesian religion is polytheistic, meaning that it contains multiple gods, many of them attributed to different aspects of physical nature and human nature, such as the gods of the sea, the sun, and warfare. To personify these deities, the people of Polynesia began carving them out of wood (and sometimes stone), giving them menacing facial expressions to scare off evil spirits.

In the early 1930s, young Ernest Raymond Beaumont-Ganntt from Louisiana sailed throughout the South Pacific, visiting various islands. Upon returning to the United States, he changed his name to Donn Beach and opened a restaurant named Don the Beachcomber in Hollywood. The restaurant was themed to the Tiki culture of the Pacific Islands and served various dishes and beverages reminiscent of the flavors and images that made up a culture that was not yet well-known by Americans. Don the Beachcomber became extremely popular, especially to the rich and famous of southern California. In the late 1930s, entrepreneur, Victor Bergeron, opened another Tiki-themed restaurant in Oakland, California, called Trader Vic's. The California World's Fair in 1939 was also themed in a similar way, showcasing "the pageant of the Pacific." However, both restaurants and the world's fair seemed to cater to the rich and famous of California.

As Europe and America began to colonize the world in the late nineteenth century for economic gain, new colonies were established in Polynesia and the South Pacific, providing the mother nations with resources such as sugar, pineapple, and other items only found in tropical climates. However, in the late 1930s and early 1940s, Japan began to take over many of the colonies owned by Europe and the United States throughout the Pacific. Trying to halt the spreading influence of Japan, now allied with Fascist Italy and Nazi Germany, the United States halted oil sales. In retaliation, Japan attacked the American base at Pearl Harbor on the Hawaiian island of Oahu, on December 7, 1941. President Franklin Delano Roosevelt declared war on Japan, starting a four year war, lasting until August 15, 1945, and ending only after America dropped atomic bombs on the Japanese cities of Hiroshima and Nagasaki.

While fighting the war on the different Pacific Islands, American servicemen became exposed to the native cultures of the various island peoples, including the complex Tiki culture of the southern Pacific islands,
such as New Zealand, Hawaii, and Fiji. In 1947, James Michener wrote a
book called *Tales of the South Pacific*, which would later be made into the
popular musical, *South Pacific*. As American GIs began returning home
from the islands in the late 1940s and early 1950s, they brought with
them ideas about the culture of the Pacific Islands and the Tiki culture.
One of the popular forms of culture included Hawaiian music using the
ukulele, because of its supposed de-stressing quality; also, the tropical
feel of Hawaii led to a feeling of relaxation, which was much needed in
the 1950s to combat the stress of commuting and working in cubicles.
This is also the time when the Hula Girl became a popular addition to
many car dashboards, creating the exotic illusion of relaxation for the
long commutes between home and office.

Continuing the trend from Trader Vic's and Don the Beachcomber,
many restaurants, nightclubs, and lounges throughout the United States
began to incorporate Tiki themes. Often, these establishments used natural materials to transport patrons away from the concrete-and-steel
feeling of their big city lives, using decorations made of bamboo, rattan,
palm fronds, and bark. Wooden statues of Tiki gods lined the walls, and
glass lanterns suspended by rope nets hung from the ceiling as singers
dressed in hula skirts and bartenders dressed in Hawaiian shirts served
customers. These restaurants also served Polynesian-themed drinks;
both Don the Beachcomber and Trader Vic's claimed to have invented
the Mai Tai, a popular drink in these bars. Drinks were often served in
glasses or cups that were Polynesian motifs, such as an Easter Island
head, a coconut, or the bust of a hula girl. Evidence of the Tiki culture
in America also showed up in other types of businesses, including the
motels and motor lodges along Route 66 and bowling alleys, reaching

its apex with the opening in 1971 of Disney's Polynesian Village Resort, across Bay Lake from the Magic Kingdom.

* * *

The epitome of the Tiki culture's presence in Adventureland is Walt Disney's Enchanted Tiki Room; this attraction reflects the obsession over the culture of the South Pacific that many Americans had in the 1950s and 1960s. The attraction was called the Tropical Serenade when the Magic Kingdom opened in 1971, but the history of the Enchanted Tiki Room stretches back to 1963 in Disneyland and was a direct result of Walt Disney's involvement in the 1964–65 New York World's Fair. While developing attractions for the various pavilions, sponsorship money was used to innovate many new pieces of technology found all over Disney theme parks today. One of the most important technological innovations to come out of the New York World's Fair was Audio-Animatronics, which helped Imagineers to create a more life-like representation of humans and animals in their various attractions. Disney quickly found ways to use this new technology in Disneyland, for The Enchanted Tiki Room.

Walt and his Imagineers didn't originally know how the Enchanted Tiki Room would take shape; at first they wanted it to be a restaurant, where Audio-Animatronic birds would talk to guests, interrupted periodically by a tropical storm. But this idea was abandoned and The Enchanted Tiki Room show developed in its place. After Walt's death in 1966, the attraction became known as Walt Disney's Enchanted Tiki Room, since it was an attraction that he himself had helped to develop.

When Disney World's Magic Kingdom opened on October 1, 1971, a second incarnation of the show, called the Tropical Serenade, welcomed guests. Upon entering a theater located beneath a nine-tiered thatched roof, guests found the walls lined with wooden carved Tiki gods, while hanging baskets filled with flowers and perches covered with tropical birds were suspended from the ceiling. Guests were then treated to a musical show lasting approximately seventeen minutes, as the tropical birds sang songs including "In the Tiki Tiki Tiki Room" (penned by the Sherman Brothers) and "Let's All Sing Like the Birdies Sing," which featured the birds singing in styles of popular musicians of the time, including Louis Armstrong and Bing Crosby. The birds, which were voiced by such Disney legends as Thurl Ravenscroft and Wally Boag, were joined throughout the show by the Tiki carvings and flowers, who lent their own voices to the festivities.

In an effort to incorporate their many properties and films, Walt Disney Imagineering in 1998 re-imagined Walt Disney's Enchanted Tiki Room as The Enchanted Tiki Room: Under New Management. This new show featured Iago (from *Aladdin*) and Zazu (*from The Lion King*) who, according to the show's story, recently purchased the Enchanted Tiki Room to become its new proprietors. However, Iago offends the Tiki gods and is set on fire as punishment. This new attraction angered many Disney enthusiasts, who saw the refurbished version as limiting Walt's original intent for the show; ironically enough, in 2011, a fire broke out in the show building, setting fire to and destroying Iago. As a result, the attraction again went under refurbishment, reopening later in the year to its restored, albeit shorter, version.

Many guests bypass the Tiki Room on their trips to the Magic Kingdom. Because the attraction rarely has a line, many guests assume the show is closed, or may not even notice the its presence in their rush to Pirates of the Caribbean or Splash Mountain. Others may find the music annoying or the show not thrilling enough to spend twelve minutes sitting through. However, I believe that Walt Disney's Enchanted Tiki Room is a treasure hidden in plain sight: it is significant to the history of the Disney theme parks as being the pioneer for Audio-Animatronics, features great music from the Sherman Brothers, and was one of the last attractions personally worked on by Walt Disney himself.

CHAPTER FOUR

THE JUNGLE CRUISE

AN EXOTIC ADVENTURE THROUGH
A DARK PERIOD IN HISTORY

One of my favorite attractions at the Magic Kingdom is the Jungle Cruise. A popular ride in four Disney theme parks around the world, it is based on a controversial period of world history: the era of imperialism, which took place during the late nineteenth and early twentieth centuries. During this period, some of the strongest nations in the world, including Britain, France, and the United States, acquired colonies in foreign lands, exploiting the people for cheap labor and the goods as raw materials to further their respective industries. Many of these colonial landholdings would later spark major conflicts, such as World War I and the Vietnam War.

The establishment of empires is not a new concept. Rome oversaw one of history's largest empires beginning around 500 BC and lasting until about 600 AD. The early imperial movements of Europe began during the era of exploration in the mid-1400s as Portugal's Prince Henry the Navigator sponsored expeditions that sailed down the western coast of Africa, looking for a sea route to trade with India. As they sailed south, Prince Henry's patrons began establishing trading posts along the western coast of Africa, trading European goods and weapons with the native

Africans in exchange for silver, gold, and slaves. By 1492, Christopher Columbus, sponsored by the dual monarchy of Spain, began seeking a faster route to India by sailing west; according to Columbus, the world was round and if he sailed west, he would eventually arrive in India. However, the maps that Columbus had received were inaccurate, portraying North and South America as smaller than they really were, and so he arrived at San Salvador, an island in the Caribbean Bahamas. Since he believed that he had reached India, he named the people he found on the small island *tainos*, or Indians. As he went from island to island in the Caribbean looking for gold, Columbus claimed them for Queen Isabella and King Ferdinand of Spain, expanding the Spanish empire. In 1607, Britain sent a crew of men to establish Jamestown Colony in Virginia. Over the next few decades, more Europeans would travel to the American continents, establishing colonies of capitalist ventures to benefit the mother country.

The second major push for colonization began in the mid-1800s. A new philosophy, put forth by Charles Darwin and called Social Darwinism, explained that only the strongest societies would survive. Europeans considered themselves the most civilized people in the world and believed it their duty to "civilize and Christianize" any people they encountered who were unlike them in culture and religion. In 1852, Britain sent Dr. David Livingstone to the African interior to bring Christianity to the native African peoples. When many years went by without hearing from Livingstone, American newspaper reporter Henry Morton Stanley was sent to look for him. Stanley was not only told to record his search for American newspapers and to search for Livingstone, he was also commissioned by King Leopold II of Belgium to acquire territory for that small European kingdom. At the time, Belgium was a small nation surrounded by superpowers, including France and the German empire (a partnership between Germany and Prussia).

Feeling threatened, Leopold realized that in order to gain worldwide power he needed to acquire colonies to increase national wealth. As a result of Stanley's work for Leopold, Belgium established the colony of the Belgian Congo, a large, prosperous prize.

With his new empire, Leopold ruled under the auspices of spreading Christianity and civilizing the natives. He soon learned about the presence of rubber trees in his newly acquired African colony, as well as other rare and luxurious goods. Leopold began exploiting the land and the natives, leading to many deaths through overwork and abuse. Other European nations saw the wealth Belgium was acquiring through its colony and feared what might result from the opening of Africa to colonization. Kaiser Wilhelm II of Germany foresaw that the scrambling to take colonies in Africa could lead to wars between imperial powers, and called the Berlin Conference in 1884. As a result of the conference, Africa was split up into national holdings by many of the European powers. For example, Britain acquired the colonies of Kenya, Egypt, the Sudan, and South Africa; France acquired land in Algeria, Morocco, and Guinea; Germany took land in Rwanda and Namibia; and Portugal established colonies in Mozambique and Zanzibar. Around the same time, some European nations began establishing colonies in Southeast Asia, as well. Britain acquired land in India, Singapore, and Hong Kong. France established colonies in French Indochina (Vietnam, Laos, and Cambodia), whereas the Dutch established trading ports in Indonesia. Many of these colonies would not become independent nations until after the Second World War.

Walt Disney's attraction, the Jungle Cruise, is loosely inspired by two films that were released in the 1950s. The earlier film, *The African Queen*, based on the novel by C.S. Forester and starring Humphrey Bogart and Katherine Hepburn, is about two British missionaries who travel to the African interior to convert the natives. The missionaries travel on a steamboat which lends its name to the film's title, piloted by Bogart's character. However, as the small boat is traveling through a German colony, World War I breaks out in Europe. The plot of the film finds Bogart and Hepburn trying to escape the Germans who learn of the missionaries' presence in their colony. The boat encounters jungle dangers along the way, including river rapids, waterfalls, animals, and native tribes. The second film that the attraction is based on is Walt Disney's True-Life Adventure documentary, *The African Lion*, which is similar to the DisneyNature film, *African Cats*. The 1955 feature followed the feline king of the jungle through his daily life on the African savannas. This film inspired Walt Disney to create a ride-through attraction about the jungles of the world and the animals that inhabited them. Interestingly enough, Disney wanted to use real animals for his classic ride, but the unreliability of live creatures caused him to use early Audio-Animatronics, instead. This attraction was operating on opening day for both Disneyland in 1955 and Walt Disney World's Magic Kingdom in 1971.

* * *

The Magic Kingdom's version of the Jungle Cruise is set during the period of African and Asian imperialism around the 1920s and 1930s. The Imagineers have ensured that the guests are completely immersed in the time period and environment of the colonial posts of the early twentieth century, as well as the landscapes of Africa and Asia. This immersion begins as you approach the Jungle Cruise's queue building from Adventureland. Hanging from a ship's mast is a sign made of a wooden ship rudder that reads "Jungle Cruise Expedition." Beneath the rudder hangs a broken oar that describes the expedition as "exotic." As guests turn left out of Adventureland and walk down the ramp heading toward the queue building, they leave behind the general feel of Adventureland and step back in time to an imperial trading post. Posted on the outside of the building (which serves as the attraction's queue) is a sign that informs visitors they have arrived at a British jungle expedition outpost maintained by the "Jungle Navigation Co. Ltd.," which was established in 1911. Imagineers kept with the theme of the attraction by decorating the FastPass return and stand-by sign as though it were made of pieces of paper pasted to the side of the building in 1930s fashion. The FastPass distribution machines are even styled as suitcases and trunks covered with passport and expedition stickers.

As guests enter the jungle outpost building, they are greeted by period music being played over a radio station hosted by Skipper Albert Awol, known as "the voice of the jungle, broadcasting to all points unknown." Awol plays various instrumental and crooner songs in the style of 1920s and 1930s swing music, interspersed with news and jokes relating to the attraction. Those familiar with the Jungle Cruise will appreciate Awol's jokes. For example, Awol announces to skippers that "a blue jeep that has previously been reported missing has *turned up* at a nearby base camp," referencing the scene where the gorillas have destroyed a camp. Another humorous piece of advice Awol gives to skippers is that "failure to respect the animals may result in *pointed* confrontation," which corresponds to a Marc Davis-inspired scene of explorers climbing up a tree while an angry rhino tries to impale them with his horn. Davis, a Disney artist and Imagineer, was told by Walt to work on the attraction before its opening in Disneyland in 1955.

The queue is interspersed with various exotic expedition artifacts brought back by tour groups to be put on display in the jungle outpost, as well as numerous signs advertising destinations for the tourists of the Jungle Navigation Company and news for the skippers leading the tours. Near the boarding zone of the dock, a small cage sits atop a crate holding a large tarantula that jumps every few seconds, startling unsuspecting guests (myself included). Wooden crates throughout the queue are addressed to skippers and characters of the now-retired Adventurer's Club at Downtown Disney's Pleasure Island, such as Otis T. Wren and Pamelia Perkins. Near the entrance of the queue is a small empty cage explaining that it was *supposed* to be temporary quarters for a wild orang-utan and warning visitors to "keep away." However, the creature seems to have pried the bars apart and escaped; this was remediated by skippers using a piece of rope to close off the opening. A larger cage elsewhere in the queue warns visitors to "kindly keep your hands to yourself (if you want to keep them, that is!)." The sign has large claw marks scratched across it, leading guests to believe that some large animal has escaped. This may or may not be the same leopard reported by Albert Awol over the radio to have been seen in the area. Information boards posted for skippers include a "missing persons" list, complete with names like B.N. Eaton, Emma Boylen, Ilene Dover, and Ann Fellen. Other artifacts hanging about the queue include oars, pith helmets, machetes, and native masks and spears.

Midway through the queue is the office of Albert Awol, where clients of the Jungle Navigation Company can book tours down the tropical jungle rivers of the world. Awol himself is not in the office, but it looks as though he has just stepped out for a moment. A chain link gate separates the office from the queue, with a small opening for guests and the booking officer to interact. A mug of coffee sits beside a typewriter. Books have titles that reference important events of the twenties and thirties, such as the popularization of the automobile. A tobacco pipe rests in an ashtray. The office is dimly lit, allowing only the astute observer to note the framed images of colonial jungles and encased specimens of exotic insects hanging on the walls.

As guests approach the loading dock, a small shack is spotted across the river, situated along the bank. The shack has a wrap-around porch with a roof supported by bamboo poles. The roof is made of thatched

straw and is angled at a steep grade, representative of the imperial architecture of the 1930s European jungle colonies. Mosquito netting hangs
from the railings of the porch, and a gun rack holding numerous rifles is
mounted to the wall of the hut. Other props lie about the porch, including
a cane chair, a pith helmet, and a long red crutch, leading the observer to
assume that the owner of the hut may have contracted some sort of exotic
disease that has left a crippling effect. A curtain hangs in the doorway
of the cabin, behind which can be seen the foot of a bed. A sign with red
letters spelling "Keep Out!" hangs from the porch, which may reinforce
the assumption that a person with a dangerous, contagious disease lies
inside, but also warning passengers of the "dangers" that lurk ahead on
their jungle voyage.

The ride vehicles of the Jungle Cruise take the form of thirty-one passenger river boats. The boats are covered by a striped canopy, which is
covered with various "supplies" to insinuate that the ships are used to
deliver goods to colonial posts along the banks of the rivers. Passengers
sit on a bench that lines the circumference of the boat, as well as a short
bench that stretches the length of the middle of the boat. Near the back
end of the boat is a large, period-authentic (but non-functional) steam
engine with a smokestack emerging through the canopy. Robert Fulton
built the first commercial steamboat, the *Clermont*, using the steam
engine to power a water wheel that propelled the ship forward (Fulton's
Crab House in Disney Springs, formerly Downtown Disney, is named
after Robert Fulton; the restaurant is located inside a large steamboat complete with water wheel). By the 1920s and 1930s, boats were
equipped with smaller steam engines, fueled by coal. The ships were
steered by the captain through a wooden wheel, which moved a rudder
at the back of the boat. The Jungle Cruise ride vehicles have the engine
and wooden wheel, as well, except these are both for show; the vehicles
are guided along a metal track beneath the water. The sixteen boats of the

Jungle Cruise fleet have names such as Amazon Annie, Congo Connie, Ganges Gertie, Nile Nellie, and Orinoco Ida, representing the name of exotic rivers from around the world.

The guides for the jungle expeditions, known as "skippers," follow a script, but are able to personalize the spiel by injecting "Disney-approved" jokes. The skippers do not steer the boat, but are able to control it using a lever that drives the boat either forward or backward, as well as how fast or slow it travels down the river. Skippers are decked out in costumes somewhat period authentic for imperial colonizers: the cast members wear khaki shirts and pants, as well as a khaki fedora-like hat wrapped in a leopard-spotted band. Colonial officials would sometimes wear khaki clothing, as it was usually lighter in weight and did not absorb heat in the way darker colored clothing would in the hot, tropical climates of the African and Asian colonies.

The path of the Jungle Cruise takes guests down numerous rivers and across three continents, which of course is not geographically accurate. The first river that guests float down is the Amazon River, in South America. A dense canopy of foliage hangs overhead. Large, colorful butterflies with twelve-inch wingspans are perched on logs and rocks. A small waterfall to the left of the boats, named "Inspiration Falls," trickles into the Amazon, which, as the skipper explains to guests, "inspires us to travel deeper into the jungle."

Guests find themselves transitioning from the Amazon to the Congo River as they float past a beach holding three pygmy war canoes beached on the bank of the river in front of a small thatched hut. This scene is reminiscent of Joseph Conrad's novel *Heart of Darkness*, which presents the journey of a riverboat captain down the Congo River in search of for an imperial mercantilist during the height of African colonization in the 1890s. The bows of the canoes have carved heads of animals. The heads serve various purposes: one was to scare off animals or enemies along the banks of the rivers. Also, animals were an important, sustainable food source for the natives along the Congo. As a result, the natives worshipped different animal gods; the carved bows of the boats may signify a form of worship to the spirits of these gods. Across the river from the beached war canoes are a small group of pygmies, yelling and grunting, wearing carved masks and wielding spears and shields. It was not uncommon for pygmies in the 1890s to lie in wait in the foliage for an unsuspecting riverboat to come along before attacking. Keep in mind that Europeans colonizing Africa and Asia did so for selfish, economic means, exploiting the land, resources, and natives for goods and labor. In retaliation, small groups of natives would attack, throwing spears and shooting arrows at passengers of riverboats, a scene graphically depicted in Conrad's *Heart of Darkness*. While the modern usage of the word "pygmy" to describe African tribal peoples may be offensive to some, this is a term that would have been used during the late nineteenth and early twentieth century, and is thus accurate to the period in which the attraction takes place.

At this point in the ride, the skipper of the boat explains he needs to stop at his camp to pick up supplies. Upon rounding the corner, however, guests find that the skipper's camp has been ransacked by a family of gorillas. The blue jeep Albert Awol explained had "turned up at a nearby base camp" in the queue news reports is upside down to the left of the camp, the tires still spinning. This jeep, however, is not representative of a 1930s jeep, but rather looks like one from the 1960s. Supplies lay scattered about the camp, including fuel tanks, crates, and other supplies. Inside the large canvas tent, a gorilla fiddles with a gun, while another stands before a mirror, trying on a pith helmet. Pith helmets were cloth-covered helmets made of cork, and were usually white or khaki colored. These helmets are distinctly shaped, and had broad brims to keep the sun out of the wearer's face. Because they were made of cork, they absorbed water from the humidity of tropical atmospheres, which helped keep the wearer cool in warm weather. Pith helmets were generally worn by European explorers and colonizers in African and Asian colonies.

After leaving the base camp scene, the Jungle Cruise boats float onto the Nile River, where they are greeted by African bull elephants. While there is not much detail that designates this part of the attraction as the Nile River in the jungle, the foliage gives way to what is known as the African veldt. While this geographic term is not terribly accurate, as the Nile River does not pass through the African veldt itself, Imagineers attempted to give guests the feeling that they were in African grasslands and savanna. The dense trees and vines give way to an open savanna complete with scrub brushes, boulders, and a cave, interspersed with African mammals, such as lions, zebras, and giraffes. Inside the cave, a family of lions clusters around the corpse of a zebra while the other animals look on, bringing reality to the "circle of life." The seriousness of the veldt scene doesn't last long, however, as a set of laughing hyenas provides a link from the kill scene to that of a small group of men climbing up the trunk of a tree, trapped by an angry rhinoceros. The rhinoceros has a piece of cloth wrapped around the tip of its horn, which, after careful observation, guests realize is a piece of the shorts of the lowest member of the safari group on the tree. The five men, terrified, attempt to scurry up the tree each time the rhino jerks his head upwards, trying to impale them on his horn. The hyenas sit nearby, laughing hysterically. After leaving the lost safari behind, guests find a pair of Nile crocodiles along the riverbank, which the skippers explain are named Old Smiley and Ginger, who snaps. Flanking the crocodiles is a pair of ivory totems made from the same material as the tusks of elephants.

Around the bend is a large waterfall that cascades down into the river; it's named Schweitzer Falls, which, according to Jungle Cruise lore, is named after Sir Albert Falls. This is a joke, playing on the real namesake of the waterfall, Sir Albert Schweitzer, a German missionary who established a hospital in 1913 about two-hundred miles, or fourteen days, up the Ogooué River, in modern-day Gabon, Africa, then a French colony. Guests actually pass the waterfall twice, the second time passing behind the falls, to which the skipper points out "the backside of water."

After passing through a pool of hippos and the back half of a small propeller plane (the other half of which is used in the *Casablanca* scene of The Great Movie Ride at Disney's Hollywood Studios), the small boats float into a headhunter's village. The beach is strewn with bones, and spears impale totems of human skulls as a small pack of tribesmen with painted bodies dance and chant in preparation for a hunt for human heads. The thatched-roof hut, made of bamboo and palm fronds, both of which grow native along rivers in tropical central Africa, shelters the natives. The headhunters portrayed in the attraction do not reference a specific region or group of people to ensure no one is offended, even though there are still a few remote groups throughout the world today that practice headhunting. The boat makes its quick escape and quickly finds itself on another river, the Mekong, located in Laos, Cambodia, and China.

The centerpiece of the Mekong River portion of the attraction is the ruins of an ancient Cambodian temple, remnants of holy buildings from the Khmer empire of Cambodia, similar to those at Angkor Wat. Jungle Cruise legend has it that an earthquake toppled the temple into the river, which is not surprising; Southeast Asia has frequent earthquakes. To the right of the temple's ruined entrance is the stone face of the Hindu god, Vishnu, wrapped in vines. Attempting to make a joke, skippers sometimes refer to the deity as being "Shir Lee," because the boat is heading into "Shir Lee's Temple." The temple itself is complete with wavy patterns on the spires and columns that emerge from the temple, as well as a step-like pattern on the side that is similar to the architecture found at Angkor Wat in Cambodia. Upon entering the pitch dark ruins of the temple, the skipper turns on his lantern, illuminating snakes, monkeys, and a Bengal tiger. Tree roots creep down through the walls and ceiling into the river; likewise, jungle foliage has taken over many ancient Hindu temples in Southeast Asia. The walls of the ruins are painted with faded depictions of various scenes of the Hindu religion, including its three major gods: Vishnu, Krishna, and Brahma. There is also a golden statue of the Hindu monkey god, Hanuman, who sits among various artifacts in the darkened ruins.

Upon exiting the Cambodian ruins, the fanciful trip down the rivers of the world comes to a close. While waiting for the boats ahead to unload passengers, guests come alongside a lone figure standing on the left bank of the river. This man, known as Trader Sam the Head Salesman, offers guests "two of his heads for one of yours." The head salesman holds two shrunken heads in his right hand, with another attached to a necklace hanging from his neck. Atop his head sits a top hat, reminiscent of European aristocracy of the 1890s through the 1930s. He holds in his left hand a black umbrella, something that would have been wielded by the upper class of European society, but used more for shielding the sun rather than to ward off rain. However, it is evident that Trader Sam has had the umbrella and hat for a while, as they are quite beat up and the umbrella has tears in the fabric. The gentleman is probably a native of a Southeast Asian tribe due to the markings on his face, and stands amid a grove of bamboo. The Animatronic figure, who is more a stationary mannequin with limited movement than a fully realized figure like Jack Sparrow on the Pirates of the Caribbean ride, is bare-chested and, wears a red-and-white striped cloth around his waist. Could it be that Trader Sam has ambushed a Jungle Cruise boat and used the passengers and skipper to restock his head collection, then took the canopy of the boat to create a covering for himself?

Since no guests take advantage of Trader Sam's deal, the boats move forward into the docking zone, where skippers help guests out of the boats. After passing through the exit turnstiles of the queue, guests head back up the ramp into Adventureland and continue their day at the Magic Kingdom, most not realizing that they just experienced the "golden age" of one of the lesser-known and darker periods of world history.

CHAPTER FIVE

PIRATES OF THE CARIBBEAN

FACT OR FICTION?

"Yo ho, yo ho, a pirate's life for me!" These nine words constitute one of the most popular attraction soundtracks for any guest at any of Disney's theme parks around the world. Guests board twenty-four passenger boats, sail through a series of caves, past a ship battling with a Spanish fort, and through a Caribbean town being ransacked, and eventually burned, by a rowdy group of flamboyantly dressed, earring-wearing, drunk pirates.

The idea for a pirate-themed attraction began early in the developmental stages for Walt Disney's first theme park, Disneyland. Due to the success of Disney's 1950 film *Treasure Island*, starring Bobby Driscoll as Jim Hawkins and Robert Newton as Long John Silver, Walt decided he wanted some sort of attraction where guests could walk through a wax museum depicting pirates engaging in different roguish situations, such as ransacking a town. Because of the complexity and evolution of the attraction, it did not open with the park in October 1955. Shortly after the park opened, Walt and his Imagineers began working on a series of pavilions for the 1964 New York World's Fair for companies such as Pepsi, General Electric, and the state of Illinois (which would feature attractions such as "it's a small world," Carousel of Progress, and Great

Moments with Mr. Lincoln, respectively). Throughout this process, the Imagineers developed what became known as Audio-Animatronics, a form of robotic figure that looked and behaved like a human, but could perform in exactly the same way for hours on end. Walt decided to evolve his wax museum pirate attraction into a ride-through attraction with Audio-Animatronic pirates, giving thousands of Disney guests the classic attraction that exists today.

But how accurate is Pirates of the Caribbean? Are the events, locations, and characters true to history or based instead on the myths of Blackbeard, Davy Jones, and Long John Silver?

The story behind Disney theme park attractions begins before guests even step foot into the attraction building. This is no different when guests approach the Pirates of the Caribbean building in Adventureland. On the border of where Adventureland and Frontierland meet stands the area once known as Caribbean Plaza, complete with light brown stucco buildings roofed with red clay shingles. However, the focal point of this area is the Pirates of the Caribbean building, dominated by a tall clock tower. In 2006, shortly after the release of the film *Pirates of the Caribbean: Curse of the Black Pearl*, starring Johnny Depp as Captain Jack Sparrow, the ride was refurbished, featuring the addition of elements from the film. A mast featuring a black sail and the skeleton of a pirate was added to the front of the building, while a banner quoting some lyrics from the ride's well-known soundtrack was painted on the side.

EXTERIOR ARCHITECTURE

The façade of the building is loosely based on El Castillo de San Juan del Morro, a Spanish fort that dominates the coastline of Puerto Rico just outside the capital of San Juan. Also known as El Castillo del Morro, the fort was built in 1539 by the Spanish conquerors of Puerto Rico and was used to protect the city of San Juan and its harbor from sea-bound attackers. Over the next few hundred years, the fort and its walls were improved upon, adding thickness to the walls and, eventually, a lighthouse. The exterior architecture of the Pirates of the Caribbean building and the design of the buildings throughout the ride is consistent with the Gothic architecture of seventeenth and eighteenth century Spanish Caribbean colonies.

While El Castillo del Morro is located on the island of Puerto Rico, the architecture on the exterior of the Pirates building and that of the sets in each of the show scenes is most consistent with the Spanish colonial architecture found on the islands of Cuba and the Dominican Republic. For example, transverse mason arches are used throughout the façade and queue of the attraction. A transverse mason arch is an archway where blocks are arranged in an arch, running from one wall or column to another. The block at the tip of the arch is situated at a ninety-degree angle to the blocks adjacent to the columns or walls, with the blocks between the edges and tip tilted at varying degrees.

Another form of architecture that is featured in the attraction and consistent with Spanish colonial architecture during the 1700s is the nave arcade entryway. A nave arcade is a stretch of a room lined by columns linking arches. This architectural feature was often used to make a room appear larger than it truly was. The nave arcade architecture can be found in the open-air entrance of the attraction queue, leading up to the actual entrance of the building. Large columns hold up the ceiling and supporting arches, and lead up to the large double doors of the fortress.

Also common in colonial Cuban architecture was the decorative roofing and roof lines. Many of the important buildings (such as churches, palaces, and other governmental buildings) had roofs with red clay shingles, which helped keep the interior of the buildings cool during hot days. Beneath the clay shingles were long timber rafters spaced a few feet apart. Both of these architectural features can be found on the exterior of the show building.

Sitting just above the entrance to the open-air arcade of the queue, perched on the roof, is an aesthetic (and functional) feature known as a bellcote, or in Spanish, an *espadaña*. A bellcote was usually found on churches, missions, and forts, and could feature up to three large bells used to signal different events. The bellcote sitting atop the queue is not functional, of course, but rather elicits the colonial Spanish architectural feel of the attraction.

The large clock tower that stands guard before the entrance of the queue is of distinctly colonial Dominican design. Rising to twenty feet and capped with a pyramidal prism, this rectangular tower was often used as a part of church and mission architecture during the seventeenth and eighteenth centuries. These towers rarely had clocks in them, however, but instead housed large bells, similar to the bellcote, to signal parishioners and villagers of different events.

INTERIOR ARCHITECTURE

The architecture of building facades throughout the ride are also consistent with designs being used throughout seventeenth and eighteenth century Cuba, Puerto Rico, and the Dominican Republic. Take, for example, the scene where guests first see the landing party dunking the mayor in the well, trying to learn the whereabouts of the town's treasure and Jack Sparrow. The exterior of the buildings is made of a stucco material, consistent with architecture throughout the Caribbean during the Gothic period. The buildings are roofed with red clay tiles, which were used in Cuba. On the ground floor of the building behind the pirates dunking the mayor, arches crowned with transverse masonry are used once again. The windows of the building are recessed and have sash shutters, which were prevalent with architecture in the Dominican Republic. An example of the evidence of sash shutters in this scene is where the brave wife of Carlos (the town mayor) leans out of the open window above the well and yells at her husband, "Be brave Carlos, don't be chicken!" Balconies stretch along the upper stories of the buildings, lined by metal banisters and railings reminiscent of Puerto Rican architecture.

A second example of Gothic architecture in the Spanish Caribbean colonies that is accurate throughout the attraction is the "Wench-for-a-Bride" auction scene. Once again, guests find red clay tiles used for roofing behind the women waiting to be auctioned off. Sash shutters can be found covering the windows on the second floor of the buildings. Across the canal from the auction sit various pirates, attempting to bid for the potential brides. Behind the pirates, once again, are transverse mason arches, stone blocks situated in a way to evenly distribute the weight and pressure of the heavy stone walls. Balconies with decorative metal railings found in Puerto Rico are used here, as well, with sash shutters covering the doorways opening onto the balconies.

There are other architectural details that are historically accurate throughout the attraction. Covered walkways native to the Dominican Republic stretch through the town in the scene where the pirates are chasing chickens and being chased by rolling-pin-wielding women. Heavy, rectangular towers tipped with domes and supposedly housing bells, also native to the Dominican Republic, sporadically rise behind buildings throughout the town. Sash-shuttered windows, covered public walkways, balconies beneath overhanging eaves, red clay tiled roofs, and transverse mason arches can be found throughout the scene where the drunken pirates sing to the guests while the town burns to the ground around them.

Whether it is the way arches are lined with stones set in a way to equally distribute the weight and pressure of the stucco walls, the wooden sash coverings over windows, the red clay tiles on the roofs, or the balconies that hang over the show scenes, the architecture throughout the interior of Pirates of the Caribbean reflects historical accuracy of the Spanish Caribbean colonies during the Gothic period of the seventeenth and eighteenth centuries.

QUEUE AND LOADING

The queue of Pirates of the Caribbean contains highly detailed scenery and set pieces that transport guests back in time. After passing through the open-air nave arcade entryway of the attraction's entrance, guests pass through heavy wooden double doors and into the Spanish fort. The queue is lit by sporadically placed small lanterns. While these lanterns are powered by electricity, during the 1700s, these passageways would be lit by candlelight and torches, creating a similar dimness throughout the halls. Due to modern fire safety laws, real fire torches and candlelight are not used to brighten these dark halls.

Not surprisingly, transverse mason archways are used throughout the passageways, keeping the architecture of the attraction consistent. The darkness and dankness of the queue, while maintained by the modern use of dim lighting and air conditioning, creates the sense of being deep within the Spanish fort. In fact, during the Spanish colonial period, the Castillo del Morro had walls that were up to eighteen feet thick, preventing attackers from being able to blast cannon balls through the walls or easily dig their way through the walls and into the fort.

Similar to medieval castles, different portions of forts had different uses. The queue winds its way through numerous rooms, such as an armory, which contains piles of cannon balls and numerous cannons. Some of the cannons are pointed out of holes in the walls to ward off invaders. Most armories would be deep within the fort and beneath ground level to prevent enemy fire from igniting the munitions. If a cannon ball from enemy fire had entered the hole in the wall and landed amongst barrels of gun powder, the resulting explosion would have blown the entire room apart, exposing the interior of the fort to the out-side and allowing the enemy to enter. However, colonial forts also had rooms similar to this one near the exterior wall to repel invaders.

Another portion of the fort that the queue passes through is the dun-geon. This dungeon presents some historical inaccuracies. The first is its position in the fort. The dungeon is located adjacent to the exterior wall, where the queue "exits" the fort and enters the "town" where guests load onto the ride vehicles. Historically, dungeons would be located toward the middle of the fort and below ground level. If a dungeon was on the exterior wall, and a cannon ball crashed through the wall, it would create a hole allowing prisoners to escape. Also, a dungeon on the exte-rior wall would allow prisoners to escape through the windows of the cell, if the prisoner was lucky enough to saw through the iron bars over the windows. Another historical inaccuracy of the dungeon is the posi-tion of the prisoners within the cell. One of the well-known scenes of the queue is that of the prisoners' skeletons seated at a chess board. Instead of allowing prisoners to move freely throughout the cell, their jailers would chain them to the walls, either by their wrists or thumbs, their feet not touching the ground. However, to add humor to the attraction and in order to maintain its family-friendly status, the Imagineers opted to place the skeletons at the famous, unwinnable chess board.

Upon "exiting" the fort, guests find themselves in a small port town through which a canal runs inland. Because the main form of transpor-tation of goods during the seventeenth and eighteenth centuries involved shipping, towns would be located along rivers, streams, and canals. When goods were produced, they would be put onto canal boats, called *bateaux* (French for "boats"; bateau is singular form, pronounced "bah-TOE"), and shipped toward the port, a small town located where the river meets the ocean. From there, the cargo would be unloaded from the smaller boat and onto a ship bound for the Americas, Europe, or other island colonies.

A bateau was a shallow, flat-bottomed boat that is pointed at both ends. By making the boat shallow and flat-bottomed, colonists were able to load heavy cargo into it. Bateaux could also carry between one and twenty men, depending on the size of the boat. The average size of the bateau was approximately six feet in width and forty-five to sixty feet long, with an approximate depth of three feet. Bateaux were moved either by the rowing of occupants or by floating slowly on the river's currents until anchored at a destination. Bateaux could also be used to carry travelers up- or down-river to explore, or, in the case of pirates, to maraud and terrorize.

Interestingly, the ride vehicles for the attraction are modified versions of bateaux. Comparing the historical bateau to the boats in Pirates of the Caribbean, we find many similarities and a few very minor differences. The ride vehicles are also shallow, flat-bottomed boats ending in a point at both ends. The ride vehicles are able to carry heavy loads of cargo (passengers). The ride vehicles are approximately six feet wide and are about thirty feet long, with a depth of about three feet. The ride vehicles also float with the current of the ride path. While historical bateaux could carry approximately twenty men, the ride vehicles can carry up to twenty-four passengers, with four passengers in each row.

Immediately prior to loading onto the ride vehicles, guests pass a cave, situated to their right. Guests can't see deep into the cave, but rather can see flickering torchlight and hear the sounds of someone digging in the sand for treasure. This is also somewhat accurate. While burying treasure was not as prevalent as treasure being sunken in ships, there are historical records of some pirates burying their treasure. One example is that of the Puerto Rican pirate, Roberto Cofresí, who, after giving a portion of his treasure to the needy of his village and spending a portion of his own share, buried the rest in caves for safe keeping until his return.

After boarding their bateaux ride vehicles, guests pass into a series of caves and then through a "waterfall" from which Davy Jones from *Pirates of the Caribbean: Dead Man's Chest* appears and warns the guests. Because the forts along the coasts of Spanish colonies were built high up on rocky cliffs, caves leading to underground rivers and harbors were real, but were a rare find.

"RUN UP YOUR WHITE FLAG, YOU SCURVY SCUM!": THE WICKED WENCH VS. EL CASTILLO

After exiting the series of caves and taking a spill down a waterfall in the pitch dark, guests find themselves in the midst of a battle between El Castillo del Morro and *the Wicked Wench*, a pirate frigate commanded by Captain Barbossa from the *Pirates of the Caribbean* films. As guests pass between the fort and the pirate ship, they find that the two are firing cannon balls at each other, and that not every cannon ball scores a hit on its desired target. Rather, many of the cannon balls fall into the harbor, splashing torrents of water into the air and splashing the bateaux and guests as they pass by. This scene presents, once again, both historical accuracies and inaccuracies.

The Wicked Wench is classified as a frigate. A frigate was a ship whose origins were in the Mediterranean during the late fifteenth century. Frigates were used often as both pirate ships and military ships, for a few different reasons. First, frigates were built long and shallow. This reduced the amount of drag, causing the ship to be more aerodynamic. The frigate had two modes of travel: the sails to catch wind and a system of oars for days without wind. Because these ships were shallow, they had only a few decks, used mainly for storing goods and as crew quarters. As a result, cannons would be placed on the upper and lower decks of the ship. Frigates usually carried between twenty and sixty cannons for broadside warfare, and were fired by command of the gunner, a sailor whose primary roles were maintaining the cannons and ordering those firing the cannons where and how to fire. When a breeze was absent, the cannons would be retracted from the cannon wells and oars would poke out of the wells to allow the sailors to propel the ship.

Because the attraction takes place inside a building, the Imagineers had to build a smaller, shorter frigate, while at the same time maintaining the illusion of the ship being full size. Known as forced perspective, and used in numerous locations throughout Walt Disney World, *the Wicked Wench* is modified to appear longer and taller than it really is. To achieve this optical illusion, the upper deck of the ship, masts, and sails of the ship are smaller to create the look of being higher than they truly are.

The Wicked Wench appears to have two main decks: the upper deck where Captain Barbossa is standing and a lower deck where most of the cannons and the captain's quarters are located. A crewman can be seen every few seconds peeking above the railing of the ship to aim his cannon at the fort. However, no other crewmen are seen on the ship. This is not uncommon, since the rest of the crewmen are supposedly below deck firing the cannons at El Castillo. However, one inaccuracy is the role that Barbossa is playing. Those who have seen the *Pirates* films know that Barbossa is the captain of the ship. In the attraction, Barbossa is seen giving orders to those firing the cannons. Historically, the captain did not give such orders; doing so was the role of the gunner, who is not seen or heard on the ship in this scene.

The fort that *the Wicked Wench* is firing upon is, similar to the show building itself, based upon El Castillo de San Juan del Morro. The real fort is perched upon a rocky cliff, known as a morro, or promontory, on the edge of San Juan Bay, guarding the entrance to the harbor and town, as well as controlling who enters the area. Across the bay from El Castillo is a smaller fort, El Cañuelo. Throughout the years, many additions have been made to El Castillo, including a lighthouse. The walls have been reinforced multiple times; at one point, the walls were up to eighteen feet thick. Along the top of the wall are garitas, or dome-covered boxes where sentries would be stationed, watching the harbor and repelling invaders. Also along the top of the wall in different areas was a walkway dominated by cannons and piles of artillery where soldiers could attack invaders in the harbor from above.

The fort in the battle scene also has some historical accuracies and inaccuracies. Similar to the Wicked Wench, the fort was built in forced perspective to create the illusion of size and height in an area of limited space. While the blocks of the fort may be full size near the water level, the blocks get slightly smaller as they get higher to make the fort look taller than it really is. Another inaccuracy is the fact that the attraction version of El Castillo del Morro is not perched on a rocky cliff like the one in Puerto Rico. Rather, the fort is flush with the water, and in different parts, rests on a sandy beachhead. Also, while there are recessed windows on the fort from which cannons fire at the Wicked Wench, there are no soldiers seen, nor are there any cannons fired from the top of the fort's wall where, in the real Castillo de San Juan del Morro, there are many. One accuracy, however, is that there is a smaller fort across the waterway from El Castillo del Morro. While very little of this fort can be seen in the twilight of the attraction, it is possible that this smaller fort may represent El Cañuelo. However, once the guests' bateaux pass the forts, they do not sail into San Juan Harbor, but rather find themselves immediately in the center of town.

The scene as a whole presents some inaccuracies. First of all, pirates generally did not attack an opposing ship or fort unless they had the upper hand and were not outgunned. Pirates only fought if the battle was worth the risk of casualties and damage to the ship. A pirate frigate, in other words, would not attack a fort or ship for the sake of attacking. Therefore, since the Wicked Wench is significantly smaller and outgunned in relation to El Castillo del Morro, the altercation seems unlikely.

Another inaccuracy is that the *Wicked Wench* is attacking El Castillo from a broadside stance. Pirates would steer their ships in from an angle to minimize their size as a target for the enemy. The more of the ship that is visible to the enemy, the larger the target and the greater the chance for a direct hit. Thus, if a ship had its entire broadside exposed to the enemy, as in the battle scene between El Castillo del Morro and the *Wicked Wench*, the ship would not likely last very long. By turning the ship at an angle, or by approaching the enemy from an angle, it would severely minimize the chances for a direct hit. Notice that the cannons in El Castillo's window wells do not have much room to move horizontally. If the *Wicked Wench* had attacked from an angle or the side, the available artillery able to attack the ship would be greatly reduced. However, for the sake of saving space in the attraction, and the ability for guests to be in the midst of the battle, El Castillo del Morro and the *Wicked Wench* were placed opposite each other.

"PIPE THE LUBBER ALOFT": TORTURING THE MAYOR

Once guests in their bateaux pass El Castillo del Morro, they find themselves in the midst of an interrogation by a band of pirates attempting to torture information out of Carlos, the town mayor. Poor Carlos is tied up and dunked in the well, while other townsmen are awaiting their turn, frightened. After a few seconds of leaving the mayor underwater deep in the well, the leader of the attack party tells another pirate to "Pipe the lubber aloft" and Carlos is hoisted out of the well, where he spits out a small stream of water and refuses to respond to the pirates' orders to tell them where the town's treasure and Jack Sparrow are hidden. Carlos' wife pokes her head out of the window above the well, encouraging him to not tell the pirate. "Don't be chicken!" she yells to her soaked husband before he is plunged deep into the well once again.

This scene can be looked at as either historically accurate or inaccurate, depending on what diaries and records you read. While pirates are usually portrayed as being ruthless, marauding, destructive, terrorizing menaces, and some historical records reinforce this view, there are also records of pirate crews being respectable and courteous to townspeople, merely participating in acts of thievery to sustain their livelihoods.

There were many different methods pirates employed to get what they wanted from prisoners. One form of torture was to withhold food and comfort from prisoners. For example, if a captain wanted information from a prisoner, he might withhold food from that prisoner or force him to stay awake until the captain was able to get the information he wanted. Pirates were also known to maim, torture, and kill prisoners out of pleasure.

Various records and historians have attributed this radical and arbitrary violence to the fact that many pirates had extreme bouts of fury and a lack of self-control. One theory for this violence and anger is that the pirates were isolated on islands and ships for long periods of time, and as a result, had to get rid of pent-up anger and emotions, thus behaving, as one historian has labeled, like a "caged tiger." The theory goes on to explain that due to pirates having very little contact with "normal" humanity, they were severed from humanizing attachments and social conventions, and so acted ruthlessly and violently.

Another hypothesis for pirates' violent behavior is that they were simply seeking revenge on the colonists for wrongs administered by the colonists to the natives and refugees previously living on the islands. Before European colonizers settled on the islands, some of the islands were inhabited by native peoples. Prior to the age of piracy, activities occurred in the Caribbean known as privateering, which was basically legalized piracy encouraged by one European nation against another. When privateering was made illegal, many of these men decided to settle on parts of the islands not inhabited by colonists, alongside the native peoples. Over time, these ex-privateers learned to live alongside the natives, adapting their lifestyles as their own, receiving the name "buccaneers," which is French for "someone who makes smoke" (buccaneers smoked the meat they hunted before eating it). However, similar to those in the United States, many of the colonists in the Caribbean colonies decided to expand their territories, thus pushing the natives and buccaneers off their land and torturing any who refused to comply. The theory is that, furious about the awful treatment inflicted upon themselves and their native friends, the buccaneers took to the seas and began to terrorize the colonies and the people living in them in fits of revenge.

Historical records and journals also discuss that some pirate crews had the tendency to be benevolent to their prisoners. Many ships sailed under a series of rules or oaths, similar to a constitution, dictating what the crew could and could not do, as well as what the punishments for different trespasses would entail. These lists of rules were called Articles. Take, for example, the Articles for the crew that sailed aboard the *Mars*. Records indicate that these pirates were courteous to colonial citizens "as if they were Spanish." Pirates also shared their spoils of treasure with those whom they deemed needy, similar to a Robin Hood role. After a prisoner had been captured, it was accepted practice that the prisoner be given the chance to escape imprisonment. Also, prisoners would not be tortured or punished unless they put up a fight, leaving a prisoner's fate in their own hands. The Articles for the *Mars* dictate that "if any [crewmen] ... do assault, strike, or insult any male prisoner, or behave rudely or indecently to any female prisoner, he or they shall be punished." The crew of the *Mars* was expected to hold "certain operative principles of equity, justice, and protection." Also, "if at any time [a pirate of the *Mars* crew] meet with a prudent woman, that man that offers to meddle with her, without her consent, shall suffer death." Thus, the pirates that sailed on the *Mars* realized the value in respecting and sustaining their prisoners and the people they came into contact with, either for morality or for strategic reasons.

One major inaccuracy in the Pirates attraction is that the captain—in this case, Barbossa—is absent from this scene. This is a problem because pirate captains usually led boarding or attack parties, yet Barbossa is never seen throughout the attraction except in the battle scene between El Castillo del Morro and the *Wicked Wench*. Since this scene is closest to the harbor and is immediately after the battle scene, we can assume that this group of pirates is the first to arrive in the town and is thus the first boarding/attack party. The pirate giving orders to the man holding the rope is not Barbossa, and so we can assume that he is not the captain, which makes the scene itself historically inaccurate.

So is the scene of the pirates dunking Carlos the mayor historically accurate or not? It depends on what the Articles of the *Wicked Wench* state about the use of torture. Since guests have no way of knowing, it is up to them to decide.

"WHAT BE I OFFERED FOR THIS WINSOME WENCH?" AUCTIONING BRIDES

After guests in their bateaux exit the Carlos scene, they find themselves in the midst of an auction led by a pirate known affectionately to Disney aficionados as The Auctioneer. Standing before the Auctioneer is a line of homely looking women and a buxom redhead, all being auctioned off to prospective buyers seated across the canal. A makeshift banner hangs on a nearby building, reading "Wench-for-a-Bride." When the Auctioneer asks the buyers what they would like to pay for the redhead, they offer him rum, but he explains that "I'm not spongin' for rum; it be gold I'm after!"

While it is not likely that pirates received women by being the highest bidders in a twisted auction (this scene was added to bring humor to the attraction), "Wench-for-a-Bride" may be more accurate than you think. Pirate crews were usually made up completely of men, who were confined to islands and ships at sea for long periods of time. As a result, when they came across women, especially in cases where they had control of the situation, many of them took advantage of their prisoners. If a woman failed to submit to the will of her captor, the kidnapper might employ various techniques to bend the woman to his will. Some of these techniques included torture and starvation; by depriving the prisoner of food for long periods of time and promising them food once they gave in, many of the pirates were able to get what they wanted. Another way that pirates were able to persuade the women to submit to their wills was by fooling them into believing that the pirates were courteous and polite men, which ended in the women being taken advantage of when their guards were down.

However, there were some crews, such as that of the *Mars*, whose ship Articles forbade the men from meddling with the women of the towns. But the chances of crews such as the one on the *Mars* having Articles that forbade "meddling … with prudent women" were low. In fact, more than likely, if a crew had Articles similar to that of the *Mars*, the rule was probably not well enforced and likely ignored. Also, if there were too many rules that went against the men's natural instincts and desires, there was a strong chance that the captain of that crew would be mutinied against and killed.

A strong inaccuracy in this scene is that of who the Auctioneer is, or rather, is not. Generally, the leaders of a boarding or attack party got the first chance at captured booty, whether jewels, gold, prisoners, or women. Since the Auctioneer is not the same pirate who was seen torturing Carlos, one can assume that the Auctioneer is not the leader of the attack party. Also, since neither the Auctioneer nor the pirate torturing the mayor are Barbossa, we know that neither of them are the captain of the *Wicked Wench*. As a result, the Auctioneer is inaccurate; since the captain of a ship was more than likely the leader of the attack party, Barbossa should be getting first pick of the women, in particular, the Redhead, as well as the spoils from auctioning them off.

REVENGE OF THE TOWNSPEOPLE

As the bateau winds its way through the town, guests come upon a scene showing the pirates getting desperate. Things are obviously not going as well as the marauders had hoped, and worse, the townspeople are beginning to fight back. A pirate runs through a doorway, chasing a chicken. Another is being chased by an angry woman wielding a rolling pin as a weapon. Other pirates are worn out from trying to get what they want; one pirate is seen leaning up against a barrel, talking to himself and the passing guests about the treasure map he has, vowing that Jack Sparrow won't be able to find the treasure unless he sees the map. Unbeknownst to him, however, Jack is seen poking his head out of the barrel, looking over the map. Another pirate is seen offering some of his rum to feral cats.

Treasure such as gold and jewels were not the only things plundered in town. Invaders also took advantage of whatever animals, food, and drink they could get their hands on. Crews could be on the seas or on an island for weeks at a time, and during this period, food and drink ran low or began to rot. As a result, when they plundered a town, they took advantage of the supplies there, helping themselves to food and drink. Also, while onboard the ship or while at port on their 'home island,' food and drink was rationed among the crew. Pillaging a town allowed for excessive eating and drinking, with no one telling the pirates how much they were allowed to eat or drink. Because the pirates weren't recognized as belonging to a specific nation, they felt entitled to pursue enjoyment in whatever fashion they pleased against any people they encountered whenever they wanted.

Pillaging crews not only took advantage of food and drink, they also captured livestock to bring back to their ships, hence the pirate chasing the chicken. By bringing livestock back onto the ship, the crews were able to keep the meat fresher longer because it was alive. Cows could provide milk for the pirates to drink, and chickens provided eggs to eat. Pirates also captured small animals, such as cats and dogs. Cats were often used to patrol the ships, catching and killing mice. This may be the reason that Bill, the drunken pirate talking to the cats, may be acting kindly to the cats; it is possible he is trying to reassure them of his kindness and then capture them when their guard was down. It is also possible that Imagineers included this scene to simply show that Bill is completely inebriated, to the point where he is carrying on full conversations with animals.

It is not likely that villagers would fight back in the way it is portrayed in this scene. Only women are shown fighting back, and this is even more unlikely, because strong women wouldn't have gotten a chance to chase a pirate, but rather would have been captured quickly because they were seen as useful and attractive to pirate crews. Also, at this point in the attraction, the pirates are starting to set the town on fire. Rather than fighting the pirates, townspeople, especially women, would have gotten their families and valuables together and tried to make their escape before the town burned to the ground around them or they were captured by the pirate crews.

If fighting back *did* occur, however, soldiers would have led the charge. Because islands in the Caribbean during the seventeenth and eighteenth centuries were owned by European powers, they were run by a governor who was appointed by the king or ruler of the homeland, with the law enforced by that country's soldiers. These soldiers would be the ones to defend a colony in the case of an attack by an opposing nation or a pirate crew; the pillaged goods were property of the king and were counted as a loss to the nation that owned the colony. However, not a single soldier is seen fighting the pirate crew. We know that there *are* soldiers in the town, because we saw the cannons of El Castillo firing at the *Wicked Wench*, and only soldiers would have fought in a fort, not townspeople, but we do not see a single soldier in any of the other scenes, including the scene of the women fighting the pillaging pirates.

"DRINK UP, ME HEARTIES, YO HO!"
DRUNK AND CLUELESS

Immediately after passing Bill, the pirate offering to share his rum with the cats, guests in their ride vehicle bateaux find themselves in the midst of a burning portion of the town, while a number of pirates are acting foolishly, too drunk to notice that their lives could quickly come to a fiery end. To their left are a trio of pirate minstrels singing the theme song of the attraction, "Yo Ho, Yo Ho, A Pirate's Life for Me," with a donkey and dog howling along to the music. Other pirates are in the scene, arms around each other, singing along with the music. A greedy marauder has one foot on stable ground and another in a rowboat, trying to make his escape while balancing a tall tower of hats in his arms. To the right of the canal is a pirate who has fallen asleep in a pile of pigs, while another pirate swings his stein in rhythm with the music, hanging his hairy leg over the edge of the bridge he is sitting on. All of this is occurring while the city is aflame. In fact, the flames are so realistic that when the attraction opened in Disneyland in 1967, guests thought that the show building really was on fire.

The burning of towns after looting occurred frequently. After a town was pillaged and prisoners were taken, invaders sometimes set the town on fire to add insult to injury. Also, by setting the town on fire, villagers were more occupied with trying to put the fire out than fighting back at the pirates and trying to recover their possessions.

Setting a town on fire and destroying it in its entirety was not as difficult during the seventeenth and eighteenth centuries as it may seem. Most buildings in Spanish colonies during the 1600s and 1700s were made of stucco-coated bricks and clay walls. Red clay tiles were generally reserved for the roofs of the wealthy, while commoners had roofs made of straw or palm fronds. As a result, fires spread easily and were fed by a number of factors. The straw or palm frond roofing and timber rafters fed the flames, while the brick and mud walls contained and magnified the heat of the infernos, making the fire even more difficult to put out; the high temperatures also sustained the flames for a longer period of time. Also, as the roofing and timbers burned, they created glowing pieces of ash and sparks that floated into the air and landed on nearby buildings, causing them to burst into flame. Because the modern fire department as we know it did not come into being until the 1730s (founded by Benjamin Franklin), the best that colonial citizens could do to fight the flames was to fill small buckets with water and throw them on the tongues of fire. This did little to quell the blaze. Interestingly, the town of San Juan, Puerto Rico, which was guarded by the real Castillo de San Felipe del Morro, was actually set on fire and destroyed by Dutch invaders in 1625.

Drunken pirates were also a likely reality. Rum, beer, and other types of alcohol were very prevalent on ships during the seventeen and eighteenth century, including pirate ships. Fresh water aboard ships was rationed to about one quart a day. However, because water in hot, humid climates had a tendency to go bad, was not necessarily purified like the water we enjoy today, and because crews could go days without setting foot on land, something was needed to help purify the water and prevent it from becoming stale. Alcohol not only added flavor to the water, it also killed bacteria and allowed the water to last longer. As a result, pirates during the seventeenth and eighteenth centuries either made rum and beer their drinks of choice, or added it to water, meaning that every drink they took increased their blood alcohol content. The hotter the weather was and the more strenuous the work they performed, the thirstier they got, and the drunker they became.

Because they had so little and had no self-control, pirate crews were prone to participating in wasteful activities or using in excess. This was magnified when men were inebriated, as the tendency to being able to control one's actions decreases the more intoxicated one becomes. Pirate crews risked their lives to plunder a town, and quickly spent and wasted anything they had stolen, with very little hesitation in protecting their own lives. Similar to a young boy who has received money, pirates spent and used everything they had the second they got it. This is evident in this scene of the attraction. The rowdy and drunken pirate crew is seen singing their song and sleeping with pigs while the city burns down around them.

THE TOWN TREASURY

After drifting out of the burning town and past a series of jail cells where pirates are trying to convince a dog to bring them the keys to escape, guests in their bateaux pass one final scene. To the left of the canal, guests find themselves within the room holding the treasures of the town. Glistening jewels sparkle around the room, while Jack Sparrow sits on a chair at the center of the vault, singing the attraction's theme song, decked out in treasure. Sparrow is the only pirate present in this scene, which leads to the assumption that he has found the treasury alone and wants to hoard the booty for himself. This scene could allow guests to assume that the attraction precedes the first film, *Pirates of the Caribbean: Curse of the Black Pearl*, where we learn that Jack Sparrow was mutinied on the *Black Pearl* and stranded on an island with nothing but a pistol containing a single shot. Could it be that he was mutinied because he refused to share this found treasure with his crew?

The island colonies owned by Spain during the seventeenth and eighteenth centuries were known as the Spanish Main. This chain of islands was where riches and wealth from the New World were kept while ships were in port to protect the riches from being stolen by pirates. Pirate booty and colonial valuables, during the seventeenth and eighteenth centuries, was not only jewelry, gold, and precious gems. Valuables that were found in the Caribbean and transported on merchant ships included spices, coffee, sugar cane, textiles, cocoa, exotic animals, and slaves. In fact, the transportation of exotic animals may be how the parrot came to be associated with pirates; the parrot was an exotic animal, coveted by the wealthy of Europe as an addition to animal menageries. By owning a parrot, a pirate could ascribe to being "upper class."

Each pirate on a crew that acquired treasure, whether from another ship or a colonial town treasury, received a share of the booty. The captain of the ship received a share-and-a-half of the booty, simply because he was the one in charge of the expedition. Interestingly, if a crewman was injured in battle where treasure was involved, that pirate received a "bonus" share of the booty; for example, a pirate who lost a limb received four hundred pieces of eight, whereas a crewman that lost an eye might receive eight hundred pieces of eight. However, since an injured pirate served more as a hindrance to a crew, rather than a help, he was likely killed and his share of the treasure absorbed by the rest of the crew.

While many colonial towns likely had treasuries where the town's wealth was stored, guests don't see an accurate representation of pirate booty in the treasury. The shelves of the vault are lined with precious gems and gold, whereas Jack Sparrow is wearing priceless jewelry and holding a golden goblet. Nowhere in the room is there evidence of spices, coffee, textiles, cocoa, or exotic animals.

African slaves were also a high commodity in the New World during the seventeenth and eighteenth century, but not a single black pirate or townsperson is seen throughout the attraction. It was accepted practice during the 1600s and 1700s in Europe, the Americas, and the Caribbean colonies for white people to own African slaves. Yet there is no evidence of this in the attraction, most likely to avoid controversy. Around the same time that the Pirates attraction opened in Disneyland, a number of race riots were occurring throughout the nation, including in Detroit and Atlanta. By the time the Walt Disney World version of the attraction opened in 1973, the civil rights movement was less active, yet many of the events from the past fifteen years still rang in the memories of many Americans. In other words, portraying blacks as slaves throughout the attraction would have been in bad taste.

Because of the choices made by the Imagineers in what to display in the treasure room, this scene can be considered historically inaccurate. There is no presence of any of the riches that were considered valuables of the time. In fact, what Americans take for granted today, such as cocoa, coffee, textiles, and sugar cane, were considered more valuable during the 1600s and 1700s than gold or precious jewels, but none of these are present in the town's treasure room.

PIRATE LIFESTYLE

There are numerous aspects of the attraction that are consistent through-out the ride, such as the vocabulary used by the pirates, also known as their lexicon, and the pirate wardrobe. The words and phrases that the pirates are heard speaking throughout the attraction, as well as the extensive clothing and jewelry they are wearing, are actually historically accurate, and not necessarily something of legend.

The pirate lexicon is one of the things that are best known about pirates. In fact, "Talk Like a Pirate Day" has become an unofficial holiday in the United States, setting aside an entire day where people can speak the fabled vocabulary in the gravelly voice of a pirate captain, using the words "aye" and "matey" at the end of every sentence.

Along with being morally rebellious, pirates were linguistically rebel-lious, as well. One reason that pirates spoke a distinct set of vocabulary may be because many of them regularly visited island colonies in the Caribbean owned by different European nations, picking up vocabulary from each respective language they encountered. For example, Spain owned Cuba, Puerto Rico, and the Dominican Republic, while France owned Haiti, the Dutch owned Aruba, and England owned Jamaica. As a result, pirate lingo is made up of a mixture of English, Dutch, French, and Spanish words, as well as conglomerations of words in different languages and shortened versions of the words. Creole and slave language also played a role in creating the distinct vocabulary of pirate society during the seventeenth and eighteenth centuries.

Another reason that pirate language is so distinct is because they spent so much time separated from the rest of society, either on a ship or on different islands. As a result, they were not up to speed on the changing vocabularies of the colonies, dating their lexicon. Also, keep in mind that crewmen were once a part of English, Spanish, French, or Dutch societies, and so they had accents much different than we have or are used today.

Superstitions and religious vocabulary also made up the lexicon of pirate crews. Because many pirates were ex-governmental sailors or privateers, they had spent a greater part of their lives at sea. Sailors had a tendency to be extremely superstitious. Religion was also a common part of life during the 1600s and 1700s.

The vocabulary that is used throughout the Pirates attraction consists of actual words and phrases used by real pirates. For example, Barbossa calls the crew of the *Wicked Wench* "bilge rats" in the battle scene; a bilge rat, also known as a "bilgy," was a man who was forced to operate the bilge pumps at the bottom of the ships as a punishment. Barbossa also calls his crew "scurvy scum." Scurvy was a disease prominent on shipping crews during the seventeenth and eighteenth centuries that was caused by a Vitamin C deficiency. This was a common disease because of a lack of fruit on the ships, and caused spotting on the skin, bleeding, lethargy, and eventually, death. It is possible that Barbossa's crew, having been without fruit and Vitamin C for a long period of time, had contracted scurvy. A third example of a word used regularly by pirate crews is "hearties," which is heard numerous times in the attraction's theme song. A hearty was simply a friend, mate, or associate.

Pirates are also known for dressing flamboyantly, with triple-pointed hats, long coats, belts, tattoos, and jewelry. They are also portrayed as having peg-legs, hooks as hands, and eye patches. While it is possible that some pirates may have worn an eye patch, it was likely that the only ones that did so were those that required it after losing an eye in battle or an accident. The use of a peg leg is unlikely, and was probably made popular by Robert Louis Stevenson's *Treasure Island*, whereas the hook hand was popularized by Captain Hook in J.M. Barrie's novel, *Peter Pan*.

Pirates got their clothing from the colonies and towns that they sacked. This clothing could either be English, French, Dutch, Spanish, or even that of slaves. Clothing was acquired through sacking homes, ships, or even taken off dead bodies after a battle. Because clothing has a tendency to wear out quicker in a hotter, more humid climate, it was needed more often. Also, while fashion in the seventeenth and eighteenth centuries was much different than it is today, much of what was stolen was likely mismatched.

The use of golden jewelry by pirates, including earrings, is quite accurate. Earrings had a few different uses for a pirate. The first reason was simply to show off that they had acquired wealth. Jewelry during this time period was made out of gold, not plastic or painted metal. As a result, if a pirate had acquired wealth via pillaging or winning it in battle, he displayed it by wearing it on his earlobe. Another reason pirates wore earrings was for superstitious reasons. It was believed that by wearing an earring, one could prevent drowning. If a crewman was killed during battle or following an illness, it was also believed that a golden earring would send his soul into the afterlife.

* * *

Walt Disney was a master storyteller, whether it was in animation, live-action films, or theme park attractions. His philosophy toward creating a great story has been passed down through the company to present day script writers, animators, Imagineers, and theme park Cast Members. When a guest enters a Disney theme park, they are bombarded with sights, sounds, and even smells that help weave the intricate story that the Imagineers want them to believe. This is no different in one of the classic Disney attractions that have been around for almost fifty years, *Pirates of the Caribbean*. Before even getting on the ride vehicle, guests are immersed in the story by the architecture of the show building, the dankness of the fort's interior, the design of the ride vehicles, the language used by the pirates, the details of the scenes, and even the salty smell of the air within the attraction. While this attraction was inspired by the pirate lore created by J.M. Barrie and Robert Louis Stevenson, including the films Disney created during the 1950s and 1960s based on those novels, many of the details throughout the attraction are historically accurate, allowing guests to learn something interesting during their vacation at Walt Disney World.

Part Three
TOMORROWLAND

*W*hen Walt Disney began to envision Disneyland, he introduced his plans to the American public using a new forum for entertainment and education: television. As a means to acquire funding to help pay for his theme park, the television anthology series *Disneyland* first aired on ABC on October 27, 1954. The first episode of the television series, "The Disneyland Story," educated the public on what Disneyland was going to be. Each week, *Disneyland* would focus on one of four themes: Adventureland, Frontierland, Fantasyland, or Tomorrowland. Adventureland featured episodes that focused on nature, similar to Disney's *True-Life Adventures*; Frontierland featured episodes with stories of American history or the Old West, such as the extremely popular *Davy Crockett* series; Fantasyland episodes sometimes re-released films on television that had previously come from theaters (such as *Alice in Wonderland*), but also focused on the progress being made at Disneyland park; and Tomorrowland episodes, while few and far between, focused on the strides being made in space exploration and the science of rockets.

Because the *Disneyland* television show and the Disneyland park began in the mid-1950s, the theme of Tomorrowland was very different than it is today. The 1950s was the beginning of American space exploration, with the start of the Space Race between 1955–57, when the United States and the Soviet Union competed to launch the first man-made space satellite (the Soviet Union was successful, with its launch of *Sputnik I*). As a result, episodes focusing on the theme of Tomorrowland tended to educate the public on rocket propulsion systems, as well as what a trip to the moon or Mars would be like. These episodes were often fanciful, as manned space travel would not occur until 1961, when both the Soviet Union and America launched men into orbit. The first manned trip to the moon would not occur until 1969, and man has still not arrived on Mars, though we are working on the technology to achieve that milestone.

When Disneyland opened in 1955, many of the rides and attractions reflected the science and technology of the Atomic Age and the early Space Race. Space exploration and atomic energy were part of the science of the time, and both held enormous potential. As a result, rides and attractions imagined the future utilizing these technologies. Because Disneyland was so expensive to build and maintain, Disney needed sponsors for its attractions, a practice that is still seen, though rarely, at Walt Disney World. For example, when Tomorrowland opened in 1955, chemical company Monsanto sponsored a House of the Future, showing guests what living might be like in the decades ahead, specifically through the use of a new material, plastic. Another popular attraction on Disneyland's opening day was Autopia, which allowed guests to drive their own vehicles. In 1959, a new ride opened based on atomic technology, Submarine Voyage, which also found its way to Disney World's Fantaslyand, albeit with some changes, in 20,000 Leagues Under the Sea.

When Walt Disney World's Magic Kingdom opened in 1971, space exploration was still a fairly new concept, and as a result, the land's rides and attractions were still fairly concrete in terms of focus. Rather than the fantastic theming of Tomorrowland that we have had since 1994, Tomorrowland focused on the science and technology of the time.

CHAPTER SIX

TOMORROWLAND

A HISTORY OF THE FUTURE

*T*n this chapter, I'll look at two very distinct versions of Tomorrowland: the original themed land, or "Old Tomorrowland," and the strikingly new version that came after.

OLD TOMORROWLAND: 1971–1993

The Magic Kingdom's first Tomorrowland was extremely sterile, focusing on science such as space exploration. However, when the park opened on October 1, 1971, Tomorrowland was incomplete; the only two attractions available to guests on opening day were the Grand Prix Raceway and the Skyway to Fantasyland. The Grand Prix was similar to Disneyland's Autopia, allowing guests to drive their own go-cart along a metal rail. The Skyway to Fantasyland was an attraction with two loading points, Tomorrowland and Fantasyland, where guests boarded a bucket and rode to the other side of the park suspended from a wire, giving guests an aerial view.

The land itself on opening day was very different than it is today, as well. Everything looked very plain and white; upon approaching Tomorrowland from the Hub, guests were greeted by two tall, white spires on either side of the bridge, with waterfalls cascading near the spires. The track of the PeopleMover was suspended above the attrac-

tions on either side of the walkway, but was incomplete. The center of
Tomorrowland, where Rocket Tower Plaza stands today, was not yet built,
and Space Mountain would not emerge until 1975.

Two new attractions opened during late 1971: *America the Beautiful* in
November (located on the right) and Flight to the Moon on Christmas Eve
(across from *America the Beautiful* on the left). During the 1950s, Disney
refined technology for a film process known as CircleVision 360. This
allowed for nine cameras to shoot film concurrently and then be played
back on nine different screens in a circular theater, creating the illusion
that viewers are surrounded by the action from all sides. In 1955, Disney
filmed *America the Beautiful*, which opened in Disneyland in 1960 and
closed in 1984. The show also opened at the Magic Kingdom in November
1971; however, the show was much more short-lived in Florida than in
California, closing in 1974. A new show called *Magic Carpet 'Round the World*
replaced *America the Beautiful*, but it only lasted until 1975. After that, the
theater sat empty for almost ten years, when it was finally replaced by the
CircleVision show, *American Journeys*, which would last until 1994.

Flight to the Moon, which became Mission to Mars on June 7, 1975 (due
to the fact that voyages to the moon were no longer futuristic), seemed
to transport guests to outer space through a multi-sensory experience
while sitting in a theater. Guests entered the show building, where they
went through a series of different scenes setting up the attraction. One of
the first scenes involved guests looking through the window of Mission
Control while a scientist narrated the process of sending a manned space
rocket to the moon, and later, Mars. After the pre-show featuring the
Audio-Animatronics scientists at the Mission Control terminals, guests
walked into the main room of the attraction, where they chose a seat in a
tiered, circular room, at the center of which were two screens, one in the
ceiling and the other in the floor; other screens lined the perimeter of
the room on the walls. The attraction simulated a flight to the moon, and

later, to Mars, as images of outer space flickered by on the screens and the seats of the theater vibrated and moved.

In June 1972, a new attraction was added to Tomorrowland in the south building, the same building as housed *America the Beautiful*. If You Had Wings utilized similar ride vehicle technology as the Haunted Mansion, called the OmniMover. This technology, developed by Imagineer Roger Broggie and Bert Brundage, was a ride system that was continuously moving and rotated to allow the guests to see what Imagineers wanted them to see. The attraction educated guests on the various destinations they could travel to courtesy of the attraction's sponsor, Eastern Airlines. Interestingly, the attraction utilized video screen technology to show different destinations, including Mexico, Bermuda, and the Bahamas. Large dioramas surrounded the ride track, and video screens showed people dancing or displaying their cultural heritage. Many Disney fans today argue against the usage of video screens on attractions, but fail to realize that one of the more popular attractions of old Tomorrowland utilized this technology. When Eastern Airlines' sponsorship ran out in 1987, the attraction was renamed If You Could Fly and the popular theme song of the original attraction was also replaced.

In 1973, Imagineers finally had a vision for Tomorrowland, and spent the next two years constructing new attractions and themed areas for the land, focused on space exploration, as the Apollo missions of the 1970s were extremely popular. The Space Race, which was coming to a close during the early 1970s, created an interest in many young boys to become astronauts. Similar to the Dumbo attraction in Fantasyland, the Star Jets spun around central Tomorrowland, above the Space Bar. The Star Jets circled eighty feet above the ground around a Saturn V rocket, allowing guests to board one of twelve open-air rockets. A joystick in the rocket allowed guests to control the altitude of their rocket during the ninety-second flight.

On January 15, 1975, two new attractions opened to complete Tomorrowland. The Carousel of Progress, which had been open to guests in Disneyland since being shipped back to California after the New York World's Fair in 1965, was packed up in 1974 to make way for a new show in preparation for America's Bicentennial. The attraction, America Sings, utilized the same rotating theater technology as the Carousel of Progress; because of the popularity and historical significance of the Carousel of Progress to Disney history, Imagineers decided to pack the attraction up and move it to Florida to round out the Magic Kingdom's Tomorrowland. The show, still sponsored by General Electric, went through a script change, and got a new theme song. While General Electric had asked Richard and Robert Sherman to create a song for the 1964 New York World's Fair to prepare possible consumers for the innovations of the future, in 1975 General Electric wanted guests to purchase their electric appliances *today*, prompting the song "The Best Time of Your Life," which lasted until the refurbishment of the attraction in 1993.

The second attraction that opened in January 1975, Space Mountain, was sponsored by RCA. One of the challenges in building Space Mountain was that of fitting the attraction within the park. There was not enough room for the large indoor roller coaster to fit inside the confines of Disney World, and as a result, the building needed to be outside the boundaries of the park, and thus, guests needed to get to the other side of the railroad tracks. The solution to this problem was a tunnel that sloped under the railroad tracks and back up into the show building once past the tracks. Rather than leaving this area unthemed, Imagineers designed the tunnel to make riders feel as though they were in a station in outer space. Guests could look out windows to see meteors flash by, see astronauts working on a space station, and rockets fly past the windows. This was accomplished using mirrors and holographic technology.

The roller coaster itself utilized holograms and projections on the inside of the large, conical, white metal mountain to create the illusion that guests were hurtling through outer space; galaxies, stars, and asteroids flew across the night sky as guests wound and whipped through the building in toboggan-style roller coaster cars fitted out with glow-in-the-dark tape to allow for visitors to see the cars careen around the track. RCA's sponsorship ran out on Space Mountain in 1993; FedEx became the new sponsor, leading to an update of the post-show area.

In June 1975, Disney finally completed the tracks of the PeopleMover; these tracks were built into the second floors of the northern building, which housed Flight to the Moon/Mission to Mars, and the southern building, where the CircleVision shows were located. The WEDWay PeopleMover, which utilized linear induction motors to move the train of blue cars around the track (as opposed to the electromagnets that moved Disneyland's version of the ride), gave park guests a tour of Tomorrowland, taking riders through the second floor of various attractions, around the outside of the buildings, and through Space Mountain, creating a preview of sorts.

In 1989, If You Could Fly closed when a new sponsor was found for the outdated attraction. Delta Air Lines signed a deal with Disney to sponsor a new attraction where If You Could Fly was previously located, and on June 23, 1989, Delta Dreamflight opened to guests. This attraction used the same ride system and track as If You Had Wings/If You Could Fly, but eliminated most of the video screen. Instead, the attraction tried to make guests feel as though they were inside a pop-up storybook, showing a cartoonish history of flight, including scenes of barnstormers, hot air balloons, and jet planes. Delta's sponsorship of the ride lasted until December 31, 1995, when it became known simply as Dreamflight. The ride's name changed once again in June 1996, known as Take Flight, lasting until 1998, when it closed.

In 1993, Imagineers decided to refurbish and re-imagine Tomorrowland, creating a new theme for the land. This was because the theme of space flight had become stale, as expeditions into space were much more common and not as futuristic. Also, in 1982, EPCOT Center, Walt Disney World's second theme park, opened; the new park's theme was that of a permanent world's fair, exhibiting futuristic technologies, the history of different industries, and the cultures of different civilizations around the world. As a result, Disney decided that rather than using the Magic Kingdom's Tomorrowland as a display of the future to come, EPCOT Center would be a better forum for innovative ideas. This was partially because technology was moving so quickly that it was difficult for Tomorrowland to keep up with the new innovations. As a result, the land went through a complete re-imagining in 1993, reopening in 1994 with a new theme.

NEW TOMORROWLAND: 1994–PRESENT

In 1994, New Tomorrowland opened. Because it was difficult to Imagineers to keep up with the rapidly changing technology, park designers decided to theme the land around a future that never was and never would be. Taking inspiration from the stories of Jules Verne and H.G. Wells, the New Tomorrowland showed the future as one where humans, alien life forms, and robots co-existed.

In order to create a more immersive experience than what Tomorrowland evoked during the first two decades of its existence, Imagineers incorporated the attractions, restaurants, shops, and decorations into the overall story of the land. The spires and waterfalls were removed from the entrance, replaced with a sign featuring glass globes, pipes, and lasers, reminiscent of the UFOs of the 1950s and 1960s. The white and pastel color of the land was replaced by dark purple, blue, and red, and is lit by neon lights at night. The supports that held up the

track for the WEDWay PeopleMover, renamed the Tomorrowland Transit Authority, were fitted out with large bolts, gear teeth, and rivets, creating an almost steampunk look.

After crossing the bridge, guests find themselves on the Avenue of Planets, which utilize metallic structures and glass domes to create the illusion of a futuristic city. The show buildings on either side of the Avenue have taken on business-like themes; the north building (to the left) has become the Interplanetary Convention Center, and the southern building (to the right) has been given the name the Tomorrowland Metropolis Science Center, each with their own exhibitions displaying "new" technologies.

The Interplanetary Convention Center, according to the story of the attraction that was once located there, ExtraTERRORestrial Alien Encounter, has a temporary exhibit hosted by the technological transportation company, XS Tech. This clever company name could be seen as commentary on man's excessive use of technology, as XS Tech invites visitors to witness and experience their new teleportation technology. As guests sit in the circular exhibition space (previously used for Flight to the Moon/ Mission to Mars) to witness the technology being implemented, the wrong species is teleported into the theater, which happens to be a bloodthirsty alien. The creature escapes from the teleportation holding container and cuts the power, and thus, the lights to the room. Binaural audio, a special harness, and water spraying technology creates the illusion that the alien is stalking prey throughout the darkened room, oozing saliva on guests, breathing on their necks, and spraying the blood of its victims throughout the theater until, finally, it is teleported out of the room.

Across the Avenue of Planets, the Tomorrowland Metropolis Science Center became home to The Timekeeper, a show featuring a humanoid robot by the same name, voiced by the late Robin Williams. Using the CircleVision 360 technology from *America the Beautiful* and the subsequent CircleVision shows, the show followed the robotic Timekeeper as he sent one of his inventions, a floating robot named Nine-Eye (voiced by Rhea Perlman of *Cheers!* fame) who is lined with nine real-time cameras, throughout important events in history. The Timekeeper's main goal for his time machine is to be able to witness the Exposition Universelle of 1900 in Paris, specifically to witness the meeting between his two heroes, authors Jules Verne and H.G. Wells. The two authors get into an argument over the technology they describe in their novels, and Verne claims that time travel is impossible. Nine-Eye, the spunky robot, reveals herself to Verne, who, out of curiosity, grabs her and is transported into the 1990s to drive a race car, dive to the bottom of the sea in a submarine, fly in a hot air balloon, and orbit the earth on a spacewalk. The show contains brilliant dialogue, made entertaining through Williams' impersonations, and features a 360-degree view of various scenes, such as New York City, Calais, and Red Square.

Above the various buildings and exhibits of Tomorrowland was the Tomorrowland Transit Authority. The Tomorrowland Transit Authority added to the overall storyline of the land, becoming known as the Blue Line and Metro-Liner of transportation for the fictional city of Tomorrowland. While the Tomorrowland Transit Authority, also known as the TTA, still provided a tour of the land and a preview of the various attractions, thematic elements were added to the ride to add to the overall story of the area. While on the TTA, guests learned that there were two other transportation lines for the city; the Red Line provided transportation for citizens and visitors to other planets in the galaxy, while the Green Line provided transport to the Hover-Burbs, which were housing developments that hovered somewhere above the city, similar to the homes in *The Jetsons* television series. While driving through the different buildings of the land, different dioramas showed the importance of the Tomorrowland Transit Authority. One diorama displayed a hub of the

three lines, showing two robots loading onto the Red Line for interplanetary travel. Another scene showed a business that the Blue Line stopped
at, a futuristic hairdresser, where patrons simply placed a helmet on their
head, while a screen showed the machine cutting and styling the hair of
the stationary mannequin. The TTA also stopped by a window displaying
"Walt Disney's twentieth century vision of the future ... [a] model city
[that] dares to dream the perfect community in which to work, live, and
play" presented by the "Tomorrowland Metro-Retro Historical Society."
The model of this "model city" was actually a portion of the one that Walt
Disney had built for EPCOT Center before it was imagined as a theme
park after his death. The spiel of the attraction was narrated by voice
actor Peter Renaday, who also lent his voice to other Disney theme park
attractions, including Captain Nemo on 20,000 Leagues Under the Sea
and Henry the Bear on the Country Bear Jamboree.   .

The Tomorrowland Transit Authority went through another refurbishment in 2009, replacing the Renaday spiel with a new script, narrated by Mike Brassell, and replaced the fictional, futuristic theming
with a more tour-like script containing interjections by Mickey Mouse
and Stitch. The attraction was also renamed the Tomorrowland Transit
Authority PeopleMover.

The TTA loaded beneath a newly refurbished Astro Jets (renamed the
League of Planets Astro Orbiter). The Saturn V rocket was replaced with a
large tower, around which orbited a series of colorful planets encased in
metal rings. Similar in styling to the sign on the bridge welcoming guests
to Tomorrowland, the Astro Orbiter lit up at night with bright, colorful
neon lights as fantastical sci-fi silver rockets with green illuminated
lights spin around the central tower.

Other improvements were made to add to the overall theming of
Tomorrowland. For example, when General Electric's sponsorship
expired, the Carousel of Progress received an update with a new voice

cast, updates to the Animatronics, and a new final scene. The original theme song, "It's a Great Big Beautiful Tomorrow," was also restored to the show, replacing "The Best Time of Your Life." Space Mountain was updated, adding the Tomorrowland Arcade as the unloading point for the conveyor bringing guests back into the park under the railroad tracks. The arcade, becoming known as the Tomorrowland Light and Power Company, looks like an old-school power building, framed by industrial theming, including gears, corrugated metal walls, glass bubble windows, and electrical rods. Metal palm trees also emerged, creating the illusion that they caught sunbeams and stored energy; opaque glass coconuts hung from the metal fronds, turning from red to green in color, leading the viewer to believe that they collected sunlight. The energy was then transferred to lights that lined the trunk of the trees, illuminating the area. The Grand Prix Raceway was also rethemed, becoming the Tomorrowland Speedway. Other minor details added to the overall theming of the land, including a remote controlled, talking garbage can named Push and a stationary, robotic newspaper boy.

A new restaurant was added for the 1994 refurbishment as well. Cosmic Ray's Starlight Café, which sits on the border of Tomorrowland and Fantasyland across from the Tomorrowland Speedway, features three bays serving sandwiches, chicken, and other entrees. However, the main draw for many at Cosmic Ray's is the entertainment: an Animatronic alien lounge singer named Sonny Eclipse. Sonny Eclipse tells jokes and croons songs about the stars, intergalactic love, and the universe while playing on his Amazing Astro Organ, accompanied by the mysterious, invisible Space Angels. The show goes for about twenty minutes before it restarts, entertaining a multitude of guests as they eat their hamburgers and rotisserie chicken.

The shops throughout Tomorrowland also add to the overall theming. One of the main shops, Mickey's Star Traders, is meant to serve as a location for intergalactic trade and the role that Mickey Mouse plays in the merchant activity. Murals line the walls depicting Mickey as a rocket pilot, wearing flying goggles. Cityscapes of futuristic highway systems and hover trains help continue the story of Tomorrowland as a city for business, residency, and pleasure for its alien, robot, and human citizens. Astute observers will also notice that, on occasion, the Tomorrowland Transit Authority passes by overhead, allowing riders to see inside the store.

Other establishments in Tomorrowland include the Merchant of Venus, a clever play on words based on the Shakespearian play *The Merchant of Venice*, which also served as the unloading point for ExtraTERRORestrial Alien Encounter, and now for its successor, Stitch's Great Escape. Murals line the wall of various alien experiments by Stitch's creator, Dr. Jumba, from the film *Lilo and Stitch*. Stitch himself hangs upside down from the ceiling of the store, having shattered through the ceiling with a naughty look upon his face. Snack stands and small restaurants are also scattered throughout Tomorrowland, including Auntie Gravity's Galactic Goodies, serving ice cream sundaes and ice cream floats.

Throughout the 2000s, Tomorrowland has gone through various changes, many of which threaten the integrity of its theme. In 1998, inspired by the popularity of the first two *Toy Story* films and the cartoon television show *Buzz Lightyear of Star Command*, Disney introduced a new attraction, Buzz Lightyear's Space Ranger Spin, replacing Take Flight. The attraction, which utilizes infrared lasers, allows guests to shoot at targets and gain points, attempting to save Star Command's supply of batteries from the Evil Emperor Zurg.

Deemed to be too scary, the ExtraTERRORestrial Alien Encounter closed in October 2003 and was slightly modified with a new theme from *Lilo and Stitch*. The new attraction opened in 2004 as Stitch's Great Escape, under the pretense that guests are participating as prison guards in training. A new prisoner, which turns out to be Stitch, is teleported into the prison while the guests sit in the seats of the theater, held there by shoulder restraints. Stitch escapes from the prison tube and cuts the power to the theater, wreaking havoc. The technology of the attraction, including the binaural audio, shoulder harnesses, and water sprayers, all of which are similar to the previous attraction, create the illusion that Stitch is sniffing your hair, spitting on guests, and belching chili dogs into their faces. However, this attraction is controversial to some Disney fans who view it as nothing more than a watered-down version of ExtraTERRORestrial Alien Encounter.

Despite its quality, The Timekeeper was overlooked by many guests entering Tomorrowland from the Hub, who didn't notice its minimal signage. It became more expensive to keep open, and it entered seasonal status, open during the peak attendance times of the year. The Timekeeper closed indefinitely in February 2006, making way for the Monsters Inc. Laugh Floor, based on the popular Disney-Pixar film from 2001.

The Monsters Inc. Laugh Floor eliminated the CircleVision 360 format, the first time since 1971 that Tomorrowland has been without a CircleVision film. Instead, it utilized technology similar to the Epcot attraction Turtle Talk with Crush, which allowed digital characters on a screen to interact with guests in real-time through the use of cameras showing the audience to a voice actor behind the scenes. The attraction's premise is that the monsters of the Monstropolis power factory have discovered that laughter creates more power than the screams of children, and so, have decided to invite humans into the monster world to harvest laughter via a comedy club. Visitors are encouraged to text in Disney-appropriate jokes while standing in line for the attraction. The jokes are received by cast members and told by the digital monsters during the show.

* * *

As a result of the "Disneyfication" of the themed attractions of Tomorrowland, the overall theme of this area of the park has been compromised. Many frequent visitors feel that Stitch's Great Escape is a subpar attraction compared to its predecessor, and those who experienced The Timekeeper are disappointed by Monsters Inc. Laugh Floor, whose technology now seems dated and has limited re-rideability due to the same jokes often used across multiple shows. It will be interesting to see where the theming of Tomorrowland goes over the next several years, but many hope that the vision of the future will be restored, rather than the "invasion" of a once brilliantly themed land by Disney properties and film franchises.

CHAPTER SEVEN

WALT DISNEY'S CAROUSEL OF PROGRESS

A SCENE−BY−SCENE ANALYSIS

*T*was extremely hesitant to write this chapter for *A Historical Tour of Walt Disney World*. The Carousel of Progress is a fan favorite, appreciated much more by Disney fanatics, such as myself, than by the average park guest. This may be because of what the attraction means to Disney history: the literal and figurative influence of Walt Disney, the significance of the attraction to the creation of Walt Disney World and Audio-Animatronics, and an attraction that has stood the test of time. The introduction to the show informs that "the Carousel of Progress has had more performances than any other stage show in the history of American theater." As a result, many Disney fans revere the Carousel of Progress and hope that it does not change. Whenever changes or demolition are threatened, voices in the Disney fan community vow to go to the Magic Kingdom and chain themselves to the exterior of the building to prevent the destruction of their beloved attraction.

THE DEVELOPMENT OF WALT DISNEY'S CAROUSEL OF PROGRESS

Walt Disney's Carousel of Progress was initially developed as an attraction for the New York World's Fair, which occurred in Queens, New York, from April 22, 1964, through October 17, 1965. Prior to the fair, Walt

Disney was approached by four entities and asked to create attractions and pavilions for each. Each group approached Disney, outlining to him what kind of attractions they would like to see or the overall message they would want their pavilion to convey. Out of these negotiations came Great Moments with Mr. Lincoln for the State of Illinois Pavilion, The Magic Skyway for the Ford Motor Company, "it's a small world" for UNICEF and Pepsi, and the Carousel of Progress for General Electric. These sponsors, in a sense, invested in the Walt Disney Company, which used the money to develop new techniques and technologies, such as Audio-Animatronics. Walt also used this opportunity to see what the response would be to his attractions east of the Mississippi River as he began to consider a Disneyland East, what would later become Walt Disney World.

General Electric's main goal for their pavilion at the fair was to showcase many of the different products they had developed, using the Carousel of Progress as a commercial to entice prospective patrons. They hoped that the show would demonstrate the power of innovation and progress, and that even though great inventions had been developed by General Electric in the past, there was still a potential for greater innovations to come. Walt enlisted the help of two of his more talented composers in the 1960s, Richard and Robert Sherman, to develop a song that held the spirit of progress, and from this collaboration emerged the well-known "It's a Great Big Beautiful Tomorrow." However, Walt's work wasn't done; he still had to convince General Electric to adopt his idea for the Carousel of Progress theater. He set up a piano in one of his studios on the Walt Disney Productions lot and filmed himself and the Sherman Brothers singing "There's a Great Big Beautiful Tomorrow" while he explained the concept for the Carousel theater. At the end of the short pitch, Walt and the Shermans turned around, skipping away from the camera, with the General Electric logo attached to the back of their coats.

Regardless of what they thought of the pitch, General Electric seemed to like the idea for the attraction, as they adopted it for their pavilion at the New York World's Fair.

The first glimpse that the general public got of the Carousel of Progress was during the *Wonderful World of Color* television show's airing of the episode "Disneyland Goes to the World's Fair" on May 17, 1964. In the episode, Walt guides the television audience around his studio, where he shows many prominent Imagineers working on the various attractions for the fair, such as Mary Blair and Blaine Gibson. Throughout the segment on the Carousel of Progress, Walt shows a round model of the theater, explaining a synopsis of each of the four scenes. The camera then cuts to a full scale set of the scene, where Imagineers are working the scene over, manually rotating the scenes in the wings of the theater or placing props in the kitchen. Wathel Rogers, one of the men who invented and perfected Audio-Animatronics technology, sits in a chair with a series of wires and metal brackets around his forehead, shoulders, and arms. Walt then asks Rogers to demonstrate his programming of the narrator of the Carousel of Progress (the father, named John). Any movement that Rogers does with the contraption causes John to mirror that movement. Walt has a one-way conversation with the Audio-Animatronics father, reading off the newspaper in his hand and offering to light his pipe.

After the New York World's Fair closed in October 1965, the entire attraction was dismantled and sent back to Disneyland, where it was reassembled and inserted into Tomorrowland. It remained there to entertain park guests until its attraction closure in 1973, when it was once again packed up and sent to Orlando to be installed in the newly opened Magic Kingdom. Because General Electric continued to sponsor the Carousel of Progress in both Disneyland and the Magic Kingdom, they decided to overhaul the attraction when it opened in the Magic Kingdom in 1975. Disney once more called upon the talents of the

Sherman Brothers to compose a new theme song for the show; they came up with "The Best Time of Your Life," as GE wanted customers to purchase their products *now*, not "tomorrow." During this time, the casting and script was changed to update the show to reflect this new message. General Electric's contract to sponsor the Carousel of Progress ended in 1985, and they chose not to renew. When Tomorrowland was refurbished and re-imagined in 1993, the Carousel of Progress was returned to its original form, albeit with a new voice cast. Rex Allen, the original narrator in the 1964 show, returned to voice the grandfather, while the role of the father was filled by Jean Shepherd, a radio show host, who may be best known as the voice of the narrator, the adult Ralphie Parker, in the perennial classic, *A Christmas Story*. Interestingly, Mel Blanc, who voiced popular cartoon characters including Bugs Bunny and Tweety Bird, also lent his voice to a character in the show, Uncle (and later referred to as Cousin) Orville, who is seen only once in scene two, laying in a bathtub and dressed as Uncle Sam, while a General Electric fan blows over a large ice cube. Blanc's voice is also heard in scene four from the bathroom, but Orville is not physically present in the scene. The song "There's a Great Big Beautiful Tomorrow" was also updated and added back to the attraction to reflect the theme of Tomorrowland and the overall vision that Walt Disney had for progress.

Since 1993, Walt Disney's Carousel of Progress has remained relatively unchanged. The show itself is the same as it was twenty years ago, but every once in a while, keen eyes will notice the movement of a prop on stage or maintenance done to the skin or outfit of the Audio-Animatronics characters. Whether guests enter the Carousel Theater to enjoy the show or escape from the hot, humid, Florida air, the attraction presents a fairly accurate representation of the life of an average family throughout America during the twentieth century, even though some will notice that the family seems to do very little aging over time.

QUEUE AND INTRODUCTION

Upon entering Tomorrowland from Fantasyland, guests will pass Cosmic Ray's Starlight Café on the right and the Tomorrowland Speedway and Space Mountain on the left. Ahead and to the right sits a large, curved building with purple, teal, and yellow gears marking the entrance ramp to the attraction. The official title is "Walt Disney's Carousel of Progress"; Disney's name was added as an homage when the attraction was refurbished in 1993.

When redesigning Tomorrowland during the 1993–94 refurbishment, Imagineers attempted to integrate the Carousel of Progress into the overall theming of the updated land. Attempting to portray Tomorrowland as "the fantastical future that never will be," the designers created a story that portrayed humans, aliens, and robots coexisting on a distant planet. While the Carousel of Progress did not exactly fit into this new storyline, large painted gears were added to the exterior of the building, and a new sign was added at the end of the queue. A short ramp leads guests up to the level of the attraction's loading area.

The queue of the Carousel of Progress is located outside; because the theater has six different theaters, the attraction loads up to two hundred and fifty guests approximately every five minutes and so does not require a long queue or switchback. Guests can pass the few minutes standing in line watching a series of film clips about the history and origination of the Carousel of Progress. The film montage includes the pitch made to General Electric by Walt and the Sherman Brothers, as well as the clip described above from "Disneyland Goes to the World's Fair."

Upon entering the theater, guests choose a seat in the tiered theater facing a curved stage draped with a heavy curtain. In the center of the room is a large gear with the attraction's title, Walt Disney's Carousel of Progress. Colored LED lights shine on the gear, changing colors approximately every two seconds. When loading of the theater is complete, the lights dim and Jean Shepherd's voice begins narrating a brief, thirty second history of the Carousel of Progress, relating the show back to Walt Disney. He then introduces Walt's idea of progress, and his interest in following an average family throughout the twentieth century. With the cue, "May the century begin," the theater begins moving to the right, turning counter-clockwise around the stage, which remains stationary in the center of the room.

SCENE ONE: THE 1890s

As the theater rotates, a late nineteenth century kitchen comes into view while Shepherd's voice, which we quickly realize is that of the narrator, a gentleman in middle age who we soon learn is named John, sings the theme song of the attraction, "There's a Great Big Beautiful Tomorrow." The room is a simple kitchen of the late 1890s, centered around a large cast iron black stove. The smokestack of the stove rises up to the ceiling and disappears from view. Two windows flank either side of the stove, with a washbasin and water pump below the window to the left. A four-foot high wooden cabinet with a small window at the top of the door sits on the right side of the room, and John sits in a wooden rocking chair on the right with a shaggy dog at his feet. A small, round table with a red, golden tasseled tablecloth and glass oil lamp sits to John's right, with a butter churn in the corner behind him. Needlework art and framed sepia tone tintype photographs hang on the walls. A wooden crank telephone hangs over his left shoulder in the corner.

John wears a green evening coat and brown slacks. A yellow vest and red tie are beneath the jacket, and he wears his hair parted off to the side and sports a large moustache. He holds a newspaper in his left hand, a tobacco pipe in his right.

Looking out the windows, one can see a tree with pink flowers and a few small robins sitting on the branches. The other window shows a hanging clothesline with trousers and shirts hanging out to dry. A few buildings can be seen in the distance. These buildings include two-story homes covered in white siding surrounded by tall trees. A white picket fence surrounds the backyard of the Carousel family, and a dirt road, which is covered in puddled water due to a recent rainstorm, curves off into the distance.

The kitchen in which John is sitting is a fairly accurate representation of that of an average American family around the turn of the century. Maria Parloa was an extremely popular cookbook writer in the late 1800s and explained the model kitchen should be "finished in such a way that it may be washed." The kitchen of the Carousel family is finished with hardwood flooring and wood paneled wainscoting on the walls, which Parloa suggested as the best option for easy cleaning. She also recommended adequate ventilation to prevent fatigue and to air out any cooking odors, which is obvious through the two windows on either side of the large iron stove. Parloa was also an advocate for logical organization of the Victorian-era kitchen, which made cooking and food preparation as efficient as possible with quick access between the table, wash bin, stove, and food storage. This is certainly the case in the Carousel kitchen.

Because many of the modern kitchen appliances and organizational techniques had not been invented in the 1890s, many of the implements found in the Carousel kitchen look foreign to most guests. Cabinets hanging above the countertops in nineteenth century kitchens was a foreign concept, and as a result, shelves or hooks would have been used to store pots, pans, and dishes. Also, food refrigeration was not modernized in the 1890s, requiring the use of an icebox, a wooden box that was insulated to keep food cold; on a regular basis, families could have a delivery man drop off a large block of ice to put into the icebox to ensure the refrigeration of perishable foods. However, because the ice melted, especially during the summer months, a drip pan was needed to catch the leaking water below.

Because electricity was not common in most homes in the 1890s (General Electric began distributing electricity to people's homes en masse during the 1920s and 1930s), cast iron stoves were used to cook food. These stoves varied in size and shape during this period, but were often formed by using a cast. There was usually very little ornamentation on the stoves, unless the consumer decided to pay a higher premium for a fancier stove. These stoves heated using a variety of fuel sources, such as wood, charcoal, or even animal dung, and had both an oven for baking and a range for heating pots and pans. The fuel was often loaded into a lower compartment of the stove and had to be stoked and replenished to ensure that the fire stayed hot enough to cook food. To prevent smoke and carbon monoxide from filling the kitchen and the house, a pipe or shaft rose through the roof or through a hole on the side of the house to allow for the ventilation of noxious fumes. Families often spent time in the kitchen, especially during the winter, as the stove also served as a method for heating the home during cold months. This may explain why the father is located in the kitchen, as the scene takes place on Valentine's Day. The cast iron stove in the center of the Carousel family's kitchen is a fairly accurate representation of the type of stove one would find in a Victorian-era kitchen, and appears to be a higher-end stove.

There is very little indication where the home of the Carousel family is located in the United States. The voice of the father has the accent and intonation of someone from the Midwest (Jean Shepherd was born in Chicago and spent much of his life in Cincinnati and Philadelphia), and the scene outside the window leads the audience to believe that the family home is not located in a large town or city, but rather in a rural setting. This is also evidenced by the butter churner, which would be used by families to make their own butter, especially if they lived a distance from the grocer.

John begins his monologue by describing the America of the 1890s and explaining that buildings are beginning to "tower…as high as twenty stories, moving pictures flicker up on a big screen." He reports that there are approximately eight thousand automobiles in America and that it takes less than seven days to travel by train between New York and California. He also references two brothers from North Carolina who are trying to develop "some kind of flying contraption," which he scoffs at and claims will never work, and a gentleman named Tom Edison who is working on electric lights for inside the home.

John's monologue references a lot of innovations and events that were significant around the turn of the century. The first skyscraper, the Home Insurance Building, was built in Chicago in 1884, and rose to one-hundred-and-thirty-eight feet tall. By making a transition to the use of steel as the frame of a building rather than iron, buildings could now be made taller because they could support more weight. Due to zoning restrictions, height limits were placed on buildings in Chicago, allowing New York City to become the hub for skyscraper development.

Film also emerged as a popular American pastime in the late 1890s and early 1900s. In 1891, Thomas Edison received the patent for the Kinetoscope, a machine that allowed small slides to be shown; each slide had an individual picture, and when moved in quick succession, created the illusion of movement. In 1894, the first viewing parlors began opening in major American cities, charging patrons to visit and view moving pictures through Kinetoscopes for entertainment purposes. In 1896, the transition from a personal Kinetoscope experience to the use of a projector occurred. The image, on a slide, would be illuminated from behind using an oil lamp and projected onto a screen for a communal viewing experience. However, due to the limits on technology, these short films did not have sound effects or music, and so were often accompanied by a pianist playing ragtime music or an automated player piano that correlated with the action on the screen.

In this same time period, enterprising men began to popularize a new form of transportation that had already been invented in Europe, the automobile. Contrary to popular belief, Henry Ford did not invent the automobile, but rather aimed to create automobiles for the common man to afford. Ford first developed his Ford Quadricycle, testing it out on June 4, 1893, while working for Edison's Illuminating Company. Edison encouraged Ford to perfect his Quadricycle, and he built improved versions of it. Ford, however, was not the only automobile manufacturer. He was challenged by competitors including the Dodge brothers and the Cadillac Automobile Company.

While the automobile continued to be perfected throughout the last decades of the nineteenth century, they were still a luxury commodity that only a few could afford. Instead, many Americans who had to travel long distances opted to do so by railroad. The railroad system first became heavily used during the 1860s, when the Transcontinental Railroad was completed, joining the eastern and western portions of the United States together at Promontory Point, Utah. This 1,756-mile railroad allowed for quick, comfortable, and cheap transportation of long-distance travelers and cargo. Throughout the 1860s and 1870s, Cornelius Vanderbilt developed a monopoly over the railroad system, beginning by serving on the board of directors for a series of railroads in New York and New Jersey. Vanderbilt placed his son as a vice president of these railroad lines, and began to take over competing companies who threatened the success of the New York and New Jersey lines. Through the pouring of capital into these eastern lines, Vanderbilt was able to improve upon the extensive reach of railroads, which allowed for many Americans in the 1880s and 1890s to live in smaller towns, able to commute into the larger cities by train rather than by horse or wagon. By the late 1890s and early 1900s, trains were able to move at speeds up to forty miles per hour, making on average seventeen miles per hour with stops at various stations. This allowed passengers to travel from the Atlantic to the Pacific in a little under a week; as the distance between New York City and Los Angeles is approximately 2,776 miles, and trains moved approximately seventeen miles per hour, it would take passengers about one hundred sixty three hours, or 6.8 days, to get from one city to the other.

In 1900, the Wright Brothers, two bicycle repairmen from Dayton, Ohio, traveled down to Kitty Hawk, located in North Carolina's Outer Banks to conduct some experiments. It is interesting that John explains that the two brothers are "from North Carolina," which is a common misconception even to modern-day Americans. In the 1890s, Wilbur and Orville Wright began their own business, manufacturing and repairing bicycles to capitalize on the bicycle crazy of the late Victorian era. After reading news articles about experiments in Europe and America regarding flight by gliders, the brothers became interested in that technology. They packed up equipment, and in 1900, traveled to Kitty Hawk, North Carolina, to perfect their flying machine. Kitty Hawk, situated on North Carolina's Outer Banks, is home to a series of large sand dunes, which were beneficial to the experiments due to the soft landing surfaces and the sea breezes that provided lift to the man-made wings. Also, because of the relative remoteness of Kitty Hawk's sand dunes, the Kill Devil Hills, the brothers were able to conduct their experiments in privacy, away from the prying eyes of reporters and observers. The brothers mounted various experiments with their glider between 1900 and 1902, adding a motorized propeller in 1903. The first manned flight of the powered glider occurred on December 13, 1903, travelling one hundred twenty feet in approximately twelve seconds, proving John's assumption wrong when he claims that the Wright's invention "will never work."

To break up the scene, Imagineers designed two dioramas mounted on rotating turntables on either side of the stage, hidden behind a hanging curtain called a scrim. When the scenes behind the curtain are not meant to be seen, a light illuminates the curtain from the audience's side; however, when the action in the diorama is meant to be scene by the viewers, a light on the other side of the screen is illuminated, making the scrim translucent.

In the first turntable scene, we see John's wife, Sarah, ironing a garment in what looks to be the kitchen pantry, as evidenced by the large built-in wooden shelves filled with jars of food and bread. She excitedly explains how the invention of a washing machine now allows her to wash clothes in five hours rather than two days. Earlier in the nineteenth century, most laundry was conducted on Mondays, which was traditionally known as "Wash Day." This was done by filling a large bucket or washbasin with boiling water and loading it with the clothing. Each piece of clothing would be scrubbed on a washboard, which was a corrugated piece of tin. The garment would have soap or starch applied to it, and sometimes spot treated. All of the clothing in the washbasin would be stirred with a large stick with two handles, called a dolly or plunger, which mimicked the action of agitators in modern-day washing machines. After each individual garment had been scrubbed, soaked, and stirred, they would be hung on a clothesline to drip dry, which could take hours or days, depending on the temperature outside and how much sun was available.

However, in the late 1800s, a new innovation was developed, the gravity washer. This washing machine looked like a large barrel with a series of rolling pins attached to the top. Rather than using a stick for an agitator, a pulley mechanism was used to stir the clothing inside the barrel. A young girl is seen in the turntable scene next to Sarah, operating this new washing machine by pulling a lever. Washers could then put the wet garments between the rollers, which squeezed out most of the water, prior to hanging them on the clothesline to finish drying. Sears and Roebuck were so confident in their new machine that they billed it as being a savior for clothing, allowing for no more wear and tear done to sheets and garments from the old methods of laundering. After removing the dried clothes from the clothesline, one would use a metal iron to smooth out wrinkles by filling the iron with boiling water, which is what Sarah is doing as she talks to John in the scene. Sarah mentions that she needs to remove the laundry from the clothesline before the weather turns bad, but John laughs it off until it suddenly begins raining, adding a touch of humor.

On the opposite side of the stage from Sarah's turntable diorama, to John's right, emerges another scene behind the other scrim; the light illuminates a young boy sitting behind a desk in a study. The room that the boy, James (later referred to as Jimmy), is sitting in is a typical Victorian-era study. Heavy curtains hang from the window with yellow woven tassels on the edges. A thin white curtain, which allowed light to come through the window, hangs beneath the opaque curtain. Small round tables sit on either side of the study, covered in tasseled tablecloths, while a glass gas lamp sits on the desk. The desk itself is fairly small and has ornamental legs. On the wall behind James is a framed picture with four black silhouette portraits, which were popular during the mid-1800s. The portraits are of a man and woman and two young children, which may represent the Carousel family of Sarah, John, James, and their teenage daughter, Patricia. Interestingly, there is no representation of the young girl who is washing the laundry with Sarah in the turntable scene. There is also a painted portrait of an upper-class woman above the silhouette portraits, which is painted in the style of the Victorian era.

James is dressed in the traditional clothing of a middle- or upper-middle class boy; he is wearing a green button-up shirt, shorts, and knee-high socks. His blonde hair is parted off to the side. In his left hand, he holds a stereoscope, similar to the red View-Master that was a popular toy for many children in the 1990s. Users of a stereoscope would look through two lenses at a card approximately four to six inches away. The card had two identical photographs; when looked at through the two lenses, the illusion was created of a three-dimensional image. James excitedly talks to his father about the subject of the stereoscopic image, that of Little Egypt "doing the hoochie-coochee," referencing the exhibit called "The Streets of Cairo" at the Louisiana Purchase Exposition in St. Louis, Missouri, in 1904. This world's fair commemorated the one hundredth anniversary of the Louisiana Purchase in 1804, when President Thomas Jefferson purchased land from Napoleon Bonaparte of France, effectively doubling the size of the United States at the time. The Streets of Cairo was an exhibit at the St. Louis fair, and the main attraction of the exhibit was a series of belly dancers, collectively known as "Little Egypt," harkening back to a famous performer at the World's Columbian Exposition of 1893 in Chicago. For the Victorian morals of the time, the belly dancers were extremely provocative, which is why John reprimands his son, embarrassed that he found his secret stereoscope in front of the audience.

The light dims in the scene behind the scrim as John begins explaining a new invention, the phonograph, which allows for listeners to enjoy "music right here in [the] home." The turntable diorama, where Sarah was previously working on the laundry, had rotated while the audience's attention was on Jimmy using the stereoscope. A new scene is now illuminated, showing an old woman in a rocking chair listening to a tinny version of "There's a Great Big Beautiful Tomorrow" coming from the phonograph. A parrot sits on a perch and begins complaining about how the old woman, the grandmother of the family, listens to "that thing ... *all day long.*"

Also known as the gramophone, the phonograph was developed by Thomas Edison in 1877. Edison had originally used the phonograph as a recording machine to record and play back telegraph messages, as well as automated messages to be transmitted on the telephone. Edison first began his experiments of developing the phonograph by recording spoken word and sounds on a disc covered with a piece of paper embossed with magnets. A needle would make imprints in the disk based on the noise or words spoken into the machine; when placed on a phonograph machine and played back, the original recorded sounds could be heard emitting from the machine. Edison began to make recordings on a cylindrical disk covered in tin foil, first displaying his invention by speaking and then playing back the lyrics to "Mary Had a Little Lamb." In the 1880s and 1890s, disc records began being used to play music on the phonograph and were sold to consumers who were wealthy enough to be able to afford a phonograph machine.

After this short scene, dainty music begins playing and the turntable diorama where Jimmy previously had been seen is illuminated to a new scene, that of either a washroom or a bedroom that is decorated with a number of framed photographs and pink wallpaper. The entire room is not visible to the audience, but rather focused on the daughter of the family, Patricia, sitting before a mirror, curling her hair. Patricia is wearing her bloomers and a corset, and complains to her father that she is indecent before the audience. A dress is seen on a hanger attached to the wall, which would have actually been scandalous for a teenage girl in the 1890s, as the dress would stop at the knees; it was more appropriate fashion for women and teenage girls of the period to wear dresses down to the ground, out of modesty. Behind Patricia on the floor sits a mauve hatbox, which would have held a fancy hat that many women wore in the Victorian era. The use of corsets was also common to create the illusion that a woman was thinner than she really was. On the vanity before which Patricia sits a number of different Victorian-era details, such as an oil lamp and half-used candles, suggesting that there may not be enough kerosene for Patricia to consistently use her lamp at night. A small wooden table against the back wall holds a washbasin and vase, as sinks and indoor plumbing throughout the entire home were not commonplace in the late 1800s.

After the brief exchange between John and his daughter, the father reminds her to be home by nine o'clock and the lights in the diorama dim. John continues his monologue, excusing himself from the audience and explaining that he is going "to take one of those new-fangled trolleys down to the drug store soda fountain to meet the boys for a cold sarsaparilla," but quickly corrects himself, explaining that sarsaparilla has been replaced by root beer. John is likely referring to riding an electric trolley, which is a tramcar that draws electrical power from a wire suspended above the vehicle. Because the Carousel family lives outside the central business district of town, and likely does not own an automobile (as John never mentions owning one at the beginning of his monologue when he mentions that there were 8,000 automobiles in the country), it would make sense for him to ride the electric trolley into town, even if it meant walking to the trolley station.

Once arriving in the downtown area, John would likely walk down to the drug store (known today as a pharmacy), which often served as a place for community members to gather to socialize or share a beverage or meal. During the last quarter of the nineteenth century, carbonated drinks were developed, claiming to heal maladies like high blood pressure or indigestion, but later had flavors added to mask the bitter taste of the carbonated water. Seltzer or fizzy water was poured into a cup, the bubbly liquid evoking the idea of water pouring from a natural spring. Patrons to a soda fountain had multiple flavor choices they could have added to the water, including strawberry, lemon, and the popular sarsaparilla. Eventually, carbonated drinks like Coca-Cola and Pepsi would become mass produced. Soda fountains would later be added to other shops, including general stores, confectioneries (sweet shops), and department stores, and would also begin serving ice cream and hot meals to store patrons.

John ends his monologue, referring back to the notion of progress and tying it to the theme song of the attraction. He begins to sing the song as the theater again begins moving to the right into the next scene.

SCENE TWO: THE 1920S

As the Carousel Theater rotates counterclockwise, a new scene comes into view. The audience quickly realizes that they are looking at an almost identical kitchen; Disney has never officially stated whether the Carousel of Progress features the same family throughout the show or four separate, but similar families. Because the characters all have the same names, look very similar throughout the show, and are voiced by the same actors and actresses, we can assume that it is the same family throughout the twentieth century.

The kitchen is almost identical in layout, but with some cosmetic updates across the twenty-five or so years that have taken place since the first scene. The right window that previously created a nook for the stove has now been flattened against the back wall of the house. The wood paneling that stretched halfway up the wall is gone, replaced by lime green paint. Also, wires hang all over the kitchen, stretching from the light fixtures on the ceiling to the wall and various appliances throughout the kitchen. Outside the windows are a series of buildings, leading us to believe that the neighborhood that the Carousel family lives in has grown in size and become more urban over the past two decades. The exterior mural is lit as though the scene takes place in the evening or just after dusk. A large American flag hangs outside the window behind the narrator.

Once the theater comes to a stop, the audience has a moment to take in the scene as John begins his monologue. A white Hotpoint Automatic

Electric stove sits centered between the two windows. Beneath the left window, similar to the prior scene, is a sink with two taps. John sits backwards in a wooden chair, facing the audience with a kitchen table behind him, atop which sits a Singer sewing machine. To his left is a vacuum cleaner. Against the back wall of the kitchen, between the windows, are a series of shelves, upon which sit containers with labels for their contents. An herb cabinet sits beneath an electric clock, and an electric toaster and a coffee pot sit on top of the stove. In front of John is a footstool, with a tray holding a large glass pitcher of ice tea beside a full glass topped with a slice of lemon. John is dressed in a blue collared shirt and bowtie, with brown slacks. He holds a paper fan in his right hand advertising Niagara Falls.

John begins by explaining that the scene takes place on that Fourth of July, and that the day has been an extremely hot one. As a result, our narrator fans himself with the paper fan purchased at Niagara Falls. The popular destination is not one waterfall, but actually a collection of three separate waterfalls that straddle the American-Canadian border, with the American and Bridal Veil Falls on the American side in New York State and the Horseshoe Falls on the Canadian side in Ontario. As automobiles became more popular and common after World War I ended in 1918, auto tourism boomed, bringing more visitors to Niagara Falls. Judging from John's fan, we can assume that the Carousel family joined the many Americans that had recently visited the Falls due to the prevalence of automobiles; given John's new Essex car, it's entirely possible that he and his family were among these Americans.

Our narrator goes on to explain the big current events that have occurred over the past twenty years, including the solo flight of Charles Lindbergh, which, in common John fashion, he lauds as likely to be unsuccessful. He explains the growth of sports stadiums, and excitedly explains the accomplishments of a new baseball player named

Babe Ruth. John describes a new form of music called jazz, as well as a new film starring silent film actor, Al Jolson, who will talk and sing in the film, explaining how much he is looking forward to seeing this unlikely technology.

Charles Lindbergh, a pilot working for the United States Postal Service delivering mail via airplane in the 1920s, became famous on an international scale when he was twenty-five by becoming the first individual to fly across the Atlantic Ocean by himself, a trip lasting thirty hours and stretching 3,600 miles. Lindbergh took off in his plane, *The Spirit of St. Louis*, from New York's Roosevelt Field on May 20, 1927, and landed at Le Bourget Field in Paris on May 21, proving John once again wrong in his assessment. For this accomplishment, Lindbergh received the Orteig Prize, a $25,000 reward offered in 1919 by Raymond Orteig, a New York hotel owner, to any aviator who would make a non-stop flight from New York City to Paris. Because he was an officer in the U.S. Army Air Corps Reserve, Lindbergh was also awarded the Medal of Honor for his exploits. These accomplishments made "Lucky Lindy" a national hero and the subject of songs and postage stamps. He even inspired the first Mickey Mouse cartoon ever drawn (and the second released), *Plane Crazy*.

Spectator sports became popular in the 1920s, particularly baseball. A few different reasons contributed to this phenomena: games were broadcast over radio, which had become more common in American homes, and newspaper reported on the statistics of various players and events; blacks and Latinos became involved in the sport, ushering in a new pool of talent; and playing fields became enclosed, leading to the construction of large stadiums to hold the immense crowds of people eager watch the game. Also, a transition to the use of cork-centered balls rather than wound thread allowed for an emphasis on batting, rather than defensive pitching or fielding. This development led to a large fan-

following of baseball legends, such as Lou Gehrig, Ty Cobb, and Babe
Ruth. George Herman "Babe" Ruth, Jr. was actively playing for Major
League Baseball from 1914 until 1935, pitching for the Boston Red Sox
and New York Yankees. Ruth was infamous due to his reckless behavior
and public womanizing, but also was well-known for his batting average, hitting a total of seven-hundred-and-fourteen career home runs,
breaking the single-season home run record of twenty-nine home runs
in 1919, fifty-four in 1920, fifty-nine in 1921, and sixty in 1927. Ruth
became a national idol of the 1920s, serving as a hero for young men and
the envy of the middle aged during the 1920s and 1930s.

John also explains the popular forms of contemporary entertainment
of the 1920s, beginning by describing jazz as "the cat's meow." One of
the most popular forms of music of the time, jazz emerged in different
cities throughout the United States during the Prohibition era. In the
early 1920s, the United States legislature passed the 18th Amendment,
which prohibited the production, sale, and consumption of alcoholic
beverages. As a result, an illegal alcohol market developed, with booze
sold and served in illicit clubs called speakeasies. Entertainment was
offered at speakeasies, including musicians playing a new form of music,
called jazz. A few different cities, in particular Chicago and New Orleans,
became the hub of jazz music in the United States. Some of the most
famous jazz musicians are still known today, including Jelly Roll Morton,
Bessie Smith, and Louis Armstrong. With roots in the slave spirituals of
the 1850s and 1860s, as well as the ragtime and blues music of the early
1900s, jazz became a popular form of music across the country and eventually inspired the swing movement of the 1940s and rock and roll music
of the 1950s and 1960s.

Jazz was so popular that film studios incorporated the music into their
films. One of the most popular films of the 1920s, released in 1927, was
The Jazz Singer, starring silent film actor Al Jolson. The film was the first

feature-length film to synchronize pre-recorded dialogue and music, bringing the end of the silent age of film and the beginning of the era of the "talkies." While *The Jazz Singer* was not the first film to have synchronized sound, which had been around since 1923, it was the first film to have synchronized speech and songs, which began approximately seventeen minutes into the film. The film only had about two minutes of actual synchronized dialogue, but the ability of speech and singing synchronization between sound and film was revolutionary. The sound for the film was recorded at the same time as the film itself, with the motor driving the cameras and audio equipment working together. Thus, when playing in a theater, both the film and sound record would be played at the same time and synced for viewers.

The plot of *The Jazz Singer* follows a young Jewish man who rejects the tradition of his family by becoming a singer of jazz music. The main character of the film, Jack Robin, played by Jolson, performed in blackface, wearing a suit and covering his face in black makeup to create the illusion that he is a black singer, a practice that was common in American minstrel shows, film, and radio shows from the 1830s until the 1950s. The film is controversial to modern audiences, as it is now seen as culturally insensitive and racist, but at the time those were non-issues and the movie was a major success. Many popular actors and actresses of the 1920s and 1930s participated in blackface performances, including Bing Crosby, Shirley Temple, and Judy Garland.

John moves away from the current events of the 1920s to discuss the technological innovations available to the common folk. He laughs to himself over a neighbor, Schwartz, who enjoys beeping the horn of his "Hupmobile." Built by the Hupp Motor Company between 1909 and 1940, the Hupmobile was produced to directly compete against Ford and Chevrolet. Unfortunately, the Hupp Motor Company and its Hupmobile came to a demise as a result of the Great Depression of the 1930s.

While Schwartz did not choose a long-lasting automobile company, John was a little luckier purchasing a car from Essex. Manufactured by the Hudson Motor Car Company, which was begun by department store owner and founder Joseph L. Hudson of Detroit, the Essex line of automobiles also competed with Ford and Chevrolet for the pocketbooks of everyday Americans. In fact, sales of Essex automobiles were third among auto manufacturers in the United States in 1925. Essex automobiles would be phased out in 1938, with the name changed Terraplane. John explains that as a result of his new Essex automobile, he is able to easily start his car using the electric starter, whereas in previous vehicles he had to start his engine by turning a hand crank, which was an inconvenient, difficult, and dangerous process.

John continues to explain the accomplishments of travel in the United States in the 1920s, mentioning that travelers can get from New York to Los Angeles by train in only three days. Trains were able to travel at speeds up to one hundred miles per hour, with averages of approximately forty-miles per hour, including frequent stops. Technology had developed during the early decades of the twentieth century, making train travel more common for passengers on cross-country trips.

At this point in the scene, John finally addresses the tangled mess of wires hanging throughout his kitchen, attributing to "new electrical servants" who "add life to [the] home," courtesy of Thomas Edison. Suddenly, fast-paced music begins and the lights begin to flicker as the appliances come to life: the vacuum inflates and begins to sweep back and forth in the corner, the oven door of the stove begins to open and shut, the kitchen appliances on top of the stove begin moving around, and the door of the refrigerator opens while the light inside is illuminated and extinguished. Suddenly, the lights to the home go out, which John attributes to the appliances blowing a fuse. Unfortunately, he also blows a fuse for the entire neighborhood, which evokes angry protests from his neighbors. John sends his son, Jimmy, who we have not yet encountered in this scene, outside to reset the fuse box and restore power to the home.

During the early decades of the twentieth century, a flood of new inventions were developed bringing electrical appliances into the home. However, because no one had yet come up with the concept of an electrical outlet, and because it cost so much to embed new wiring into the walls of a home or building, new electric wires were strung throughout the home, connecting into the lighting fixtures in order to provide electrical power to the various appliances. With electricity now readily available, new machines were developed to make chores and the everyday lives of Americans easier and more efficient. Electric vacuum cleaners were invented to allow for fewer steps in sweeping the floor. Rather than constantly adding to and stoking a stove fueled by wood or charcoal, electric ranges and ovens were developed with coils that became red hot from electrical currents. The ice delivery men had become obsolete, as electric refrigerators built by General Electric and Kelvinator began using compressors, fans, and sulfur dioxide to cool the inside of the refrigerator, allowing for the home manufacturing of ice cubes and longer food preservation. However, because consumption of electricity was not regulated by power companies, and because technology had yet been developed for grounding and preventative shortages, overusing electrical power in the home often led to the blowing of fuses, as evidenced in the Carousel family home.

After Jimmy resets the fuse, the lights come back on, illuminating not only the kitchen, but also the scene on the turntable diorama behind the right hand scrim. We see Sarah, John's wife, sitting on an enclosed porch, sewing a white shirt. She is wearing a red dress and white cap, in the fashion of the late 1700s. We soon learn that the Carousel family is participating in the 4th of July parade in town and that John and Sarah will be dressing as George and Martha Washington. Because of the mid-summer heat, Sarah is sewing on the porch to benefit from the evening breeze, while fireflies flicker outside the screened windows. John does not seem thrilled with the idea of dressing up, blaming the evening's festivities on Sarah's Ladies' Club.

Ladies' Clubs, also known as Women's Clubs, began in the 1850s in the United States as the female counterparts of various men's clubs, such as the Freemasons, Elks, and Rotary clubs. Women gathered on a regular basis to advocate for the improvement of many social issues, including temperance (limiting the consumption of alcohol), women's rights and suffrage (the right to vote), educational and prison reform, and working conditions for women and children. Because this scene takes place in the 1920s, after World War I has concluded and women received the right to vote in 1920 as a result of the Nineteenth Amendment to the U.S. Constitution, it is not surprising that the local Ladies' Club would be sponsoring an Independence Day celebration, as patriotism, especially among women, was rampant during this decade.

Sarah goes on to explain that their son, Jimmy, chose the music for the fireworks show; the diorama on the left is illuminated to show the young man standing in the parlor on a footstool, dressed as a young patriot, leaning against a record player while John Philip Sousa's "Stars and Stripes Forever" plays. The record player in this scene does not look like a typical phonograph of the 1920s; however, it is likely that this player was of the sort that shared the cabinet with a radio during the early decades of the twentieth century. Sitting to Jimmy's left in a rocking chair is the family's grandfather, dressed as Benjamin Franklin, and holding a red firework rocket in his hands.

John begins commenting on the record player/radio combination set that Jimmy is playing the music on, explaining that their new Crosley radio set allows them to get news and entertainment from all over the country, even from Pittsburgh. Crosley was a large seller of radios in the mid-1920s, becoming a top manufacturer for combination radio and record players of 1924. This reference is made to the first commercially available radio station, KDKA, which began in Pittsburgh, Pennsylvania, on August 20, 1920. Jimmy changes the radio station, which features an announcer discussing the festivities in town for the evening of Independence Day.

While the audience's attention was on Jimmy listening to the Sousa march in the diorama on the left, the right hand diorama where Sarah was sewing on the porch has rotated and illuminated to reveal the daughter, Patricia, dressed as the Statue of Liberty. Patricia is sitting on a bench in front of her window, and proceeds to complain about how her new boyfriend, Theodore, will feel about her being dressed as Lady Liberty. The scene behind the scrim obviously takes place in Patricia's bedroom, and we can assume that she is in her final years of high school career due to the college pennants. There are also black-and-white photographs hanging on the wall and a record on the ground, leaning against the wall.

After laughing at his daughter's vanity, the scene behind the scrim dims and John changes subjects, describing the new innovation of indoor plumbing, as the scene behind the left scrim lights up to reveal a man laying in a bathtub reading a newspaper, while wearing a red, white, and blue top hat. It soon becomes obvious, due to the outfit hanging behind the bathtub, that the older gentleman will be dressing as Uncle Sam for the 4th of July celebration. John explains that the man, Uncle Orville, has invented something that he calls "air cooling," which the audience realizes through Orville's setup of a Westinghouse fan blowing across a large block of ice pointed at him in the tub. On the other side of the tub from the fan and ice block, Orville has a glass of iced tea sitting on the closed lid of the toilet, complete with a wooden toilet seat. Closer examination of the bathroom reveals other details: glass bottles of various soaps or elixirs sit on a wooden shelf on the back wall of the bathroom, and shaving implements and soap sit on a shelf above the porcelain sink. Wooden paneling stretches halfway up the wall to allow for easy cleaning.

There are many different pieces of evidence from the scene to suggest that it takes place on July 4, 1926. We know that the scene occurs prior to 1927, as that is the year Charles Lindbergh makes his journey across the Atlantic; it's also the year that *The Jazz Singer* was released to theaters, and both of these events are things John is looking forward to. We also know that the Carousel family's Crosley radio was manufactured in 1924, at the earliest. July 4, 1926, was a significant date; it was the one-hundred-fiftieth anniversary of American independence against the British. This may be why the entire family is dressed as significant American historical figures or characters, as the 4th of July festivities include a large parade and fireworks display in the downtown area. Patricia dressed as the Statue of Liberty likely has historical implications, as well. In 1924, President Calvin Coolidge used his presidential authority to declare the Statue of Liberty and Liberty Island a national monument, to be protected under the Antiquities Act. This caused the famous statue located in New York Harbor to become a popular tourist destination.

Uncle Orville reprimands John with an angry, "No privacy at all around this place!" and John apologizes for his insensitivity. He is quickly interrupted by Sarah announcing that his costume has been completed, urging him to prepare for the Independence Day celebrations. John excuses himself, sending the audience on their way by once more singing "There's a Great Big Beautiful Tomorrow" as the theater begins to rotate to the right, transitioning into the next scene.

SCENE THREE: THE 1940S

As the theater continues rotating to the right, a third kitchen comes into view. This kitchen is still reminiscent of the one from the 1890s and 1920s scenes, but with some very obvious changes. The kitchen is now a mixture of blue cupboards, a yellow refrigerator, and a flowered wallpaper around the dinette area. The right hand window has been recessed out into a U-shape, allowing for a blue rubber booth to be built against the wall surrounding the far side of a table covered in a yellow tablecloth. John sits in the booth, facing the audience; he is wearing a red sweater on top of a collared shirt, and his moustache has been trimmed down to the shorter style of the 1940s.

The kitchen of the Carousel family is a fairly typical kitchen of the late 1940s and early 1950s. Linoleum, which became very popular for middle-class homes in the 1940s and 1950s, can be seen throughout the kitchen; the floor seems to be made of shiny linoleum, rather than the hardwood of the first two scenes, and both the lower and upper cabinets seem to be covered in linoleum. New paint colors began to be used in the 1940s, as well, especially blues, yellows, and pinks. This was a new change, compared to the standard earth tones that were used in homes earlier in the century. The refrigerator and the stove in the Carousel family kitchen are also yellow, the same color as the lower cabinets. A blue tile backsplash lines the wall behind the kitchen sink and stove, which match the color of the upper cabinets. A copper range hood hangs over the stove, allowing for ventilation of food odors. On a ledge behind John sits an old radio, measuring approximately two feet long by six inches tall, a far departure from the family's radio in the second scene that was housed inside an entire cabinet. Over John's left shoulder, hanging on the wall, is an old wooden Black Forest cuckoo clock, which was popular during the 1940s.

John begins his monologue by explaining that the scene takes place on Halloween "in the fabulous forties," which guests can see by the pumpkin in the corner and the ceramic jack-o'-lantern on the table. He explains the new innovations that have taken place over the past two decades, mentioning that the "refrigerator holds more food than ice cubes. And thanks to our new automatic dishwasher, I don't have to dry the dishes anymore." While electric refrigerators were used in the 1920s, as evidenced by the refrigerator in the second scene, they were still fairly small, requiring consumers to travel into town to get their meat and vegetables on a regular basis. This was mainly because refrigeration technology for home units was fairly new and could not maintain refrigeration of as many items as would be possible in the 1940s, when freon began being used more commonly as a refrigerant, instead of sulfur dioxide. The yellow refrigerator in the scene was manufactured by General Electric, a nod back to the original sponsor of the attraction at the 1964 New York World's Fair, and also a popular producer of refrigerators in the 1940s. The decade also saw the beginning of the domestic use of electric dishwashers. This mainly occurred because of new technology and innovations that developed in the home, like the common use of indoor running water and the heat drying of dishes and silverware in the electronic dishwasher unit.

John continues to speak to the audience, explaining that he is a member of a new concept discussed on the radio called "the rat race." This term describes the dull, monotonous commute on a twice-daily basis with seemingly no end result that became common after the end of World War II. Upon returning from the wars in Europe and the Pacific, many GIs decided to purchase prefabricated homes that were located outside urban centers, beginning the push for urban sprawl. In order to commute to their workplaces, many families began purchasing cars, leading to the daily commute into town for jobs, many of which were in the new sphere of office work. We know that this scene of the Carousel of Progress takes place after World War Two, not only because of the use of the term "rat race," but also because John mentions that a man delivers news daily on the television named John Cameron Swayze. The right turntable diorama becomes illuminated, showing the grandparents of the family watching a television program.

Swayze began his career in radio, reading off news broadcasts to audiences. However, in 1947, he began his career on New York television, reading news to the small television audiences. Commercially available television did not become available to American audiences until 1948, bringing programs to homes, such as the news, orchestral performances, boxing matches, and comedic variety shows. Therefore, we can assume that the scene takes place in the late 1940s, which may be why the kitchen looks more like a stereotypical kitchen from the 1950s, similar to those in the 50's Prime-Time Café in Disney's Hollywood Studios.

After the scene with the grandparents sitting in front of the television behind the right scrim, the left turntable becomes illuminated showing John's son, Jimmy, in his bedroom, carving a jack-o'-lantern. Jimmy is dressed as a werewolf, similar to the title character from the 1941 horror film, *The Wolf Man*. The use of Halloween and Jimmy's costume for the 1940s is significant, as this decade is around the time when costuming and trick-or-treating became popular in the United States; the term "trick-or-treating" was first used in this country around 1934 and first found in print in 1939.

Jimmy's bedroom is typical for that of an American boy in the 1940s. Although few details can be seen in Jimmy's bedroom, it is obvious that a bed is behind him, and that he is standing at a desk beside a bookshelf topped with a lamp and globe. Photographs of cowboys hang on the back wall, evoking the popular cultural influence of the Old West; cowboys, Indian raiding parties, and outlaws permeated the culture of the 1940s, as depicted in novels, films, and radio shows of the era.

After the short scene, the lights dim, and John asks the audience if they hear the noises coming from Patty's bedroom, explaining that she is using "that old exercise machine she saved from the attic." The right turntable diorama lights up to reveal Patty, now a college student, standing with her back to the audience, talking on the phone. She is wearing a short, floral dress and nylons, while the belt of a Vibrating Belt exercise machine is strapped around her waist.

The Vibrating Belt Machine became popular between the 1920s and 1960s and was sold by popular retailers such as Sears & Roebucks and JC Penney's. The idea behind them was that the vibrations would cause the fat cells to break down or redistribute throughout the body, causing weight to be lost or the area with the vibrations to become slimmer. Early research into the implications of applying vibrations to the body began in the 1880s, when John Harvey Kellogg utilized vibration on patients at his sanitarium (or home for mentally ill patients) in Battle Creek, Michigan. Russians later studied Kellogg's research and began to use vibration technologies on athletes in order to help stretch and limber their muscles prior to athletic competitions. Machines similar to those that were being used began to find their way into catalogs and department stores to be purchased by consumers, and eventually entered the homes of consumers. However, these machines gained criticism, as advertisements and popular belief dictated that the machine alone could help the user to lose weight or reap the health benefits of the vibrating belts; instead, positive results were more common when the machine was used in conjunction with other healthy activities, such as caloric reduction and other physical activities.

The audience is again not quite able to guess the room in which Patty is "exercising," but the assumption is either a bedroom or powder room. No furniture is in the scene, except for a vanity table, the exercise machine, and the table on which the telephone sits. Framed photographs of various flowers and young men, some of them in military uniform, hang on the wall above the vanity, so we can assume that we are in a room that Patricia spends the most time in. A shag rug lines the floor, as well as a carpet-covered scale for the young woman to weigh herself on to determine how much weight she "still has to lose." Glass blocks form a window along the back wall, something that was beginning to become popular in homes during the 1940s.

While she is exercising, Patty and her friend, Babs, discuss the boys they are taking to the Halloween Party; the two girls then insult each other's dates. John, listening in on the conversation, feels sorry for Babs' date, wondering what Sarah's friends thought about him while he was dating his future wife. Keen guests will notice that the response to this question is the song of the cuckoo bird, chiming the hour, insinuating that Sarah's friends thought John was crazy.

John quickly moves on, trying to draw attention away from the cuckoo clock, by discussing how the late 1940s began a "do-it-yourself craze," and how the family has begun transforming their basement into a "rumpus room." At the end of World War II, thousands of young men returned home to the United States, collecting their salary and bonuses for fighting in Europe and the Pacific. Many of them used their soldiers' pay to purchase new homes, and many returned home to sweethearts they had married prior to being deployed or whom they had promised to marry upon their discharge. As a result, the population of the United States exploded during the late 1940s and early 1950s, as these sweethearts, separated for four or five years, began spending a lot of "alone time" together, and started families. Known as the "Baby Boom," this era lasted from the late 1940s until the mid 1960s when women began to move into the workplace in force, which ultimately led to fewer children. Because families were so large in the 1940s and 1950s (some having as many as ten or more children), they needed additional room for the children to play, and so many families began to expand their livable space into the basement of their homes. Because technology allowed for in-home refrigeration of perishable items through the use of the refrigerator and freezer, the subterranean level of the home was no longer needed for food storage and preservation. This opened up space for entertainment and relaxation purposes.

Sarah can be seen in the basement rumpus room standing on a ladder and applying vertical striped wallpaper to cinder block walls. Because wallpaper in the 1940s was not manufactured with pre-applied adhesive on the reverse, as it would be decades later, it needed to be applied manually with a liquid adhesive, such as starch or methyl cellulose. She throws John a tongue-in-cheek compliment for the "clever automatic paint stirring machine" he has created out of her food mixer. The lights dim in the room as the sounds of the paint mixer become louder and faster. Suddenly, a wet explosion is heard as Sarah screams, indicating that the liquid adhesive has splattered all over her. John laughs off Sarah's frustration and encourages the audience to sing along to the theme song as the theater once again rotates right into the last scene.

SCENE FOUR: THE TURN OF THE TWENTY-FIRST CENTURY

As the theater rotates into the last scene of the show, guests realize that the home that the Carousel family has lived in over the last hundred years has changed drastically. Rather than the scene centered on the kitchen with the two dioramas on either side, this scene depicts the home as an open floor-plan concept, with no physical separation between the kitchen, dining room, and living room. The entire family is present in the scene (excluding Orville, who we will learn about later). Grandpa and Patty are sitting in chairs on either side of a Christmas tree in front of a brick fireplace on the left side of the stage. Jimmy and Grandma are center stage, wearing a digital glove and headset, while John stands behind the kitchen counter and Sarah sits at a desk on the right side. The family dog, Rover, sits near the edge of the stage wearing a red bow around his neck.

Each of the six family members is dressed in fashion styles popular for the re-imagining of the attraction in the early 1990s. Patty wears a pink knit sweater and teal pants, with a hairspray-curled hairstyle. Her pants are tucked into her long white socks, which may be due to the white and pink ski boot in her lap. Grandpa is wearing brown slacks, a brown vest, a blue collared shirt and a red tie. He is wearing brown tennis shoes on his feet. His wife, the grandmother of the family, is wearing a floral dress with a belt around her waist. The formality of the grandparents compared to the informality of the grandchildren indicate the generational differences. Jimmy sits on a barstool and is the only member of the family who seems to have changed significantly in age over the past hundred years of the show, growing from middle school aged in the third scene to late high school in the fourth. He is wearing white tennis shoes, blue jeans, and a shirt with large, bright colored stripes that was characteristic of the fashion of the 1990s. John is standing behind the counter, his pants (if indeed he is wearing any) not in view. However, it is obvious that he is wearing a blue knit sweater that was typical winter garb for the late twentieth century. He is also wearing a green Christmas apron covered in red poinsettias; aprons became more appropriate for men to wear in the 1990s as women entered the world of work and men began taking more of an interest in the goings-on of the home. He has lost his moustache since the previous scene, as clean-shaven men became the norm during this time. Sarah is dressed in a professional manner, wearing a red blouse tucked into gray slacks, held up by a black belt. She is also wearing a fashionable scarf around her neck and a pair of glasses, again making her look like a professional, rather than a stay-at-home mom.

While Disney has never given the date intended for the scene, the living space of the family home could take place in either the late 1990s or early 2000s, even though different references made in the scene make it obvious the attraction was updated in the 1990s.

Although the home has an open floor plan, the scene is split into three distinct areas: the dining room, the living room, and the kitchen. The dining room is set in the rear of the scene, along the back wall of the house. Floor-to-ceiling windows and a sliding door line the back wall, allowing for natural light to filter in during the day. A very modern dinner table with matching chairs is centered in the dining room, decorated with a centerpiece and red candles for the Christmas dinner that is being prepared.

The living room, in the left half of the scene, has very little furniture: a television is in the center, and Grandpa and Patty sit in easy chairs with their backs to a brick-and-mortar fireplace. A tall, decorated Christmas tree stands between the two chairs, presents piled beneath the boughs.

The kitchen is very open to the rest of the home; countertops line the back wall, while a U-shaped island separates the kitchen from the living room. Four bar stools stand against the island. On the right wall of the kitchen are a black refrigerator and a glass-front oven that is set into the cupboards, off the ground. A pan rack hangs from the ceiling in the center of the kitchen, and recessed lights illuminate the room. Nearest the audience, Sarah sits at a desk working on a laptop computer. The wall is lined with shelves, which hold a large computer screen, books, and other knick-knacks. A dry-erase whiteboard hangs over the desk with notes on it, indicating that Sarah is a working mom who is trying to balance her career and motherhood. Various decorations hang on the walls and sit on shelves, such as plates, framed illustrations of vegetables, potted plants, and even a ceramic rooster.

As though the audience hadn't already figured it out, John introduces the scene as taking place on Christmas, attributing the day to peace and quiet, when Jimmy suddenly interrupts him by reporting he has scored three hundred points on a virtual reality video game. Jimmy is wearing an electronic glove on his right hand and a set of goggles over his eyes. He invites his grandmother to play the game with him; she is also wearing the electronic gear. Virtual reality gaming was extremely popular in the 1990s. Nintendo was the first company that released virtual reality technology into the home. The toy company, Mattel, manufactured the glove, partnering with Nintendo in selling the Power Glove to consumers in 1989. This glove, which looked like a winter glove, had a video game controller on the forearm to manipulate the settings for the game. Only four games were released that directly utilized the technology of the Power Glove, and so the technology was considered a failure. However, it cleared the way for other virtual reality technology to come. In 1991, Sega released a headset for their arcade games and Mega Drive console, which was also known as the Sega Genesis. This set of goggles was wired into the console and tracked the movement of the player's head, responding accordingly. They improved upon the technology and released the Sega VR-1 motion simulator arcade game in 1994, which transported players into the world of the digital video game environment. Nintendo released the Virtual Boy in 1995, a portable, table-top game, with a controller that was connected to a set of goggles on a tripod, allowing the game to be played anywhere. Other toy companies began to manufacture virtual reality games for both home use and arcade use. A few Disney connections to virtual reality gaming include *Aladdin's Magic Carpet Ride* and *Ride the Comix,* video games at DisneyQuest that utilize virtual reality technology to put gamers in the worlds of Agrabah and comic book battles, respectively.

After Jimmy's game, he raises the goggles from his face and invites his grandmother to participate as well. She is at first reluctant, but quickly accepts the challenge. At first, her coordination of the technology is rocky, but she quickly gets the hang of the game and starts destroying the enemy space rockets.

While Grandma is playing the video game and Jimmy watches, Sarah explains that she has finished programming the home's voice activation technology that will cause all the "household items [to] do anything we tell them to." She demonstrates the technology by requesting that the Christmas tree lights brighten, and they do in response to her prompt. She goes on to explain that the oven is also programmed to respond to John's instructions, and he tries it out by telling the oven to set to 375 degrees. The oven responds by confirming the temperature.

Voice recognition technology was first developed in 1936 for AT&T's Bell Laboratories to do initial research for taking instructions via verbal input to early computers that were part of their emerging telephone technology. Over the twentieth century, voice recognition technology improved. For example, in the 1960s, a speaker was required to pause between each word to allow the computer to recognize what was being said. This became obsolete in the 1970s, as pausing between words was no longer required. Today, speech recognition technology is used most commonly on smart phones, utilizing programs that let the speaker do Internet searches and make phone calls or text messages by speaking to their cell phone. However, this technology was still a long way off for adaptation in a home during the 1990s.

Patty, referred to as "Trish" in this scene, discusses the technology of the late twentieth century with her grandfather, who begins an "In my day … " story. He explains to her that he can remember a time without car phones, laser discs, and HDTV. Ironically enough, Patricia should also remember, since she has aged very little over the past hundred years. This interchange between Grandpa and Patricia dates the show; out of the three types of technology that the grandfather lists as being common in the scene (car phones, laser discs, hi-def television), only one is still in use today.

Because cellular telephone technology has changed so dramatically over the past twenty-five years, many young people today are not familiar with what a car phone was. The first car phone was developed in 1946 and used radio technology to transmit messages across three different frequency bands. Many could not afford the eighty-pound system, and so the car phone was not immediately popular. The technology became cheaper and more compact throughout the twentieth century, until it became suitable for consumer use in the 1980s and 1990s. Using radio band technology similar to that used in the 1940s, the signal was transmitted by a removable radio antenna that attached to the roof of the car via suction cup or heavy duty magnet. This allowed for calls to be made and received while on the road. The car phone quickly became obsolete in the United States in the mid and late 1990s as cell phone technology improved and became cheaper, as well as being more mobile than the car phone.

The second piece of extremely outdated technology that Grandpa references while talking to Patricia is laser discs. While laser discs were used concurrently with video cassettes and BetaMax cassettes, it never really caught on in the United States due to the high cost of purchasing a laser disc machine, as well as the high cost associated with purchasing a film on laser disc. Although laser discs did provide a higher definition viewing experience than competing VHS tapes, technology for video cassettes and VCRs improved, prices dropped, and laser discs went into decline. The price for laser disc films was as expensive as purchasing a VHS player, which deterred most consumers. Another disappointing factor of laser discs and their players was that they could only be used for play-back function, not for recording; because the film rental industry was not as common in the 1980s and early 1990s as it would be during the late 1990s and early 2000s, many families liked to record television programs and films on tape to watch them again later, something that was offered by VCRs but not laser disc players. Also, the discs, similar to CDs or DVDs, had a tendency of skipping or "blipping" if dust or fingerprints got on them. Even though VHS became the norm for home film viewing, evidence of laser disc technology can still be seen due to the market for DVD and Blu-ray films today.

The scene continues with very little historical references. In true Disney fashion, however, something goes wrong, adding tension and hilarity: as Grandma continues to score more and more points on the virtual reality video game, John compliments her high scores. Believing that John is instructing it to raise the temperature, the oven heats itself higher and higher each time John says a number until, unfortunately, the turkey catches fire and the oven explodes. The family laughs off the mishap and begin looking toward the twenty-first century and to technology that "can read our minds" to prevent John from "burning [the] Christmas turkey," something that has become an annual tradition for them.

The family begins singing the attraction's theme song together as the theater rotates counterclockwise one last time into a room similar to the one guests loaded into, with heavy curtains draped over the stage and a large gear in the middle. John's voice comes over the intercom and thanks guests for experiencing Walt Disney's Carousel of Progress, which he explains is a "tribute to the Carousel of Progress from the 1964 New York World's Fair." He encourages guests to gather their personal belongings and to exit the theater through the doors at the rear, bidding farewell to the audience by wishing them a "Great Big Beautiful Day." As guests step back out into the bright, Florida sunlight, whether they realize it or not, they have spent the past twenty minutes learning about how America has "progressed" throughout the twentieth century, proving how subtly Imagineers can capture the imagination and interest of park guests through the use of historical detail.

Part Four
OTHER ATTRACTIONS

Disneyland would be a world of Americans, past and present,
seen through the eyes of my imagination—a place of warmth
and nostalgia, of illusion and color and delight.

— *Walt Disney*

When Walt Disney created Disneyland during the 1950s, he opened it as a man who had red, white, and blue running through his veins. In fact, when he dedicated the park on its opening day in 1955, Walt explained that "Disneyland is dedicated to the ideals, the dreams, and the hard facts that have created America, with hope that it will be a source of joy and inspiration to all the world."

Walt, of all people, had a reason to be proud of his country as an American patriot.

His father, Elias Disney, worked as a carpenter, and was hired to help build the temporary structures that would house the 1893 World's Columbian Exposition, better known as the Chicago World's Fair, which served as a way for America to showcase its industrial strength and cultural dominance over the rest of the world.

As a boy, young Walter moved to Marceline, Missouri, which had sprung up in the late 1800s along the Santa Fe Railroad line. During the late 1800s and early decades of the 1900s, the railroad served as the backbone of American economics, acting not only as a method of long-distance transportation for passengers, but also as the main method through which raw materials and products were transported across the country. Many of the towns through which the railroad ran and the surrounding areas provided resources and raw materials to help the railroad function at full capacity, as well as any goods that those traveling along the railway may have required, something that Walt participated in during his teenage years in Kansas City, selling newspapers and snacks to railroad patrons. Walt's love of trains developed at this young age, and would later manifest itself when he would build the Carolwood Pacific Railroad in the backyard of his home, and later, the passenger railroad that would encircle Disneyland.

Young Walt was also employed by his father to deliver newspapers after the family moved to Kansas City, leading to a transition in Walt's life from the backbone of American industry working on the railroad to delivering newspapers, the lifeblood of American culture in the era of his youth. While Walt often discussed the hard times he endured twice daily delivering the *Kansas City Star* for his father, including the bitter cold of Midwest winters and the utter exhaustion from beginning his deliveries before dawn, he also recognized that the experience developed in him a strong work ethic and helped him to become the man he eventually would become.

During the latter days of Walt's teenage years, he was finally able to escape the growing dullness of the Midwest and his father's high expectations. After three of Walt's older brothers, including Roy, joined the armed forces in 1917, when America entered World War I, Walt also desired to enlist to defend the country he loved and follow in his brave brothers' footsteps. Being only sixteen, Walt was too young to enlist in the infantry forces, and instead applied to become an ambulance driver for the American Red Cross. When Walt and a friend were rejected, he changed his birth date on his passport to 1900, instead of 1901, explaining to his parents that he didn't want his grandchildren to think he was a "slacker" for not supporting his country in the war. Elias and his wife, Flora, finally relented, and Walt traveled to Chicago, where he was stationed, awaiting deployment.

Before he could be deployed overseas, Walt contracted influenza during the epidemic of 1918 and had to return home to be cared for by his parents. When finally he returned to Chicago, the war had ended, but he was chosen to be sent to France to help the nation recover in the war's aftermath.

While stationed in France, Walt was employed as an ambulance driver, but did very little transporting of the sick or injured. Instead, he ran errands for the hospitals and those who were enlisted, as well as providing tours of the region for visiting dignitaries. During downtimes, Walt drew cartoons of a doughboy character he had created, a young soldier fighting on behalf of the Americans against the regime of German Kaiser Wilhelm II.

After a year in France, Walt returned to America where he would soon begin his work in animation. Serving his nation as a military representative, even though he did not fight in battle, helped to deepen a sense of American pride in the young Midwesterner.

Walt carried his American pride into adulthood, making it a key part of Walt Disney Productions. During the 1940s, Walt would once again have the opportunity to serve his nation when he turned the Disney studio into a propaganda production facility, employing ninety percent of the studio's animators and artists in the creation of training films for the military and animated shorts to educate the American public about ways to support the war effort.

For example, the animated short *Food Will Win the War* educated Americans about food conservation, as well as helping to encourage farmers of their significance in defeating the Axis powers of Germany,

Italy, and Japan during World War II. Another short film, *Education for Death*, showed a young German boy, Hans, as he grows from childhood innocence and, after being indoctrinated by Nazi ideology, becomes a Nazi soldier, ultimately dying for the German cause in war. A more light-hearted look at the war featured Donald Duck in numerous propaganda films, including *Der Fuehrer's Face*, which portrayed Nazi Germany and its radical practices in a ridiculous manner, encouraging Americans not to take the Germans too seriously while showing them how thankful they should be that they lived in a nation of freedom.

Disney was also called upon by the United States government to help increase good will toward the country in Latin America. In the early 1940s, Walt Disney and some of his best artists and animators were sent to Latin and South America, where they made observations of and created art based on Latin American landscapes, peoples, and customs. Out of this trip came two important, but lesser-known Disney animated films, *Saludos Amigos* and *The Three Caballeros*, released in 1942 and 1944, respectively.

Many of Disney's animated shorts and feature films, as well as numerous live-action feature and television films focused on American themes, as well. For example, in 1948 Disney released *Melody Time*, featuring two animated shorts that were based on historical American legends: Johnny Appleseed and Pecos Bill. In 1957, Disney released *Johnny Tremain* to theaters, which would later air on *The Wonderful World of Disney* television anthology series. The film, based on the novel of the same name, followed a young man living in Boston during the events of the American Revolution.

However, the most popular of Disney's history-based projects was *Davy Crockett: King of the Wild Frontier*, a five-part miniseries that aired on his *Disneyland* anthology television series from 1954–1955. This show helped to bring the coonskin cap into the American consciousness, and even made its way into Disneyland when it opened in 1955 through the introduction of the Davy Crockett Frontier Museum, featuring wax figures of many of the show's popular characters as well as the Davy Crockett Explorer Canoes and the Mike Fink Keel Boats, which allowed guests to navigate the Rivers of America surrounding Tom Sawyer Island.

One of the most interesting ways Walt Disney contributed to Americana, however, was also significant to the history of The Walt Disney Company and Disney theme parks throughout the world today.

From April 22, 1964, until October 17, 1965, the New York World's Fair was held in Flushing Meadows Park in Queens, New York. While many different nations contributed to world's fairs, these expositions were generally meant to glorify the host nation and its accomplishments and technological innovations. Three American companies (General Electric, Ford, and Pepsi) and the State of Illinois called upon Walt during the planning stages for the fair. Walt and his crew of Imagineers focused on highlighting American ingenuity, the American dream, and American liberty for three of these pavilions.

In the Ford Magic Skyway attraction, Walt himself narrated a ride through history, highlighting man's past, the invention of transportation, and the future of vehicles. Walt's partnership with Ford featured a fitting dynamic, as both Henry Ford and Walt Disney were true American visionaries, focusing on how they could improve the lives of Americans during the times in which they lived.

The second pavilion, General Electric's Carousel of Progress, highlighted American ingenuity and the progress of technology, as a family pursued the American dream from the late nineteenth century through the near future.

The third pavilion, sponsored by the state of Illinois, highlighted the most famous of the state's historical figures who exemplified American freedom and liberty, Abraham Lincoln.

The fourth pavilion, hosted by Pepsi as a salute to UNICEF, featured the now classic attraction, It's a Small World, and worked to instill a message of acceptance, tolerance, and love between the nations of the world.

These four attractions provided Disney with the finances and motivation to develop the fledgling technology of audio-animatronics, which would soon be used in his growing theme park empire.

Walt's newest project, the Experimental Prototype Community of Tomorrow, more commonly known as Epcot, would never come to fruition in its original concept due to Walt's death in 1966. However, in addition to his goals of achieving the utopian ideals of city planning and eradicating the problems of slum living and infrastructure and transportation issues, Walt understood what it meant to be an American. In everything that he did, he attempted to improve upon things, to make life better for himself, his children, and the families of America.

As I researched the topics of this book, I realized that each of them, while not necessarily influenced by Walt on a personal level, were influenced by the ideas and American beliefs of Walt Disney. The attractions and venues discussed in this volume reflect the American ideals and beliefs that Walt held dear:

§ The Country Bear Jamboree was to be an entertainment offering at the Mineral King Ski Resort that Walt had initially planned on developing in the Sequoia National Forest in 1965.

§ Casey's Corner, a small counter-service restaurant located on the west side of Main Street, U.S.A., in Walt Disney World's Magic Kingdom, is based on the animated segment "Casey at the Bat" from the 1946 package film *Make Mine Music*, and reflects the turn-of-the-twentieth-century sports culture that Walt may have experienced while living in Marceline.

§ Storybook Circus, a mini-land attached to New Fantasyland in the back of the Magic Kingdom, harkens back to family entertainment, as well as influence from numerous circus-themed shorts and films produced by Disney, including *Dumbo* and "Bongo," which was a part of the package film *Fun and Fancy Free*.

§ Spaceship Earth, the attraction located inside the iconic geodesic sphere located at the entrance to Epcot, represents the American spirit of innovation and improvement of technology, even while looking at key points of human history, beyond that of the USA.

§ Sunset Ranch Market, an outdoor food court located on Sunset Boulevard in Disney's Hollywood Studios, and themed around World War II, features different insignias designed by Disney animators to represent different units of the United States military during that war.

While Walt Disney has been gone for almost fifty years, his legacy of innovation, pursuing the American Dream, remembering and honoring our past, and appreciating the freedom and liberty we have in our nation continues to live on in numerous films, lands, and attractions as the result of his effort to showcase the best of America.

CHAPTER EIGHT

COUNTRY BEAR JAMBOREE

*E*very trip my family and I made to Walt Disney World when I was younger included one of our favorite shows, the Country Bear Jamboree. I'm not sure what it was about the show that we enjoyed so much, whether it was the audio-animatronics, the corny jokes, the music, or the air conditioning, but it was an attraction we made sure to experience on a regular basis. However, being a child, I was more often mystified by the illusion that real bears were on stage, singing songs and playing instruments, rather than understanding the music itself or even the historical implications of the show.

As I got older and developed my passion for the intricacies of Walt Disney World, I began investigating the digital resources available to me in terms of Disney websites and media. One afternoon, early in my high school years, my dad came home with a gift for me, which I still have: two burned CDs loaded with songs and soundtracks from Disney World parks and attractions. Having these two audio CDs, including the entire ride-throughs of Pirates of the Caribbean, the Haunted Mansion, and song clips from "it's a small world" and the Carousel of Progress, transformed my love of the Magic Kingdom into an obsession (thanks, Dad), as I could now relive my Disney World memories while driving to school or sitting in my bedroom. However, it was the first track on *Walt Disney World Songs, Volume 1* that I had on repeat, the full soundtrack to the Country Bear Jamboree.

With nothing but the audio from the attraction and my memories of it from our last trip there (YouTube wasn't around yet), I focused more on the banter of the hunting trophies, the lyrics to the songs, and the musical styling that made up this popular Disney World show. I quickly had the songs and dialogue memorized, which brought my appreciation of the attraction to a higher level during my next trip and future trips to the Magic Kingdom.

However, it wasn't until my high school and college years, as my interest in American history began to develop, that I began to realize that the Country Bear Jamboree wasn't meant to be set in the modern day era, but rather sometime in America's past. While the country songs that the bears sang were similar to those my maternal grandfather listened to as he and I would make trips to his farm in Newaygo, Michigan, the setting for the show was obviously meant to evoke a time and place more in the past than the 1960s and 1970s.

Interestingly, the story behind the attraction's development and the show itself exemplifies a part of the American Dream: Americans who are trying to improve entertainment, to bring happiness and pleasure to a wider range of people. The musical genre of the show is also distinctly American, a style that has been developed solely in the United States, and similar to the melding of cultures that have made American culture through the metaphor of the "melting pot" since the early twentieth century. Country music has pulled attractive aspects from many different musical genres from all over the world to create something new.

The story of the development of the Country Bear Jamboree is filled with controversy that still gets many people fired up today, in an age when environmentalism is a hot political issue. Disney fans lament what-could-have-been, while many nostalgic fans of Disneyland are bitter that the country bears no longer exist at Disneyland. While the storied history of the attraction is fascinating and often full of surprises, its historical backstory is just as intriguing.

"THERE WAS ... BLOOD ON THE SADDLE": MINERAL KING

After the success of Disneyland in 1955, Walt Disney began looking for other projects to expand the scope of both family entertainment and his growing entertainment empire. In 1964, he sponsored four different pavilions for the New York World's Fair, held in Queens, New York. Disney and WED Enterprises (the new Imagineering branch personally owned by Walt) created attractions for General Electric, Ford, Pepsi, and the State of Illinois, leading to classic Disney attractions like Walt Disney's Carousel of Progress and "it's a small world."

The success of Walt's attractions at the New York World's Fair led him to turn his attention to creating an East Coast version of Disneyland, and as a result, Walt and WED began to investigate a remote area of central Florida. However, Walt did not plan on simply replicating Disneyland in the swampland of Florida, but rather wanted to create a "vacation kingdom," ultimately purchasing forty-three square miles of land to house the new resort.

While the Magic Kingdom opened on October 1, 1971, this was not Walt's true intention for the Florida property: in 1966, he presented a film to the Florida legislature to convince them to allow him to use the land to build what he called Epcot, or the Experimental Prototype Community of Tomorrow. Immensely interested in city planning, Walt intended on creating a futuristic city, which would allow for people to vacation and live in the metropolitan center, facilitating interaction between different cultures and revolutionizing urban infrastructure, including transportation and waste disposal. For example, Epcot would function without automobiles; a multi-tiered highway would run beneath the city, allowing for traffic to pass through, while visitors and residents of Epcot would utilize WEDWay PeopleMovers and monorails to get around from place to place.

Unfortunately, after Walt's death in 1966, his plans for Epcot fell apart, and in haste to develop the Florida property, the company decided to build a larger version of Disneyland, known as the Magic Kingdom, and two resort hotels, the Contemporary and the Polynesian. Many of these revolutionary technologies and city planning techniques, however, would be incorporated into Walt Disney World's property when it opened in 1971, including the underground utility corridors, known as the Utilidors, as well as the monorail transportation system around the Seven Seas Lagoon.

However, it was shortly after the opening of Disneyland in the 1950s that Walt began to develop ideas for one of the most controversial Disney projects in the history of the company. While on location in Europe filming the live-action film *The Third Man on the Mountain* in the late 1950s, Walt fell in love with the rugged terrain of the Alps. In fact, his interest in the European Swiss Alps led to the creation of the Matterhorn Bobsleds attraction at Disneyland. However, another direct result of Walt's interest in snowcapped mountainous vistas led to his involvement in producing the opening and closing ceremonies of the 1960 Winter Olympics, held in Squaw Valley, California. Together, the production of *The Third Man on the Mountain* in the Swiss Alps and his involvement in the Squaw Valley Winter Olympics caused a deep interest in winter sports and the mountain ranges of California, which would ultimately manifest itself in the years before and after his death.

In early 1965, the National Forest Service issued a statement requesting proposals for the development of a ski resort in Sequoia National Forest, a region surrounded on three sides by Sequoia National Park, located in central California in the southern Sierra Nevada Mountains. Established in 1908 by President Theodore Roosevelt, the Sequoia National Forest was intentionally separated from the adjacent Sequoia National Park because of the future possibility of using the land for its mineral resources. In the 1870s, silver was discovered in Mineral King, a portion of which would later become the Sequoia National Forest.

Virtually overnight, hundreds of prospectors flocked to the valley to mine the precious metal. However, the mineral riches were quickly depleted and the area became a ghost town, home only to a few seasonal cabins, occasional hikers, and various forms of wildlife. In an effort to encourage conservation of the area and to foster the return of native flora and fauna, Congress named Mineral King a national game refuge, withholding the status of national park in case more silver was discovered in the area in future years.

In 1948, the Sierra Club, an organization aimed at environmental protection founded by famed conservationist John Muir, proposed the building of a ski resort in the Mineral King region of Sequoia National Forest. However, access to the proposed area would require the building of a road through the national forest, which would result in the displacement of trees and the destruction of the habitats of various forms of wildlife. This idea was revisited by the United States Forest Service in 1965, and after receiving six proposals for the development of a ski resort, the forest service awarded the contract to Walt Disney Productions.

Disney and his team immediately began to work on permits for the building of his newest endeavor, the Mineral King Ski Resort, which would be located on the valley floor of the Mineral King area. The resort land would utilize approximately forty percent of that area, while the village itself would take up only twenty percent of the game refuge. Given three years to present plans for the new resort, including its effect on the local environment, Disney got to work on a set of blueprints.

With a lease on the land for thirty years, the ski resort would feature two individual resort hotels. A series of ten restaurants, including the Sky Crown, which would sit atop Eagle's Crest Ridge at 11,090 feet above sea level, would feed the one million projected annual visitors. The resort would be home to numerous ski runs, but would also provide entertainment and activities to non-skiers, such as swimming, tobogganing, sledding, and ice skating during the winter, and hiking, horse-back riding, fishing, cave exploration, and camping during the summer. The resort village of Mineral King would also feature specialized shops, a chapel, and a small movie theater to cater to visitors. Disney was able to acquire all necessary permits in 1968, and intended to open the resort to visitors in 1973, although with portions incomplete. The resort was to be fully operational by 1976.

Drawing upon his plans for Epcot, Walt Disney incorporated many of his ideas on urban planning in order to preserve the natural beauty of the area, as well as to help conserve the natural environment. For example, automobiles would not be permitted for guests staying at the Mineral King Ski Resort. Upon arriving at the resort, visitors would park their vehicles in an underground parking garage, which would hold 3,600 cars. They would then board an old-fashioned steam-powered cog loco-motive, also known as a rack railway, which would transport them from the foot of the valley, through the mountains, to the resort itself. Often used in areas where a steep grade is present, rack railways are similar to modern locomotives, except that they utilize a center rail that has teeth; a cog located in the center of the railcar meshes with the center rail, reducing the chances of sliding backwards and giving the wheels some-thing to lock onto as the train climbs uphill. Disney also developed tech-nology for what was called WEDLifts, which were a series of fourteen ski lifts that could be converted into a skyway during the summer months, allowing for aerial transport of skiers and non-skiers alike. In order to preserve the natural beauty of the area, these lifts would be camouflaged.

The developers of the Disney resort also planned on utilizing sight lines of the mountain peaks to make the resort unseen from outside the resort property at the entrance of the valley. Because the resort was located a distance from any major metropolitan areas, Disney also planned on providing its own electricity to power the resort, as well as water storage tanks and sewage treatment facilities, mirroring some of the revolutionary ideas proposed by Walt for Epcot.

The Mineral King was for many a welcome addition to Disney's properties on the West Coast. In fact, Walt Disney and his company were actually given two distinctive awards. The team of designers from WED received the Outstanding Service in Conservation of American Resources award for their efforts to build a tourism facility while maintaining the natural environment in the region. Walt himself was awarded the Hans Georg Award posthumously, which is given to the one person who has made the largest contribution to the sport of skiing each year, as a result of Walt's work designing the ski resort. Unfortunately, however, one group was staunchly against the addition of the tourist destination to Sequoia National Forest: the Sierra Club.

Founded in 1892 by conservationist John Muir, the Sierra Club was created to advocate for the protection of earth's natural resources and environments. The modern-day Sierra Club focuses on advocating for renewable energy and looks for ways to reverse global warming. When Walt Disney Productions announced the creation of the Mineral King Ski Resort in 1965, the Sierra Club became the company's most vocal opponent. Conservationists Jean and Richard Koch spent over a decade resisting the influence of Walt Disney Productions in building the ski resort, holding hike-ins in the game refuge, submitting petitions to state and federal legislators, and even marching in protest at Disneyland.

The main argument of the Sierra Club centered around the building of a road through Sequoia National Park that would bring visitors to the underground parking garage at the foot of the valley. After being presented a plan by Walt Disney Productions, Interior Secretary of the United States Stewart Udall gave permission to the company to build the road through the national park on the stipulation that the road would "not result in the removal of a single redwood" tree. The Sierra Club objected to the building of this road, which would upgrade the pre-existing one-lane dirt path into a multi-lane, high speed, all-weather highway that would cut through the Sequoia National Park to bring guests to the parking location. The conservationist society argued that this would displace eight million cubic yards of rock and dirt, causing erosion in the draining of the roadway during rainstorms and displacing the natural habitats of local wildlife. They also argued that the ease of access would lead to overcrowding of the area, and could ultimately lead to the destruction of the natural beauty of Sequoia.

Disney explained that the destruction of Sequoia National Forest and the Mineral King region was not their intention, but rather its conservation and benefit. For example, a nearby horseback riding company was polluting the nearby river with bacteria from horse droppings; evidence of this was present downstream in the Kaweah River, which Disney promised to remediate if given the chance to build the Mineral King Ski Resort. However, this was not convincing enough for the Sierra Club.

The efforts of the Sierra Club were not sufficient to win the National Park Service to their agenda. With Udall's approval of the building of the highway through Sequoia National Park, the organization decided to go to court. In 1969, the Sierra Club sued the leadership of Sequoia National Forest and Sequoia National Park, as well as the secretaries of Agriculture and Interior at the federal court level, asserting that "the project improperly handed control of too much national forest land to Disney" and that "the highway through the national park was illegal." In order to quell the complaints of the plaintiffs, the judge ordered an injunction, halting the building of the highway while the matter was investigated.

The case went to the United States Supreme Court in *Sierra Club v Morton, 1972*. The court ruled against the Sierra Club 4–3, explaining that the organization did not have a valid reason to sue, since the building of the road and the ski resort would not harm any individuals or individual property. The court cited that the argument of the Sierra Club, rather, would simply "vindicate their own value preferences." The justice who wrote the verdict on behalf of the Supreme Court, Potter Stewart, did note that "aesthetic and environmental well-being, like economic well-being, are important ingredients of the quality of life ... [and are] deserving of legal protection." This statement led the Sierra Club to believe that if they simply amended their argument and evidence, they would still prevail.

On January 1, 1970, President Richard Nixon signed the National Environmental Policy Act, which required all federal agencies to study the environmental effects of proposed actions, a direct result of an oil spill that occurred in Santa Barbara, California, in 1969. Ultimately completed in 1976, the United States Forest Service completed their report on the Mineral King area, looking at effects on the region of water flow, the visitation of millions of people annually, snowfall, and other factors.

More than a decade old, the idea for the Mineral King Ski Resort began to lose steam. No longer finding it worth the effort to fight the Sierra Club in the matter, Disney abandoned the idea of building a ski resort at Mineral King. The final nail in the coffin came in 1978, when President Jimmy Carter signed the National Parks and Recreation Act, which officially made the Mineral King area and Sequoia National Forest a part of Sequoia National Park.

"AND NOW, HERE IS A SPECIAL TREAT OUT OF BURBANK": DEVELOPING THE COUNTRY BEAR JAMBOREE

While in the planning stages for the Mineral King Ski Resort, Walt Disney realized that not all guests would be interested in participating in skiing or the other recreational activities of the valley. In true Disney form, Walt and his Imagineers at WED began to develop various theming

and entertainment offerings to enrich the experience of the resort's visitors. Because Walt was a firm believer in theme and story, and because
Mineral King was located in the Sierra Nevada range of California, he
decided to theme his entertainment offerings around the local residents
of the region—bears. This may have been a result of the popularity of
the Humphrey the Bear cartoons produced by Disney, a character created in the early 1950s to promote tourism in the national park system
(interestingly, the grunts and utterances of Humphrey were provided
by Disney sound effects technician, Jimmy MacDonald, who would later
voice Mickey Mouse after Walt's smoking made it difficult for him to continue voicing the mouse in 1947).

In an effort to keep visitors at the Mineral King Ski Resort after fin-
ishing their day's activities, Walt decided to create an entertainment
offering that would feature "lots and lots of bears." Fresh off the success
of his most recent attraction, Pirates of the Caribbean (which opened in
1967 in Disneyland), Walt tasked one of his best Imagineers, Marc Davis,
to develop some sort of show for evening entertainment at the Mineral
King. Originally an animator who worked on films such as *Snow White
and the Seven Dwarfs* and *Peter Pan*, Davis is well known by Disney fans
as someone who added humor to his work and often portrayed his animated and animatronic characters in a caricatured style. Throughout
the many weeks and months after being charged by Walt to develop the
show, Davis spent time developing concept art for what the show could
be. Davis drew pictures of various species of bear in an anthropomorphic manner, performing in humorous situations like riding bicycles,
wearing formal clothing, singing, and playing instruments. After seeing
Davis' work, Walt encouraged him to develop the idea of a show where
animatronic bears sing and play music.

However, with the focus being on developing the resort and addressing the challenges against the Mineral King by the Sierra Club, creating a

show for the ski resort was put on the backburner. Ultimately, the attraction was developed for Walt Disney World's Magic Kingdom, entertaining guests on the park's opening day in 1971. While Davis developed the show and the style of the bears along with Imagineer Al Bertino (who worked on the Humphrey the Bear cartoons), composer George Bruns and Imagineer Xavier "X" Atencio, who also wrote the lyrics for "Yo Ho (A Pirate's Life for Me)" and "Grim Grinning Ghosts," wrote or adapted the songs for the attraction.

The development of the visuals for the show, which would take the form of audio-animatronic figures, happened concurrently with the development of its soundtrack, as the song choices for the attraction often inspired the design of the characters. The show features eighteen audio-animatronic bears on five stages, while audio-animatronic busts of a buffalo, a buck, and a moose hang on the wall to the right of the stage. The show runs approximately fifteen minutes and features twelve songs, most of which were adapted from previous musical artists, though some are original works by Atencio and Bruns.

The show itself takes place inside Grizzly Hall, which is a union hall set somewhere in the West around the late 1920s or early 1930s, although a sign above the attraction's marquee lists Grizzly Hall as being established in 1898. Another sign commemorating the founder of the local performance hall, Ursus H. Bear, lists his death as 1928 (the term "ursus" refers to a genus of bear, which includes the brown bear, and is what the bespectacled subject of the portrait looks to be). In 1928, vaudeville was at its heyday as a form of stage performance akin to the modern variety show featuring dance, slapstick comedy, and musical acts, which is the type of show that the attraction is supposed to represent.

Originating in France in the valley of Vire (vaux de Vire, replacing Vire with "ville" when it arrived in America, hence "vaudeville"), vaudeville's roots stretch back to the 1850s and 1860s, when musical and comedy acts traveled from frontier settlement to frontier settlement, or visited the circuits of men's clubs in large urban areas. Often made up of obscene comedy acts and bawdy musical numbers, these shows targeted men, and often provided alcoholic beverages to help the patrons escape the problems of life on the frontier or the troubles of the big cities. The shows sometimes featured women wearing immodest clothing, at least for the time, with extremely short skirts (hemmed at the knees, oh my!), sheer cloaks, and flesh-colored tights. Another popular genre of vaudeville shows had white actors ("minstrel comedians") painted in blackface and speaking and singing like blacks—an act considered racist today, but an accepted part of culture in the antebellum America of the 1850s.

One of the most famous of these minstrel comedians, Bert Williams, was a black man who used his race to not only perform as a minstrel, but also make fun of the genre itself. A well-known bit featured Williams dressed in a bird costume, acting as a "submissive" black man named Jim Crow, poking fun at the harsh discriminatory practices against blacks in the South following the Civil War. These shows continued throughout the latter part of the nineteenth century, becoming more popular as cities sprung up to entertain masses of men.

One famous acting troupe of the mid-nineteenth century was the Jolly Corks, a drinking club made up of comedians that entertained groups of men in New York City who would later become the Elks club. After attending a funeral for a friend, the group gathered to reflect on the life of the deceased member of the Jolly Corks and one member, George F. McDonald, suggested that the comedic troupe become a "protective and benevolent society." The Jolly Corks visited local theater owner Tony Pastor, who owned the opera house at 201 Bowery. There they began a partnership with the proprietor, ultimately establishing the first Grand Lodge of the Order of Elks.

Spending most of his life as an entertainer, Pastor was sent away from his home in the city while a teenager by his father to "curb his boyhood penchant for performance," but was quickly sent back home because he distracted the other field hands with his comedy bits. He routinely performed for P.T. Barnum, and even sang and made jokes at various saloons. Involved in show business during the Civil War, Pastor was well known for ending his routines by hosting a sing-along of "The Star-Spangled Banner."

In 1865, he decided to make the bawdy men's shows more appropriate for family audiences and opened his New York theater, Tony Pastor's Opera House at 201 Bowery. It held multiple performances of variety shows each evening, with the earlier shows more appropriate for women and families, while the later shows catered more toward male audiences. In 1867, McDonald and the Jolly Corks approached Pastor about performing in these more chaste acts, wishing to reach a wider audience. The success of Pastor's Opera House Bowery led him to move his performance hall to Broadway in 1875, resulting in the popularization of vaudeville as an American pastime.

The last few decades of the nineteenth century were a peak time of European immigration to the United States, specifically from the central and eastern European countries around the turn of the century. Upon arriving to the United States via ship, these immigrants entered the country through an immigration station located in Upper New York Bay called Ellis Island. After disembarking, they would go through a series of tests, medical examinations, and interviews to determine whether they were fit for admission to the United States or were to be sent back to their place of origin.

Because many immigrants were extremely poor and had spent most of their life savings for passage to America, plus the fact that many of them came from agricultural regions and had very few industrial or work skills, most of them settled in major urban areas of the Northeast and Midwest, such as New York, Detroit, and Chicago. The settlement of these large numbers of immigrants often led to racism and discrimination against European immigrants by Americans, an idea known as Nativism, or favoring native-born Americans. In an attempt to help their families financially, as well as to overcome the racism that they often experienced, some immigrants utilized skills from their home countries in performance. One example of this is Yiddish theater, which featured stories from traditional Jewish culture. Another example is the well-known Marx Brothers, who got their start on vaudeville as a musical and slapstick comedy act that later translated to film.

Flo Ziegfeld, the producer of the *Ziegfeld Follies*, put on an annual show that featured sexualized women and other popular acts, and promoted a strongman act from Germany, Eugen Sandow, during the 1890s. Sandow, known as the father of bodybuilding, performed feats such as lifting a horse or large barbells to amaze theatergoers. Ziegfeld would later go on to employ famous performing artists for his *Follies*, such as Will Rogers, W.C. Fields, and Eddie Cantor.

During the 1920s and 1930s, vaudeville began its decline as new mediums for entertainment began to emerge. The New York vaudeville scene was slowly replaced by the shows of Broadway theaters, such as musicals and plays. With the invention and popularization of the radio, many vaudeville acts began to perform on the radio in serial shows, such as those starring Jack Benny and Ed Wynn. Other vaudevillian actors and comedy troupes starred in film or film shorts, including the Marx Brothers, W.C. Fields, Charlie Chaplin, Buster Keaton, and Larry, Moe, and Curly of the Three Stooges.

"AN ASSORTED ASSORTMENT OF EXECUTIONERS OF MUSIC AND SONG"

The Country Bear Jamboree can take its roots from vaudeville, albeit it focuses on musical acts rather than slapstick comedy routines, magic, or acrobatics. As noted above, the show takes place sometime after 1928, as that is when Grizzly Hall founder, Ursus H. Bear, died. This would fit into the period when vaudeville was at its peak in popularity.

The intended location of the attraction can be deduced from clues in the show itself. The show building, Grizzly Hall, is located in Frontierland, which represents the spirit of the American West, so it can be assumed the show takes place somewhere west of the Mississippi River. Also, one bear is referred to by its subspecies: Zed, a brown bear playing the fiddle for the Five Bear Rugs, is referred to as a bruin (a Dutch word for the species brown bear). The "Grizzly" in Grizzly Hall is the name of a subspecies of brown bear. The brown bear and the grizzly are now mainly located in the Pacific Northwest region of the United States, which includes Montana, Wyoming, and Washington. Also, one of the busts on the wall is that of an American bison, which live in a similar area, with some of the largest concentrations being in Wyoming. However, the emcee of the show, Henry, does introduce some bears as being from the Sunshine State (Florida) and "a special treat out of Tampa," which is approximately seventy miles west of Walt Disney World. With the number of references to regions in the American West (including a bear referred to as the "dimpled darling of the Dakotas"), it is likely that the bears from Florida have simply traveled out west to participate in the musical revue.

Grizzly Hall itself is themed as a building constructed from logs. Its high peak and balcony harkens to the architecture of the American Pacific Northwest. Old-fashioned kerosene lanterns hang on the pillars supporting the balcony, while a long sign advertises to passersby the current performance featuring three bears playing their instruments and singing. Short catchphrases hint to guests what they are about to experience: "singin' & stompin', clappin' & growlin', Country Bear Jamboree, a Wild & Wooly Good Time!"

To the right of the entrance door is a pendulum clock listing the minutes until the next show, helping to set the time period, rather than the face or digital clocks used for wait times for attractions elsewhere on property. This clock looks similar to a Regulator Pendulum clock, which used the weighted, swinging pendulum to keep the clock wound, rather than having to be wound by hand like a face clock.

The waiting area for the show is fairly simple and relatively unthemed; horizontal wooden panels line the wall up to a chair rail, above which is plaster that is painted pale yellow. Gas lamps are mounted to the wall, as well as gas chandeliers hanging from the ceiling. Wooden pillars spread throughout the room help to hold the ceiling up, which is supported by heavy wooden beams that stretch its length. The extent of the detail and backstory in the waiting area are oval portraits of the different performers of the show in cartoon, rather than animatronic, form; these portraits may actually be reproductions of the conceptual art for the characters drawn by Davis and Bertino as they developed the ideas for the attraction. The floor of the waiting lobby, however, reveals its most interesting detail: small black scratches approximately three to four inches long are featured over the wooden planks that serve for the flooring of the room, leading the observant guest to realize that this show is not only performed by bears, but also patronized by bears, whose claws gouge the floor as they walk into the theater every night.

When the next show is ready to begin, guests are funneled through heavy, wooden doors down a relatively unthemed hallway through a velvet curtain into the theater, where wooden benches await them. Each of the four stages flanking the middle stage have turntables, which allow multiple audio-animatronic bears to appear individually throughout the show.

The theater features five stages, each draped with a red velvet curtain.
Each stage is capped with ornamental woodwork, featuring gold inlays
and scrolling sculpting that includes curlicues and carved images of trout
and cherubic bears. The center stage has a plaque and portrait commemorating the founder of Grizzly Hall, Ursus H. Bear, listing his birth and
death dates as 1848 and 1928, respectively. The ornamental nature of
the stage leads guests to assume that this is no small town, rinky-dink
theater, but rather a theater managed by a well-to-do community. The
central stage is also lit at stage level by a series of gas lanterns. First used
in the 1800s, footlights, or lanterns lit by gas at the edge of the stage, were
controlled by the turning of valves, which allowed the show technicians
to raise and lower light levels based on the amount of gas that was burning. The light was magnified by reflecting off a concave mirror, throwing the light forward onto the performers and set pieces on stage, rather
than backward into the audience. Eventually, these gas lamps would be
converted to electric light bulbs, but this didn't happen en mass until the
early decades of the twentieth century.

A scrim curtain hangs over the stage, hiding the performers from
the audience. Emblazoned across it are a number of advertisements,
including "Unicycles for Trick Bears" from the Bruin Cycle Company (a
reference to the Disney animated short "Bongo" where the titular character, a circus bear, rides a unicycle), and "The 'Dump,' Continental
Cuisine" with booths available for bears. Surrounded by the bear-
themed advertisements is an image of two bears, a male and female,
sitting in a canoe under a moonlit sky. This type of curtain was common
in vaudeville theaters, where it was used to advertise local products
and companies, including physicians and grocers. These drop curtains
also included images or paintings of a nature or cultural scene, such as
the one of the bears in the canoe, which defined the local community's identity and favorite scenery from the area. While the introductory

roll-drop curtains provided an image with advertisements, they also provided the background scenery for the acts or scenes in a vaudeville or stage performance. Because the painting on the advertising scrim shows a bare, snow-capped mountain on the right, and because painted roll-drop curtains often portrayed the activities and backdrop of the area, we can assume that the theater likely takes place somewhere near the craggy Rocky Mountains rather than the more eastern Appalachian Mountains, which are covered in trees. This further proves that the location of Grizzly Hall is somewhere in the northwestern portion of North America.

As the show begins, the lights dim and a spotlight illuminates three hunting trophies hanging on the right-hand wall: a bison, a white-tailed buck, and a moose. The three busts come to life and begin to have a conversation. The buffalo, voiced by Thurl Ravenscroft (who provided a lot of voice work for Disney films and attractions, as well as being the original voice for Tony the Tiger), begins to harass the bears backstage, impatiently telling them to hurry up and start the show, while the moose and buck tell him to be patient and make jokes to try to lighten him up. The jokes and comments of the three trophies, which occur throughout the show, is reminiscent of of the vaudeville era, when audience members—especially those in the bawdy men's shows—would yell and mock the performers, sometimes resorting to throwing tomatoes at them. This is also exemplified by the comments of Statler and Waldorf in episodes of *The Muppet Show* and the *Muppet*Vision* 3D attraction at Disney's Hollywood Studios, another example of a vaudevillian-type variety show.

The fifteen minute show is a combination of both pre-existing songs and original songs written by George Bruns and X. Atencio. In fact, only two original songs were written for the show: "The Bear Band Serenade" and "Come Again." The remaining eleven songs were popular during the 1940s, 1950s, and 1960s, and represent subgenres of country music, including bluegrass, folk, blues, the ballad, Western music, and rockabilly. One of the main inspirations for the show was a Appalachian family musical group of the 1960s, the Stonemans, who not only recorded much of the instrumental music for the show, but even provided some of the singing voices of the characters.

While the show features thirteen songs, some of the songs have more interesting historical implications than others. For example, a bear named Ernest, his fiddle bearing his stage name, "The Dude," sings the third song, "If Ya Can't Bite, Don't Growl." While the modern term "dude" describes a cool guy, the word in the latter years of the nineteenth and the first half of the twentieth centuries had a very different meaning. During the period of American history known as the Gilded Age, lasting from the 1870s until the 1920s, metropolitan areas began to grow exponentially as the populations of urban areas began to explode; blacks fled racism and discrimination in the south by moving to northern cities, technology began making previous agricultural practices obsolete, and large amounts of immigrants began flooding into America. As a result, in an effort to portray an aura of dominance, a group of upper class men, known as dudes, began to wear flashy clothing, such as tall hats, crazy colored (for the time) pants, and other extravagant outfits, attempting to outdo each other through their flashy attire. Because of the big city nature of these dandies, they were often seen by the rest of American society as only being able to function in the cities, eventually getting the title of "city boys."

The latter years of the nineteenth century led to the popularization of the Old West, with the rise of Western circuses such as Buffalo Bill Cody's Wild West Show, and many city dwellers began to travel out west to experience its culture and practices. This led to the creation of dude ranches, which gave visitors from the cities an opportunity to learn how to ride horses, herd cattle, and learn the "ways" of a cowboy. This often led to a miserable vacation, as depicted so well in the 1991 film *City Slickers*.

It is obvious that Davis and Bertino were mocking the dude of American cities during the Gilded Age in the show, as even Ernest's song features content about a city boy who got in over his head when he visited a men's club; when approached by a go-go dancer, Ernest refuses because of his marital status, and is reprimanded by the dancer for being at a men's club instead of being faithful to his wife.

The next song, "My Woman Ain't Pretty," is performed by country singer Tex Ritter, through the audio-animatronic bear, Liver Lips McGrowl. The song shows the connection between blues music and country music, explaining that Liver Lips' wife is not attractive, but is a moral woman, and that while he's in the relationship begrudgingly, he is faithful to his wife and as a result stays with her. Ritter also sings another song in the show, "Blood on the Saddle," lip-synced by one of the best known characters of the show, Big Al. Big Al is a large gray bear wearing a cowboy hat with an upturned brim. He is obviously under the influence, as a corked jug sits on the ground next to him as he sings his tragic song about a cowboy who has been crushed by his horse and lies dying on the ground. Big Al's drunkenness causes him to interrupt the show while Henry sings "The Ballad of Davey Crockett," only stopping when his inebriation causes him to fall off his stool and through the curtain, leading Henry to close out the show before things get further out of hand. Interestingly, Big Al was modeled after Al Bertino, one of the show's co-creators, both in image and namesake.

Another song with an interesting historical backstory is "Mama Don't Whup Little Buford," sung as a duet by emcee Henry playing guitar and another bear, Wendell, playing the mandolin. When the attraction opened in 1971, another Henry-Wendell duet ("Fractured Folk Song") was in the show, but was removed during a refurbishment in 2012. Both of these songs were originally performed by comedic bluegrass singers Henry Haynes and Kenneth Burns, better known as Homer and Jethro. In fact, the banter between Henry and Wendell at the beginning of "Fractured Folk Song" came directly from the Homer and Jethro song on their record by the same name. When Marc Davis designed the characters of Henry and Wendell, it appears he even modeled the image of the bears on Homer and Jethro: Henry is significantly taller than Wendell, just like Jethro was taller than Homer. When comparing conceptual art of Wendell to a photograph of Jethro, physical similarities are also evident, such as the overbite and toothy grin, as well as the large smile that causes their big cheeks to make their small eyes disappear.

Because Homer and Jethro took on the persona of hillbillies when performing, as well as made self-deprecating jokes about their appearance, the modeling of Henry and Wendell after the bluegrass singers helps to further the illusion and story of the two country music-singing bears. In order to set the scene for Henry and Wendell's hillbilly bluegrass song, a roll-drop curtain is lowered to show the scene of a wooden shack across from a run-down barn. Chickens mill about in the dirt path between the two, while a pair of worn long johns hangs from the porch of the shack, drying in the breeze.

Out of all the songs in the show, only three are sung by female characters, which may be a sign of the times in which Davis, Bertino, Atencio, and Bruns developed the attraction; very few women sang country music popularly during the 1950s and 1960s. This was significant, because like many professions in America at the time, men dominated the country music scene during the mid-century years. While more women eventually became country singing stars in their own right, they often were relegated to songs about relationships and the world of women and emotions. As a result, it is interesting that all three songs performed by the female bears are about relationships and heartbreak.

The first female act is by Trixie, an extremely large bear who wipes her eyes with a handkerchief with one hand and holds a glass of wine in the other. Another of the acts features a made-up bear, Teddi Bara, wearing a hat and holding a parasol, draped in a feather boa and swinging on a swing wrapped with flowers hanging from the ceiling. She sings of all the effort going into trying to win over a guy, but ends with the famous Mae West line, "Y'all come up and see me sometime, ya hear?" leading to excitement from Henry and the busts on the wall. Patty Stoneman of the Stoneman family voices Teddi Bara.

A third act by female performers is performed by the Sunbonnet Trio of Bunny, Bubbles, and Beulah, triplet sisters who also sing about heartbreak. Rather than a painted roll-drop curtain, however, the Sunbonnet Trio is accompanied by projected slides featuring an illustrated song. First used in 1894, the illustrated song was used occasionally in vaudeville acts, but became more common in nickelodeons—early cinemas that charged five-cent admission. The illustrated song used images on glass slides that were then projected using the Magic Lantern, a gas lamp that with a lens that projected the image onto a screen. An operator changed out the slides in time to the music being sung or performed on stage. The illustrated song was the precursor to silent films, which were accompanied by piano music. They were eventually replaced when censors deemed them too "suggestive."

This is certainly the case with the illustrated song performed by the Sunbonnet Trio, "All the Guys That Turn Me on Turn Me Down." The triplets sing about their disappointment with not being able to find a beau, no matter how many men they approach that they are attracted to. The song features one of the triplets approaching multiple male bears, all of which either have a disgusted look on their faces, are holding a hand up in rejection, or even walking away from her. The images are accompanied by the lyrics of the song, which during the height of the illustrated song would allow the audience to sing along.

After Big Al's drunken ditty, Henry appears on a stage to the right, wearing a coonskin cap atop his top hat. Quickly, however, guests realize that the hat is not merely a coonskin cap, but a real raccoon that begins singing along with Henry. The two sing "The Ballad of Davy Crockett," which was popular during the show's development in the late 1960s and may have been one of the first instances of cross-marketing in Disney's entertainment history. First airing on the *Disneyland* anthology television show in 1954, the legend of Davy Crockett was split into five one hour-long episodes tracing the life and myths of the character, leading to his death at the Alamo. Throughout the 1950s and 1960s, Davy Crockett and his famous coonskin cap became a national phenomenon, as young people throughout the country fell in love with the American hero. As a result, when the Country Bear Jamboree opened in 1971, many of the children who had participated in the Crockett fever of the 1950s would be young parents bringing their children to the park and would have a personal connection to the show through this song.

Unfortunately, Henry and Sammy, the raccoon, are quickly interrupted by the inebriated Big Al, who once again begins singing "Blood on the Saddle." In a sort of dueling banjos, Henry calls upon the entire cast of the Country Bear Jamboree to outdo Big Al's drunken ditty by singing "Ole Slew Foot," a pre-existing song about bears originally recorded by rockabilly singer Johnny Horton. As the song reaches its peak intensity, the theater becomes dark, a loud crash is heard from Big Al's stage, and his curtain flutters closed. While many believe this signifies Big Al being so drunk that he's fallen off his stool, the official backstory of the attraction that was released in 1971 explains that the cast of the show was distracting the audience with the rousing rendition of "Ole Slew Foot" while the members not present on stage jumped him to end his embarrassing, drunken performance.

Henry and Sammy try to recover, but quickly dismiss the audience before more embarrassing things occur. To get people moving out of the theater, the two begin to sing "Come Again," an original song composed by Atencio and Bruns specifically for the show. The three hunting trophies, Max, Buff, and Melvin, say goodbye to the audience and make sarcastic and occasionally mocking comments to various audience members as they file out of the theater.

While not the most popular attraction at Walt Disney World, the Country Bear Jamboree has made a big impact on popular culture, spoofed in such television shows and films as *The Simpsons* and *A Goofy Movie*. Throughout the years there have been multiple versions of the show, such as Country Bear Vacation Hoedown and Country Bear Christmas Special, which ended their runs in 1992 and 2005, respectively. The Disneyland version of Country Bear Jamboree, which originally opened in 1972 and featured twin theaters running two shows consecutively, due to the popularity of the show, closed in 2001 to make way for The Many Adventures of Winnie-the-Pooh.

Taking its inspiration from a beloved form of entertainment, the vaudevillian variety show, the Country Bear Jamboree continues to stand as a contemporary among popular shows and franchises including *Saturday Night Live* and The Muppets. As a result, while it is certainly not the most attended attraction in Frontierland, let alone the Magic Kingdom, the Country Bear Jamboree at Walt Disney World will not be going away any time soon, not least because it is cheap and easy to maintain, and there is no obvious alternative for the space.

The popularity of the show, such as it is, stems not from the show itself, but rather from the humor, the fun music, and the shared American social history of music and performance, as well as the nostalgia felt by return visitors to the Magic Kingdom who have grown up with this opening day attraction.

CHAPTER NINE

CASEY'S CORNER

*W*henever I think of true Americana, three things come to my mind: hotdogs, Disney, and baseball. Many don't realize that there is actually a connection to all three when they visit Walt Disney World, and it may be the most "American" part of the Magic Kingdom. Located at the west end of Main Street, U.S.A., sits Casey's Corner, a quick-service dining location that provides portable, sports stadium fare, including hotdogs, cracker jacks, cotton candy, nachos and cheese, and other distinctly American-themed foods.

The theming of Casey's Corner literally takes a page from American history. Although the restaurant is influenced by the 1888 poem "Casey at the Bat," the restaurant also pays tribute to the 1946 animated Disney film, *Make Mine Music*. All three—the poem, the animated short, and the restaurant—offer much for guests to discover about American culture and the game of baseball.

BASEBALL: AN AMERICAN GAME

Baseball is one of the most popular sports in the United States today. In fact, the game is commonly known as "America's pastime." Many different playing levels exist. From a young age, children enroll in tee ball, a simplified version of the game. If they are good enough, they can play for a recreational league or even a traveling league in elementary school, middle school, high school, and college. There are hundreds of minor league teams of differing ability levels, and thirty teams compete each year for the World Series trophy as part of the two leagues of the American League and the National League, which make up Major League Baseball. The game has become an ingrained part of the American identity: families make annual pilgrimages to their favorite major league teams, such as the Detroit Tigers, or root for their favorite minor league teams, such as the West Michigan Whitecaps or the Greensboro Grasshoppers. The game has even become part of American culture: numerous films, such as *Field of Dreams, The Sandlot,* and *A League of Their Own* have become immensely popular, and songs including "Take Me Out to the Ball Game" can be heard being sung by school children. Even food such as hotdogs and peanuts can trigger memories of visiting a favorite baseball stadium each summer.

While there is evidence of humans hitting rocks and balls with sticks as early as the ancient Egyptians and Carthaginians between 2000 and 4000 years ago, the game of baseball as we know it today began to take shape in the 1700s. Originating in England, schoolboys often played the game of rounders; after hitting a ball, players would run from milking stool to milking stool, which acted as modern bases. Runners could be tagged out by being hit by a thrown ball. Eventually, the stools were replaced by poles embedded in the ground as the game became more developed with rules similar to the way the game is played today.

During the 1830s and 1840s, the game became a pastime for boys in large cities as well as young men at gentlemen's clubs, organizations akin to modern-day country clubs. One of the most popular gentlemen's clubs, the Knickerbocker Base Ball Club, headquartered in New York City, developed a set of rules that became common throughout the United States in the 1840s, including the rule that a runner could be tagged out or forced out, rather than having a ball thrown at them. The game quickly became a method for the upper classes of New York to compete with one another and show off their skill in leisure activities, akin to games such as croquet and tennis; the game was dominated by the wealthy because they could afford time to playing sports, rather than having to work to support their families.

During the late 1840s and 1850s, newspapers and magazines began reporting on the results of the games played in the gentlemen's clubs. Interested readers began to take time to watch for the games, and a close following of baseball in America began. During the 1860s, baseball leagues began to form, leading to a more organized system of competition between teams. In the 1880s, a series of songs, novels, and events began to turn the baseball player into a hero to be admired. Stadiums were built in urban areas, which drew those plagued by the problems of the cities away from their worries for three or four hours on occasion. Players began to be idolized, as well as the teams, and as a result, the various leagues began to require them to wear different colored stockings in order to tell the teams apart; many teams began to be referred to by the color of their socks, such as the Boston Red Sox and the Chicago White Sox.

Americans who are unfamiliar with the game of baseball are at least familiar with its great heroes, including Babe Ruth, Jackie Robinson, Ty Cobb, and Lou Gehrig. During the 1870s through the mid-1940s, the Negro League featured professional black players, ending only after the creation of the Major League Committee on Baseball Integration and the signing of black player Jackie Robinson to the Brooklyn Dodgers in 1947. During World War II, as hundreds of thousands of American men enlisted in or were drafted by the military, women stepped up to the plate to continue America's pastime, with the creation of the All-American Girls Professional Baseball League.

Luckily, the game of baseball survived these controversies, continuing to be a key part of the American social consciousness today, even as it was during the creation of the modern game, around the turn of the twentieth century.

"CASEY AT THE BAT: A BALLAD OF THE REPUBLIC SUNG IN THE YEAR 1888"

During the first heyday of baseball, which took place from the 1880s until the early 1900s, the game burst into the American consciousness as a favorite afternoon activity for the residents of America's cities. In 1908, the well-known song "Take Me Out to the Ball Game" became popularized. Sports stadiums began to spring up, leading to a high amount of advertising and marketing aimed at American consumers. Dime store novels about the game began flying off the shelves of drug stores, and stories of the deeds of the sport's heroes became the things of American legend.

One of the most popular examples of baseball lore was the 1888 poem "Casey at the Bat," written by Ernest Thayer. The poem was first published in *The San Francisco Examiner*, a newspaper owned by William Randolph Hearst. Originally a humor writer, Thayer, a college friend of Hearst, penned the poem with very little fanfare from readers of *The Examiner*. However, in August 1888, after the poem's printing in *The New York Sun*, New York resident Archibald Gunter clipped out the poem and shared it with his friend De Wolf Hopper, a comedian who put on shows to theater patrons. Later that month, Hopper performed the poem during a show for players of the Chicago and New York baseball clubs, and the it became wildly popular.

The poem features the fictionalized team from Mudville playing against a rival team. Mudville, unfortunately, is two runs down against the opposing team, and the game is in its last inning with two outs. The two players before the titular character's turn at the bat, teammates Flynn and Jimmy Blake, each get hits, placing them into scoring position; Flynn ends up on third base, while Blake reaches second. Cue the star of the team, Casey, to the plate. Casey is described in the poem to be the favorite of the crowd:

> *Then from five thousand throats and more there rose a lusty yell;*
> *It rumbled through the valley, it rattled in the dell;*
> *It knocked upon the mountain and recoiled upon the flat,*
> *For Casey, mighty Casey, was advancing to the bat.*

The pitcher throws the first pitch, but in his arrogance, the batter watches the ball go by, claiming that the pitch "ain't my style." In response, the umpire, or game official, calls the pitch a strike, giving Casey only two more chances to hit the ball. The crowd, furious at the call, threatens the umpire's life. Casey simply raises his hand to quiet the spectators as the pitcher sends the next pitch over home plate. Again, Casey watches the ball sail over the plate in a haughty manner, proving to the crowd and himself that he doesn't need three chances to win the game. The hero becomes serious, "the sneer … gone from Casey's lip, his teeth are clenched in hate," swinging the bat so hard at the pitch that "the air is shattered by the force of Casey's blow." The last stanza of the poem explains that somewhere people are happy, children are shouting in joy, and bands play in the gleaming sun. However, the poem concludes that that somewhere is *not* Mudville, because "mighty Casey has struck out."

BUT THERE IS NO JOY IN BURBANK— MIGHTY DISNEY HAS STRUCK OUT!

The popularity of "Casey at the Bat" inspired many spinoffs and references, both during the early part of the twentieth century, as well as in popular culture today. One example of this was an animated segment by the same name in the 1946 Disney film, *Make Mine Music*. Recited by comedian and singer Jerry Colonna and animated by a number of Walt Disney's Nine Old Men (such as Eric Larson, Ollie Johnston, and Ward Kimball), the short was set to music composed by Ken Darby, who composed numerous other scores for Disney films and shorts, such as *Song of the South*, and wrote the Elvis Presley song, "Love Me Tender."

"Casey at the Bat" was one of ten segments in *Make Mine Music*. The film, released in 1946, was the eighth full-length animated film by Walt Disney Productions. Unfortunately, it did not make much of an impact on American and foreign consumers. Released shortly after World War II, many fans of Disney films throughout the world were more concerned about rebuilding after the war than watching movies. Cities like London, Munich, and Berlin were destroyed as a result of the intense bombings carried out by both the Axis Powers and the Allies during the conflict. Homes had been destroyed, families torn apart, and millions of individuals had been executed as a result of racial genocide. Entire governments and economies in Europe and Asia had to be rebuilt, soon to be assisted by America's Marshall Plan, whose monetary assistance was used to help stimulate agriculture and business as a result of the lack of finances of the European governments and population. As a result, watching American films was far from the minds of most in Europe in the years after 1945.

Make Mine Music was the third film released as what was known as "package films" by Walt Disney Productions during the 1940s and 1950s. Shortly after the outbreak of World War II, the American government required Disney to begin making propaganda films for the American public and military. As a result, much of the finances and animating staff usually reserved for making animated shorts and full-length films were required to produce propaganda films for the United States, including *Der Fuehrer's Face* and *Education for Death*. After the Japanese attacks on

Pearl Harbor on December 7, 1941, many of the talented Disney animators were either drafted into the military or enlisted voluntarily. Also,
foreign markets, such as France and Britain, were occupied trying to
fend off the invasion of Nazi forces, and as a result, many of the citizens
in those countries were unable to spend money on seeing American
films, leading to less money being made by Walt Disney Productions.

In an attempt to win the Latin American countries to the side of
America and her allies, the U.S. government established the Good
Neighbor policy in the 1930s; as a result of this program, the White House
sent musicians, singers, athletes, movie stars, and other celebrities to
nations like Mexico and Brazil to convince them to resist communist
and fascist influences. Walt Disney himself traveled to many Central and
South American countries, bringing with him some of his best artists
and animators to research the culture and styles of the different nations.
From this trip came the first two package films, *Saludos Amigos!* and *The
Three Caballeros*, which were intended to inform the American public
about the rich culture of Latin America, as well as show those nations
that America was willing to partner with and validate their societies.

Continuing the experimentation and low budgets of the Good
Neighbor package films of the early 1940s, Walt Disney Productions
would release four more package films during the late 1940s: *Make Mine
Music* in 1946, *Fun and Fancy Free* in 1947, *Melody Time* in 1948, and *The
Adventures of Ichabod and Mr. Toad* in 1949. Most of these films continue to
be some of the least familiar animated films in the Disney canon to mod-
ern American consumers, likely seen only by some of the most hardcore
Disney fans. However, many of the segments from these films, including
"Peter and the Wolf," "Mickey and the Beanstalk," "The Legend of Sleepy
Hollow," and "Pecos Bill" became popular with Disney fans when they
were released through other formats, such as the television shows *The
Ink and Paint Club* and *Walt Disney Presents*. Unfortunately for Walt Disney

Productions, while new techniques would be developed during the war years through the creation of the package films, the films were ultimately a failure, as they were quickly butchered, the segments split apart, and the more popular of the shorts shown in various television programs throughout later decades.

As the "Casey at the Bat" segment of *Make Mine Music* begins, its title card is shown. A set of stadium bleachers is in the distance, while a wooden fence stands in the foreground with two hollowed-out knotholes near the bottom. Ragtime piano music plays in the background as an invisible hand begins to paint "a Musical Recitation" in red letters across the fence and a pair of eyes peeks out through the knotholes. The lettering continues, explaining to viewers of the short that the segment is sung by Jerry Colonna, using the peeking eyes as the two O's in Colonna's name. The painted letters and eyeballs disappear and are covered by a broadside showing the title of the short, "Casey at the Bat," in red letters centered around a baseball bat.

The screen fades as trumpets blow a musical transition and a chorus of singers begins the musical storytelling of the short. The first stanza of the song does not feature lines from Thayer's poem, but rather are original to the film and are used to set up the background of the story. While the chorus sings about the locals streaming to the stadium to watch Casey play, a series of still paintings shows a number of men and women traveling through a natural landscape. The first painting features individual horses pulling black carriages, some of which are plumed, while suited men and women in Victorian-style dresses walk along a dirt path. The second still image features more people on their way to the ballpark, many of whom are riding bicycles or running toward the ball field. This image also shows small children holding pinwheels and flags following their mothers carrying parasols as they head to the ball field. The third still shows the stadium surrounded by a wooden fence, plastered with broadsides explaining that the game will be pitting the home team, Mudville, against the visiting team, Burbank, a reference to the location of the Disney studio. Throngs of visitors stream into the stadium, as vendors stand outside selling balloons. The next still shows numerous fans of Mudville sitting in the stands in top hats, beautiful dresses, and bonnets, holding canes and parasols, showing the upper-class leisure activity that was attending a baseball game. The grandstands are draped in red, white, and blue bunting, representing that the game was a truly American pastime and that attending a baseball game both around the turn-of-the-century and in the present day is a way to express the American identity. The final still shows the baseball field with the players standing in position around the field, as the camera zooms in on the scoreboard in the outfield.

As the camera begins focusing on the scoreboard, Colonna begins singing the story of Mudville and their star player as written in the poem by Thayer, starting the actual recitation one minute into the animated short. As Colonna sings the poem, bits of dialogue, such as that of the coach lecturing his players, are interspersed between the lines of Thayer's story. Colonna provides all dialogue in the segment, including that of the various characters and the singing narrator. In order to provide the animated short with more of a narrative structure, as well as the opportunity to interject bits of humor, the team who created "Casey at the Bat" decided to summarize and add bits of narration and dialogue, and as a result, the poem is not recited verbatim in the short. However, the writers of the segment do adhere closely to the original text by Thayer once Casey steps up to the plate.

Colonna sings and narrates the segment in an Irish accent, while Casey himself has red hair and mutton chops. This may be a result of the rumor that Ernest Thayer based the character of Casey in his poem on an Irish acquaintance, or the assumption that the inspiration for the character was Mike "King" Kelly, an Irish-American player of the time. Colonna himself was born in America and of Italian ancestry, so the accent he uses to perform the recitation of the poem is added intentionally to create depth to Thayer's poem.

The animated segment keeps with the general feel of the culture of the late 1800s and early 1900s; many of the men, both on and off the field, wear moustaches, which were in vogue during the Victorian Era. The moustache craze spread to America via England; from 1860 through 1916, England required that all soldiers enlisted under the British Crown grow and maintain a moustache, as it created a sense of manhood, strength, and aggression in a military filled with young men who were often inexperienced in military maneuvers. As a result, the wearing of this style of facial hair became associated with the upper-class sophistication of both northern Europe and the United States during the reign of Queen Victoria and Prince Albert. Other members of the crowd and Mudville's band wear mutton chops, another popular facial hair style of the late nineteenth and early twentieth century. The women sitting in the stands carry parasols, which signified their upper-class culture as well.

Parasols, being made of cloth or silk, often cost a tidy sum of money to have made, and were used to prevent the carrier from becoming touched by the sun; wealth during this time meant having pale skin, a result of not having to work outside for a living. Also, one can assume the audience is part of the upper classes because they cannot only afford to pay admission to the game, but also can take time out of their schedule to partake in a leisure time activity like baseball. Some members of the crowd, especially the most vocal of the fans who demand Casey step up to the plate, are obviously part of the working class, as they are dressed in suspenders, something that would have been used by factory workers, not the well-to-do.

The uniforms and equipment used by the players of the game also signify that baseball was a gentleman's sport. Neither the umpire nor the catcher wears modern protective gear, but rather a pad to protect their chest. The umpire, obviously a part of the middle or working class, wears a bowler cap and suspenders, while a rudimentary mask covers the catcher's face. The uniforms of the players also signify the game as being a more sophisticated venture. While the visiting team wears plain yellow-and-red uniforms, their shirts are collared and their pants are pulled up at the knees with long socks. Mudville, on the other hand, wears blue-and-white uniforms with a red necktie tucked between the buttons of their outfits, something that would be unheard of in the modern game of baseball.

Interestingly, the Disney short does not take place in 1888, even though the poem was written in and represented events of that year. As the chorus of singers introduces Casey as he comes up to bat, Colonna compares Casey to being "the Sinatra of 1902," which places the short as taking place fourteen years after Thayer intended the poem to occur. The reference to Frank Sinatra is meant to show how popular Casey is as a player, likening his celebrity to that of one of the most popular solo artists of 1946.

After Casey takes his third swing after his two strikes, the music transitions to a sweet melody performed by the chorus, going through a montage of bluebirds in a tree, beams of sunlight, a band playing on a bandstand, and playing children, as the singers and Colonna explain that "somewhere" everyone is happy and joyful in the sunlight. The image quickly transitions to the city of Mudville and the ballpark, which is enduring a thunderstorm with driving rain as Colonna leaves the viewers of the segment with the famous line, "But there is no joy in Mudville, Mighty Casey has struck out!" A sobbing Casey stands at home plate trying to hit the baseball and continually missing, as the chorus sings the ironic line, "Casey the pride of them all!"

Unfortunately for the Disney studio, the animated short based on Thayer's poem, as well as the film it was part of, were failures in 1946. As a result, the outcome for Mudville's game can be seen as an allegory for Disney's attempt at success with *Make Mine Music* and the other package films of the 1940s.

CASEY'S CORNER: A HOMERUN FOR HOTDOGS!

Originally opened as the Coca-Cola Refreshment Corner in 1971, the restaurant located at the corner of Main Street, U.S.A. and the park hub was refurbished and renamed Casey's Corner in 1995. The eatery, one of the most popular in the park, sells "designer hotdogs," including chili-cheese dogs, corn dog nuggets, and the barbecue slaw dog. While there are still a few slight nods back to the Coca-Cola Refreshment Corner through the use of Coca-Cola signage and advertisements, the theming of the restaurant leans heavily toward the game of baseball, specifically around the turn of the century.

As guests approach the restaurant from the hub, they find an outdoor seating area across the sidewalk against the wrought-iron fence sur-rounding the gardens of flowers, which is often occupied by the fami-lies of ducks that frequent this area of the Magic Kingdom. These tables, covered by red and white umbrellas, offer additional seating. A pianist playing ragtime piano often performs beneath the canopy of the restau-rant. Attached to the canopy, on the corner of the building, is the sign for the restaurant, a large red "C" outlined by clear electric light bulbs, with the restaurant's name, Casey's Corner, printed in blue letters along the curves of the sign. The large red C is shaped in the same style as that on the opening scene for the animated short in the segment from *Make Mine Music*. Inside the hollow part of the sign is a figure of a baseball player swinging at a pitched baseball. The baseball is hollow on one side, and on windy days causes the figure to spin in a circle as though the player is striking out, like the baseball hero in Thayer's poem. A six-foot-tall wooden figure of a baseball player wearing a white uniform with vertical blue stripes and the restaurant's name scrolled across his chest welcomes guests as they walk into Casey's Corner through its Main Street, U.S.A. entrance.

The white entrance doors show the opening date of the restaurant, engraved on a baseball, as 1888. This date fits into the overall story of the town of Main Street, U.S.A., but also connects back to the year that Thayer published "Casey at the Bat." Upon entering the small counter-service restaurant, guests find the ceiling painted red, with red-and-white striped wallpaper. Above the service counter is an ornate wooden awning, similar to something that would have hung over the box office or concession stand of a baseball stadium in the 1880s. Stained glass lamps featuring the Coca-Cola logo hang from the ceiling, making the room feel even more a part of the era it is meant to represent.

The menu, attached to the wooden awning over the counter, features the fateful scene from the Disney short, with Casey standing haughtily on the left while the opposing pitcher stands on the right in mid-pitch. The room is decorated with framed photographs and magazine advertisements featuring baseball players and ladies in Victorian dress drinking Coca-Cola out of glass bottles. A wooden cabinet on the left wall of the room, which serves as a condiment station for the hot dog fixin's and other supplies, including napkins and straws, is decorated with baseball-themed props, such as a metal basket full of baseballs and cardboard popcorn buckets. Similar supply cabinets throughout the restaurant feature other memorabilia, including beer steins emblazoned with baseball team logos, glass bottles of Coca-Cola, baseball caps, and glass jars full of peanuts.

To the right of the main entrance of Casey's Corner is the small main dining room. Above the entryway into this dining room is a large white banner reading "BALL GAME TO DAY," beneath which hang five small American flags featuring a circular pattern of thirteen stars. This flag is out of place here, as the flag of the United States in 1888 would have been a similar pattern of stars in the rows that we have today, but would have forty stars for the forty states, rather than the thirteen stars on the flag that was adopted in 1777. The flag that flies atop the building on Main Street that the restaurant is located in is actually a more accurate representation of what the flag would have looked like in the period of the restaurant's story: it features forty-five stars organized into six rows, leading us to believe that our visit to the restaurant is taking place sometime between 1896 and 1907, which is when the forty-five star flag would have flown. The flag would not have forty-six stars until 1907 when Oklahoma became a state. This flag may place the restaurant in the year 1902, as this is the date referenced in the animated short when Colonna explains that Casey is "the Sinatra of 1902."

The main dining room has red painted walls featuring photographs, advertisements, portraits, and artist renderings of the game of baseball during America's Victorian era. A wooden chair rail stretches about three-and-a-half feet off the ground with square wainscoting below, adding to the Victorian elegance of the restaurant. Felt banners and pennants hang from the crown moulding along the ceiling of the room commemorating different baseball clubs from the turn-of-the-century, including St. Louis, Lehigh, Downer, and Lockport. Red and white tables with decorative metal chairs litter the room, sitting atop black-and-white tiled floors. Electric lamps hang from the ceiling featuring upturned glass fixtures and Tiffany lampshades.

On the left hand wall of the room is a scoreboard that seems to just be another decoration fitting in with the baseball memorabilia. Astute observers will realize that the scoreboard actually references the poem and Disney short: the teams on the scoreboard at Republic Field are listed as VISITORS and MUDVILLE, with Mudville trailing by two runs. The ninth inning scores list both teams as having scored zero runs; a number is only placed on a scoreboard in baseball after the completion of the inning. As a result, we can assume that the scoreboard is showing the final score of the game, referencing Casey's failure to win the game for his team in the bottom of the ninth inning. Also, the scoreboard explains that the game is taking place at Republic Field, although neither the animated short nor the original poem named the field on which the game was played. Instead, the field's name listed on the scoreboard in the restaurant is likely a reference to the full title of Thayer's poem, "Casey at the Bat: A Ballad of the Republic Sung in the Year 1888."

The main dining room of Casey's Corner features many different pieces of baseball memorabilia that may be of interest to baseball, history, and Disney fans. The back corner of the room features a small nook with a table over which is strung a series of baseball pennants all labeled Mudville, an obvious reference to the home team from Thayer's poem and the Disney short. Racks of wooden bats hang on the wall below the pennants, as well as a series of pegs holding baseball caps. Shadowboxes featuring baseball equipment from the early twentieth century hang around the room, including one displaying catchers' pads, a worn-out home plate, an umpire's brush, and photographs of mustachioed ball players.

Growing up, my family was one that watched the Detroit Tigers play on television on a nightly basis. We made pilgrimages first to Tiger Stadium and later to Comerica Park in downtown Detroit to root for our favorite players. We even visited Lakeland, Florida, on occasion to watch the team play spring training games at Joker Merchant Stadium. As a family fascinated by the game of baseball, and as someone who personally loves history, visiting Casey's Corner restaurant on the northwest corner of Main Street, U.S.A. has always been an enjoyable experience. Not only is

it a well-themed eating environment, it also makes one feel the connection between baseball and all things "American." Even visitors who are
not baseball fans will find themselves learning about American history
when visiting the restaurant, whether it deals with the early game, styles
of turn-of-the-century fashion, or even the role baseball has had on our
national identity over the past hundred and fifty years.

CHAPTER TEN

STORYBOOK CIRCUS

*E*lephants, daredevils, sideshows, peanuts, large tents, spot-lights, and calliope music. Ask any American what they think of when they hear the word circus, and these are the words that come to mind. The circus has been a popular form of entertainment for Americans for as long as America has been a country, showcasing daz-zling feats of strength and courage, as well as animal acts and (the subject of many of my nightmares) clowns. The institution of the circus has even entwined itself in the popular culture of American history, portrayed in books like *Water for Elephants* and films including *Big Top Pee-Wee* and *Dumbo*. The circus itself portrays a similar aspect of the American Dream to that of the vaudeville-style entertainment of the Country Bear Jamboree: increasingly family-friendly entertainment that showed how individuals could push their bodies and abilities to the limits, going fur-ther than others expected them to go.

In 2012, a new land at the Magic Kingdom known as New Fantasyland began to open in phases. This expansion was the largest of its kind in Magic Kingdom history, and added seven new attractions, new shops, and new restaurants. The land, now the largest in the park, is organized into three sections:

§ The Enchanted Forest has attractions based around some of the more beloved Disney princess films, with new attractions and experiences such as Under the Sea: Journey of the Little Mermaid, Be Our Guest restaurant, and the Seven Dwarfs Mine Train.

§ Fantasy Village, the original Fantasyland, features classic attractions like "it's a small world," Peter Pan's Flight, and the newly built Princess Fairytale Hall

§ Storybook Circus, which replaced Mickey's Toontown Fair, retooled some existing attractions in order to create a more cogent storyline by rewriting the story of Goofy's Barnstormer around the idea of Goofy being a circus daredevil, while the well-known Dumbo the Flying Elephant attraction was moved to this part of the park, adding a second spinner in what would become known by the Disney fan community as "Dueling Dumbos."

The theme and story of Storybook Circus is well fleshed out and full of details, even to the point of the design of the floor in Big Top Souvenirs looking like the tarped ground of a circus tent. While the mention of the word "circus" evokes all sorts of images and senses to millions, many don't realize the rich history that inspired the theming of this new mini-land.

THE HISTORY OF CIRCUS TROUPES

The modern circus began centuries ago in Ancient Rome, where the term "circus" first was used. The word, of Latin origin, literally translates into "circle," which describes the shape of the ring in which the action of the show took place. The early circus featured acts from different areas of the Roman Empire, as well as acts from the regions with which the empire traded: acrobats from Asia, animals from Africa, and gladiator fights and chariot races from Rome and Gaul. Created to distract Roman citizens from political and economic issues, the term *panem et circenses* was coined; the Roman government built a series of arenas, including the Roman Coliseum, to host events like the slaughtering of Christians in gladiator or animal fights.

During the European Middle Ages, entertainment troupes traveled the countryside, going from village to village to entertain the nobility and royalty of the region and singing ballads of the brave deeds of knights. During the late middle ages, as governments transformed from ruling through land ownership to the creation of nation-states, the nobility, who no longer served a purpose other than being wealthy, turned to tournaments to show their dominance over other noble families by participating in such activities as jousting and archery. These tournaments often would draw crowds from the surrounding countryside to root for their favorite noble.

Throughout the first thousand years of European history after the fall of the Roman Empire in 476, fairs and festivals aligned with Catholic holidays allowed for times of revelry, often tied to pagan traditions such as a celebration of the harvest. One of these festivals, May Day, took place during late April or early May to celebrate the coming of summer and the appeasement of Flora, the Roman goddess of flowers, to encourage the growing of harvest crops throughout the coming season. However, as Europe began to be Christianized, the Catholic Church began to align these pagan holidays with a celebration of various saints or Christian events, such as the birth and crucifixion of Christ.

The modern circus began shortly after the Seven Years' War, which took place between Britain and France and their allies over their respective land holdings across the globe. Shortly after the war's end in 1763, English cavalry officer Philip Astley began to hone his horse riding skills and opened a school to teach students horsemanship. In the evenings,

Astley and his fellow horsemen performed trick riding before audiences. The first recorded European circus took place on January 9, 1768, in which Astley performed trick horsemanship. In between Astley's acts, acrobats, comedy acts, and jugglers performed to entertain the masses. As a result, in 1782, Astley opened the first circus, the Aphitheatre Anglois. Throughout the eighteenth century, the circus began to become more popular, as cities began to build permanent structures to house circuses, such as the London Hippodrome. In 1793, John Bill Ricketts began his own trick horse-riding circus, which was so popular that dignitaries, including President Washington, traveled to Philadelphia to see the show.

The nineteenth century in American history is known as the century of Manifest Destiny, referring to the idea that God granted the United States the entire North American continent to expand from the Atlantic to Pacific seaboards. With the discovery of precious metals during mid-century, large numbers of people began migrating westward. In an effort to entertain Americans on the frontier, Joshuah Purdy Brown began using temporary canvas tents to house his circus as it traveled from place to place. During the 1860s and 1870s, free blacks and farmers fled the South and began moving west to find a way to improve themselves financially. As a result, tales and feats of heroes of the west became legendary. Buffalo Bill Cody capitalized on the frenzy by creating his Wild West show, complete with skilled horse riding, sharp shooting by Annie Oakley, and even re-enactments of famous historical battles between Americans and Indians. There was also a sideshow that featured cowboys and Indians, including Sitting Bull, a Lakota holy man who helped defeat General George Armstrong Custer and his forces at Little Big Horn in 1876 and who would later be captured and killed at the hands of Americans who wanted to stop his effort to remove white men from Sioux land.

The best-known American circuses are the Barnum and Bailey and Ringling Brothers circuses of the late nineteenth and early twentieth centuries. While the three circuses merged to be one single circus troupe known as the Ringling Bros. and Barnum & Bailey Circus in 1919, the three circuses each began independently and slowly merged over time to become the traveling organization that it is today.

The origin of the Ringling Bros. and Barnum & Bailey Circus began with Phineas Taylor Barnum, who possessed a penchant for entertaining people through the exhibition of the strange. In 1835, when he was only twenty-five years old, Barnum purchased a slave woman named Joice Heth, who was paralyzed and blind at eighty years old. Barnum, in an effort to make some money and to make himself famous, claimed that Heith was 161 years old and was actually the nurse of George Washington. Barnum and Heith traveled throughout the northeast United States over the next few years, ultimately earning him a profit of $1,500 per week, a small fortune in those times.

Barnum continued exhibiting his oddities and, in 1841, he purchased Scudder's American Museum, located in New York City. A precursor to the modern Ripley's Believe It or Not! museums, the rebranded Barnum's American Museum operated for twenty-four years and invited patrons to view numerous "attractions" showcasing the strange. Two of Barnum's best-known attractions were the Feejee Mermaid and Tom Thumb. Purported by local newspapers to have been caught by Dr. J. Griffin of the British Lyceum of Natural History, Barnum convinced Griffin to show-case the mermaid in the American Museum. Barnum advertised the natural oddity in the papers, showing the creature as being a bare-breasted woman with a fish tail, but when guests paid their quarter admission to the museum, they realized that the mermaid was simply a withered monkey torso sewn onto the tail of a fish. J. Griffin was not actually a doctor, but rather a fake name used by an accomplice of Barnum, who together conspired to make money off the hoax. Barnum acquired the "mermaid" from an acquaintance, showman Moses Kimball.

Another of Barnum's well-known hoaxes was that of General Tom Thumb, a small boy who, according to advertisements of the time, was "a dwarf of eleven years of age, just arrived from England!" Barnum explains in his personal diary the reality of Tom Thumb: the boy was not eleven, but rather five years old, and was named Charles Stratton. Barnum heard of Stratton's dwarfism, putting the boy at less than two feet tall and under sixteen pounds, and convinced the boy's mother to let him travel with the showman throughout New York and the New England area in 1842. Barnum paid the boy three dollars per week and covered all expenses, but once again combined a physical oddity with a hoax that included a hint of reality. Although Barnum claims in his diary that he had proof that the boy had not grown since he was six months old, he also realized that very few people would come to the American Museum to see the exhibit if they found out the boy was only five, instead of the advertised eleven years old.

Barnum's American Museum continued successfully until 1865, when it burned to the ground. Barnum opened a second location of the museum shortly after the fire, but that building also burned to the ground, in 1868. Barnum spent the next two years developing P.T. Barnum's Grand Traveling Museum, Menagerie, Caravan, and Circus, with circus entrepreneur William Cameron Coup, which opened in 1870. The traveling museum was an opportunity for Barnum to display his oddities, and was so popular that in its first year Barnum made over $400,000 in revenue, equivalent to almost eight million dollars today. This immense popularity caused Barnum to refer to his exhibition as the Greatest Show on Earth. In 1874, the New York Hippodrome became the permanent home for the Grand Traveling Museum, covering five acres of land in New York City and seating ten thousand audience members at any given time.

While Barnum's show focused to some extent on acrobatics and feats of strength and daring that many attribute to the circus today, his show was really an opportunity to showcase the strange and uncommon, better known as the modern-day sideshow.

The immense popularity of the circus as one of the main forms of entertainment in post-Civil War America caused Barnum and Coup to rethink how the circus operated. In the early 1870s, Coup developed a method to transport the show by rail throughout different parts of the country, allowing the show to reach more people and wider audiences. Still used to this day, circus animals and performers were loaded onto trains, allowing for easier transport of the circus to different areas of town, and also allowing for the promotion of the show as the different exotic animals and performers were offloaded from the train and paraded through town on the way to the show's location. Coup also encouraged Barnum to create a second performance ring, ultimately expanding to a seven-ring show focusing on the spectacle of circus acts rather than the artistic feats of the show. This increased the number of performers and animals needed for the show, especially between acts. For example, with more rings, more clowns were needed. However, because of the large amounts of clown performers used between acts, it became too difficult for crowds to be able to discern what the numerous voices were saying, and as a result, circus clowns became silent and began miming their slapstick humor instead of telling jokes.

In an effort to continually make his show greater and grander, Barnum teamed up with James Bailey and James Hutchinson in 1881. Bailey, born James Anthony McGinnis, an orphaned boy from Michigan, was adopted by Frederic Harrison Bailey, who worked in various circus shows. After the death of his parents, the young man worked as a bellhop in a hotel in Pontiac, Michigan, when he was given a job by Frederic Bailey to hang handbills for the Somers Menagerie, which was performing in Pontiac

one evening. Bailey was so impressed that he hired young James to travel
with him and the show, ultimately adopting the boy and giving him his
surname. After serving in the Civil War, Bailey began to establish his own
circus show, buying or merging with various shows throughout the latter
decades of the nineteenth century. In 1880, Bailey decided to challenge
P.T. Barnum's show and actually outsold it, selling double the number
of tickets that Barnum sold. Foreseeing his circus empire falling apart,
Barnum proposed a merger with Bailey's show, creating P.T. Barnum's
Greatest Show on Earth, and the Great London Circus, Sanger's Royal
British Menagerie, and the Grand International Allied Shows United,
which would later become known as the Barnum and Bailey Greatest
Show on Earth. Barnum focused on the talent and acquisition of acts for
the show, while Bailey took over the management of the show.

The first major attraction for Barnum and Bailey's Circus was an elephant named Jumbo, acquired from the London Zoo in 1882. The star
of the Greatest Show on Earth measured eleven-and-a-half feet tall and
weighed a whopping six-and-a-half tons. Once again using the media
as a way to hype up his acts, Barnum published stories about how difficult it was to get Jumbo into the large box that would hold him while
transporting the mammoth elephant to America from Great Britain.
Upon arriving in New York, the Greatest Show on Earth paraded Jumbo
down Broadway and across the Brooklyn Bridge before heading to the
Hippodrome, drawing enormous crowds that would eventually patronize
the show to see what the elephant could do. Jumbo would die in 1885,
causing the Greatest Show on Earth to dissolve, only to be re-established
in 1888 until Barnum's death in 1891. The Barnum and Bailey show began
touring in 1888, expanding its locations across the United States.

After Barnum's death in 1891, Bailey expanded the show in an effort
to carry on the showman's legacy. With the expansion of the show across
the United States, Bailey used eighty-five railroad cars to transport the

Greatest Show on Earth to its various locations, as well as using over one thousand employees and performers. The show consisted of five rings for performances, three more than were used in 1881 when Bailey's show merged with P.T. Barnum's.

As Bailey began aging, he began to think about retirement. Sometime during the first decade of the twentieth century, Bailey built an estate in Mount Vernon, New York, and in 1905, he sold half of his shares of his show to another up-and-coming circus show, Ringling Brothers. After Bailey's death in 1906, the Ringling Bros. purchased the Greatest Show on Earth for $400,000, creating the most popular circus troupe today, the Ringling Bros. and Barnum & Bailey Circus.

First established in 1884, the Ringling Bros. Circus initially featured five of the seven Ringling brothers, Alf, Al, Charles, John, and Otto, acting as the founders of the show, with the other two brothers, Henry and Gus, joining the show in 1886 and 1889, respectively. The Ringling Bros. United Monster Shows, Great Double Circus, Royal European Menageries, Museum, Caravan, and Congress of Trained Animals began entertaining visitors in their tented show in Baraboo, Wisconsin, playing to over four thousand guests in different areas throughout Wisconsin and Illinois. Near the end of 1889, the Ringling Bros. circus took to the rails, giving them the opportunity to reach wider crowds.

After Bailey's death, the troupe purchased Barnum and Bailey's Greatest Show on Earth, respecting both James Bailey and P.T. Barnum so much that they toured the two shows throughout America separately until 1919, rather than completely absorbing the circuses. However, with the outbreak of World War I in 1914 and the start of American involvement in the war raging in Europe in 1917, the Ringling Bros. made the decision to completely merge with Barnum and Bailey's shows in 1919, cutting back on the traffic that three separate traveling shows would create on the railroad system needed for the transportation of troops and wartime materials.

Feeling threatened when a major competitor, the American Circus Corporation, signed a contract to perform in the New York Hippodrome, John Ringling purchased American Circus in 1929 for $1.7 million, becoming the largest circus troupe in America. Shows would continue to rake in profits until 1956, when the Ringling Bros. and Barnum & Bailey circus gave its last performance in Pittsburgh, Pennsylvania, due to financial troubles, beneath the canvas tent of the big top. The show was quickly revived, however, when Irvin Feld, the head of the show, began to promote it in enclosed arenas, rather than tented big tops. Feld eventually purchased the show in 1967.

Today, circuses take all sorts of forms. While the Ringling Bros. and Barnum & Bailey circus still makes routine stops in major cities across the United States, other troupes have emerged. For example, the Canadian circus company, Cirque du Soleil, entertains visitors through a variety of traveling and permanent shows throughout the world, drawing upon such inspiration as the music of Michael Jackson and Greek mythology. One of the more popular shows of Cirque du Soleil, La Nouba, performs on a regular basis at a permanent theater at Disney Springs. Although Cirque du Soleil does not utilize animals, the shows often tell stories through the use of acrobatics, feats of strength, and storytelling through the use of dance and miming.

While straying some from the original form of the circus, many modern "circuses," such as Cirque du Soleil and the Blue Man Group, hold true to the original vision of Barnum, Bailey, and other circus forerunners, through the promotion of acrobatics, humor, and the odd.

"MEET THE WORLD'S MOST AMAZING CURIOSITIES!"

The history of the circus includes numerous types of acts used to amaze those who were willing to part with their hard-earned money for a few hours of entertainment beneath a big top. While many think of the animal and acrobatic acts, they are only some of the many attractions that made up the circus.

Animal acts began first being used as circus entertainment as early as the circuses in Ancient Rome. During the latter years of the Roman Empire during the first few centuries of the first millennium, Christians were targeted because they did not worship the Roman deities. While worship of Roman gods and goddesses was not terribly important, the religion of Rome was tied heavily to the leadership of the Roman Empire. Thus, by refusing to worship the deities of Rome, Roman leadership accused Christians of not revering the emperor with the honor and respect he deserved. As a result, Christians were targeted for persecution and were often forced to participate in gladiator battles and battles against animals, such as lions and bears. These spectacles would be held in the great Roman arenas, such as the Roman Coliseum, where thousands of citizens would gather to watch the butchering of the Christ-worshipping men and women.

Animal acts were also popular during the years when the modern circus took its form. Philip Astley, the British cavalry officer who performed acts of daring trick horsemanship during the 1780s, and Buffalo Bill Cody, who exhibited his Wild West show throughout the late 1800s, both used animals, specifically horses, in their shows. These acts showed the power of man over beast, displaying the civilizing role that God has given men over creation. However, with the prevalence of horses throughout America and Europe at this time, many circus-goers were not overly impressed with the equestrian acts, as horse riding was commonplace and often seen by many individuals on a day-to-day basis. In an effort to create more of a shock factor and to draw larger crowds, circuses began to utilize exotic animals. In the 1800s, the German Hagenbecks began to import exotic animals to be used in circus and menagerie shows, specifically large cats. In 1812, the Cirque Olympique, a French circus performing in Paris, exhibited the first trained elephant, Kioumi. In 1833, Isaac A. Van Amburgh performed various acts while locked in a cage with lions and tigers, gaining notoriety in circus history as being the first American trainer of large circus animals. Circus acts continued to use exotic animals throughout the nineteenth and twentieth centuries, including lions, tigers, elephants, and other creatures, thus exhibiting the power of man to tame wild animals. However, with the movement toward animal rights in the 1970s and 1980s, many circus acts began to limit the use of exotic and wild animals for their shows, instead focusing on acts featuring domesticated animals, like horses and dogs.

Another type of act distinctly associated with the circus is acrobatics, such as the high wire, trapeze, juggling, and other gravity-defying performances. Initially a part of equestrian acts, acrobats would do trick horse riding, switching their riding position as part of the performance. Eventually, floor acrobatics began to become popular, as pantomiming clowns and acrobats began to perform tumbling and feats around the circus rings. During the seventeenth and eighteenth centuries, tight-rope walkers were very important, but it was the invention of trapeze artistry in the 1850s that brought acrobatics to the role of headlining acts for the circus. In 1859, Jules Leotard gained the nickname of The Flying Trapeze (inspiring the song by the same name) when he swung from one trapeze to another to the horror and admiration of the audience. Interestingly, while the Frenchman may not be known to the layperson for his acts on the trapeze, his name will be forever recognized for the invention of his performance outfit, the leotard.

In 1917, during the height of World War I, revolution erupted throughout Eastern Europe, as Vladimir Lenin overthrew the Russian tsar, giving the power in the country back to the working class. In an effort to eliminate all social class and the ruling power of the Russian nobility, Lenin nationalized industry throughout Russia, placing the government in complete and direct control over the production of industrial goods and services provided to the citizenry. In 1919, Lenin nationalized the Russian circus industry. Because of this direct government control, many performers who were not Russian fled their jobs working in the circuses, bringing with them many of the acrobatic skills they had learned while working in Russia. These performers fled to Western Europe or even America, leading to acts such as German strongmen, Russian acrobats, and French trapeze artists performing in American circuses.

Daredevil acts also became synonymous with images conjured at the mention of the circus. Numerous risky activities, including parachuting, airplane stunts, and human cannonballing began to be billed to draw larger crowds during an era of fierce competition between circus troupes. For example, French daredevil Jacques Garnerin began performing stunts as early as 1797, when he performed a series of jumps from great heights using the first non-rigid framed parachute, at one point jumping 3,200 feet out of a hot air balloon. Because of his feats, Garnerin is seen as the founder of modern skydiving.

During the 1870s, a hoax employed by P.T. Barnum, called the Human Cannonball, began to delight audiences at shows. In 1871, a man dressed in drag with the stage name Lulu was first launched, but used a catapult instead of a cannon. Nine years later, Zazel, a British woman, was employed by Barnum to be shot from a faux cannon. While taking the shape of a cannon, the contraption was actually a series of springs that launched the performer and firecrackers that simulated a cannon blast. After the coiled springs released, throwing Zazel out of the mouth of the cannon, she was caught by a net. Unfortunately, during one performance, she missed the netting, resulting in a broken back and the end of her career with Barnum's circus.

Another form of daredevil artistry dealt with a new form of technology during the first few decades of the twentieth century, the airplane. The

main form of airplane stunt was known as barnstorming, and often featured World War I fighter pilots performing death-defying stunts in open
cockpit airplanes. After the end of the war, many fighter pilots had no
opportunity to use their skills, as commercial aviation had not yet become
popular. The United States had decided to reinstate their foreign policy
of isolationism, with many in Congress hesitant to become involved in
foreign affairs after the money and lives lost fighting Europe's war. These
pilots often flew at high speeds, performing barrel rolls and loops in battle
to evade enemy gunfire. Unfortunately, because America was officially a
peacetime power, soldiers were no longer needed. As a result, those who
possessed specific skills in aviation, including the ability to fly their planes
at high speeds (for the time), as well as the ability to perform successful
barrel rolls and loops, were out of work. Also, with wartime production
ending and consumer society resuming, a surplus of airplanes became
available on the market. With nothing else to do, these fighter pilots often
became daredevils, showing off their skills at circuses and other events.

Barnstorming not only featured trick flying, but also many different
stunts that the audience perceived as risky or dangerous. One of these
stunts was known as wing walking, in which pilots would climb out of
their open-air cockpits to hang from ladders below their wings, walk
from wingtip to wingtip, or even do handstands on the wings as they
flew through the air. One wing walker, a U.S. Army pilot named Ormer
Locklear, became the first wing walker when he had to climb out of his
cockpit in mid-flight to fix his plane's radiator. Other pilots saw this feat,
and as a result, Locklear's commanding officers in the army encouraged
him to continue to keep spirits high. Locklear was eventually released
from the army and became a well-known stuntman, but later died
while performing. Other dangerous stunts performed by barnstormers
included climbing from one plane to another while flying at high speeds,
strapping one's feet to the wings while the pilot did stunts, and even

stunt parachuting. Barnstorming was so popular during the 1920s that historian Don Dwiggins wrote that "flying circus[es] turned out more famed pilots than the Army and Navy put together."

Another famous aspect of the circus was the sideshow, more popularly known as the freak show. As explained above, Barnum actually got his start exhibiting the strange and uncommon, drawing crowds with the Feejee Mermaid and General Tom Thumb. While visitors to the circus often enjoyed the daredevil, acrobatic, and animal acts, it was the strange people of the sideshow that actually drew them to the circus.

While exhibitions of the strange occurred as early as the seventeenth century, the sideshow began to resemble the form as we know it today during the 1800s. One early sideshow promoter, Tom Norman, was a contemporary of Barnum in the 1870s. Norman exhibited various freak show attractions, but was best known for his employment of some of the most famous "freaks," including the Elephant Man. Born in 1862, John Merrick, better known as the Elephant Man, had genetic defects that caused him to be covered with tumors and growths, which eventually led to his head and hands becoming swollen and large and his hair to fall out. Merrick's family and doctors attributed his malformation to be a result of his mother being startled by an elephant while she was pregnant with him. Norman discovered Merrick after he had become acquainted with Dr. Frederick Treves at the London Hospital.

American circuses also featured sideshows. Barnum first entered show business when he opened Barnum's American Museum, but transitioned to more circus-centered attractions after the museum burnt down in 1865 and again in 1868. However, the sideshow continued to be an integral part of Barnum's shows until the 1960s and 1970s when attitudes toward people with genetic malformations and physical differences became more accepted and the exhibition of people with differences became less politically correct.

Many of the modern-day freak show acts originated in the sideshows of the Ringling Bros. and Barnum & Bailey circus. For example, Schlitzie Surtees, a young man who was born with a condition called microencephaly, causing the human skull and brain to develop at a smaller size, was known as a pinhead. Surtees was billed as being "The Last of the Aztecs"; because of the nature of his developmental disorder, he was unable to communicate or perform complex tasks.

Another famous set of performers of the Barnum sideshow were the original Siamese twins, Chang and Eng Bunker. These two men were born conjoined by a piece of cartilage on their sternum and a pair of fused livers. Born in Thailand in 1811, the brothers were discovered by a Scottish fisherman who realized their potential while the eighteen-year-old boys were swimming. After speaking to their parents, he convinced them to allow the boys to travel the world. Upon visiting North Carolina, the twins purchased a plantation, complete with slaves, and married a pair of sisters after retiring from Barnum's show in 1839.

Another stereotypical "freak" that was a mainstay of the sideshow was the bearded lady. Touring with Barnum when she was nine months old, Annie Jones was actually kidnapped from her parents by a physician who saw her on display in a church in Virginia. By the time she was five, Jones had a full moustache and sideburns, and spent a large period of her life working for Barnum as the Bearded Lady.

Barnum's sideshow acts became immortalized in the 1932 film *Freaks*. Considered a horror film because of the physical deformities portrayed, the film follows the lives and relationships of various sideshow stars. Many of the film's stars were actual performers in Barnum's sideshow, including Surtees, Prince Randian the Living Torso, and Peter Robinson the Human Skeleton. Because of the shocking nature with which the individuals were displayed, the film was banned in many countries shortly after its release.

"THE LITTLE ELEPHANT WITH THE BIG EARS, THE WORLD'S MIGHTIEST MIDGET MASTODON: DUMBO!"

While Walt Disney never seemed to have a defining moment that relates to the circus, it is obvious that he was influenced by the Greatest Show on Earth, having grown up and lived through the height of the show's popularity. A number of films and shorts were inspired by the circus. Disney films featured a variety of circus-themed subjects, such as the animated short "Bongo," which was a segment in the 1947 animated film *Fun and Fancy Free*, and the live-action film *Toby Tyler*, in 1960.

Fun and Fancy Free is one of the package films that were released as a result of World War II, when foreign markets, especially in Europe, declined as a result of the conflict, and many working for Walt Disney Productions left the studio to participate in the war effort. The film featured two segments, "Bongo" and "Mickey and the Beanstalk." Based on a story by Sinclair Lewis, "Bongo" is about a unicycle-riding circus bear who has become disenchanted with performing and longs for a life in the forest with other bears. After escaping the circus train as it travels to a new town, Bongo finds himself vying for the affection of a girl bear by attempting to prove himself a true wild bear rather than tame bear.

Toby Tyler follows the adventures of a young orphan boy who runs away to the circus, where he sells concessions and eventually rises to become a circus performer.

Although both of these films were popular during their time, the one Disney film centered around the circus that continues to be popular to this day is *Dumbo*, released in 1941. It is one of the shortest Disney animated films, clocking in at only sixty-four minutes. Because director Ben Sharpsteen was ordered to keep the film simple and inexpensive, the film took on a cartoonish look. As a result, RKO Pictures, who distributed the Disney films in the early days, demanded that Disney change the film to either make it longer or shorter so they could make more money.

When Walt refused, RKO gave in and distributed the film anyway, making *Dumbo* the most successful Disney animated film of the 1940s.

The film features a baby elephant born with unusually large ears whose mother performs for the circus. A namesake of his father, Jumbo Junior is labeled "Dumbo" by his mother's peers, who mock him for his ear size. Dumbo becomes a spectacle for the circus owners, paraded through town and put on display for guests, but when one boy mocks and pokes fun at her baby, Dumbo's mother becomes very angry and begins to tear the circus tent apart. She is thrown into a cage marked "mad elephant" and separated from her child. In order to replace his mother in the circus, the ringmaster forces Dumbo to perform as part of an elephant pyramid. However, the stunt goes horribly wrong, injuring all the other elephants. Embarrassed, Dumbo sits in the night, crying, when a small mouse named Timothy finds him and attempts to cheer him up. The pair accidentally knock a bottle of champagne into a water bucket from which Dumbo is drinking, getting them both drunk and leading to hallucinations about pink elephants.

When the friends wake up the next morning, they find themselves asleep on the high branches of a tree. Timothy explains that as a result of the baby elephant's ears, they probably flew to the upper reaches of the tree. When Dumbo is terrified to get back down, a group of passing crows provide Timothy with a "magic feather," which allows Dumbo to believe he has the power to fly. Back at the circus, and dressed as a clown, Dumbo is forced to jump from a burning building façade as a stunt. However, as he plummets toward a bucket of water, he loses his grip on the feather and begins flying on his own. He instantly becomes a national celebrity and wins the release of his mother, touring the country as Dumbo the Flying Elephant.

Like most Disney films, *Dumbo* was not an original story written by Walt or his team of storytellers, but rather adapted from a book. Co-authored in 1939 by Helen Aberson and Harold Pearl, *Dumbo, the*

Flying Elephant was not a standard book, but rather a Roll-A-Book. These books consisted of pages that were stitched together top to bottom, rather than pages stitched left to right, creating something similar to scrolling through a modern-day web page. Each page featured an illustration and text, and pages advanced by using a series of rollers that wound the pages past a cut-out screen. Roll-A-Books were created in the late 1930s to serve as a novelty version of books and printing, giving readers a different way to experience stories than the standard bound book. This "revolutionary" method was meant to become an alternative method of storytelling, allowing consumers to save space by storing small scrolls that would go into the Roll-A-Book case, rather than large hardcover books. This new textual medium also helped to make the act of reading a book a more visual experience, as though readers were *watching* the story rather than reading it. After seeing the book, Walt purchased the rights to *Dumbo, the Flying Elephant* and began to develop it for theater audiences.

While still holding to the overall themes of the book, Disney's adaptation included some distinct differences from Aberson and Pearl's original. For example, while the baby elephant is given his nickname soon after exposing his large ears in the film, in the story angry circus guests give him his nickname after he brings the tent to the ground when botching a stunt. Also, Disney thought it would make the titular character more innocent if they portrayed him as a newborn elephant, whereas the story featured Dumbo as a "midget elephant whose ears were extra big." In the book, after he is labeled Dumbo, the poor elephant befriends a robin, named Red, who brings him to an acquaintance named Professor Hoot Owl, a psychiatrist, who encourages him to pursue his dream of flying. Red brings Dumbo to a cliff, pushes him off, and tells the small elephant that he needs to start flapping his ears or it will be his demise. Dumbo begins flying and decides to employ his trick at the circus. The movie version differs by telling the story of Dumbo learning to fly as part of a circus act. Dumbo instantly becomes a celebrity and begins touring America with his mother and Red as his manager.

Walt Disney's *Dumbo*, being set in the culture of the circus, highlights many of the aspects of the circus previously discussed. At the beginning of the film, a number of storks deliver bundled babies to the circus in the middle of the night, flying to its winter home in south Florida. Animals that received their babies were common circus animals, including lions, tigers, bears, hippopotamuses, and kangaroos. Many of these animals would have been used as parts of menageries, displaying odd or exotic animals that many circus-goers likely had not seen in person before. Animal trainers who showed off their skills in taming or controlling large African cats displayed other animals, such as lions and tigers. Still other animals, like the elephants or bears, would be trained to perform specific tricks, such as balancing acts or riding on a unicycle, respectively.

Shortly after the animals receive their babies, the scene changes to the next morning, when the circus begins loading onto the train, something pioneered by Barnum shortly after the Civil War. The train in *Dumbo*, known as Casey Junior, is a flatbed train, carrying the large animals and various vehicles and supplies used in the circus on flat trailers. The animals are shown riding in boxcars that fit their body shape; for example, the giraffes ride in a boxcar with holes cut out for their long necks. Casey Junior is voiced by Margaret White, an American actress.

In the 1941 Disney film, *The Reluctant Dragon*, actor and writer Robert Benchley visits the Disney studio in an effort to pitch a story to Walt Disney for an upcoming film. Through some bumbling antics, Benchley stumbles into the sound effects studio as *Dumbo* is being made, which would come out four months after the release of *The Reluctant Dragon*. Some animation for Casey Junior not used in *Dumbo* is shown on a screen as a number of sound effects engineers stand throughout the studio, ringing large bells, releasing steam from tubes, and scraping the strings of a bass with a bow. However, it is the voice of Casey Junior that is most interesting to Benchley: White is shown speaking with a device akin to two tin cans held to her throat. She explains to Benchley that the effects are stored on a device, and when the cans are held to the vocal cords, reproduce the words spoken by the actor to the sounds of the train, such as when Casey Junior whistles, "All aboard ... let's go!" in *Dumbo*.

The train, Casey Junior, is a reference to Casey Jones, who would later be depicted in the Disney animated short *The Brave Engineer*. Jones, a railroad engineer who worked for the Illinois Central Railroad, was a legendary hero of the railroad, once heralded as saving a child from the tracks of a railroad as the locomotive was bearing down. However, it was his death that immortalized him. On April 30, 1900, Jones was killed when he was unable to stop his train, *The Cannonball Express*, as it collided with another train in Mississippi. His dramatic effort to stop the train and save the lives of those in his care made him a hero; in fact, Jones, found with the whistle cord and the brake still in his hands when they pulled him from the wreck, was the only fatality, as he did not jump off the speeding train, but rather stayed to try to stop it. While there is no reference to Casey Jones in *Dumbo*, some of the animation of Casey Junior shown in *The Reluctant Dragon* shows Casey Junior avoiding collision with a speeding passenger train by calling out to the track switch to wake up and shift the passenger train to another track, only to end up as a pile of scrap metal when a bridge collapses from a raging thunderstorm, a more accurate reference to the animated train's namesake.

Another historical reference in the film is the name given to the baby elephant by his mother. While the name "Dumbo" is given to the young pachyderm after his sneeze reveals his unusually large ears, his mother originally named him Jumbo Junior, after the baby's father. While we never see the father of the titular character, students of circus history would realize that it is likely a reference to Jumbo, the large elephant purchased from the London Zoo by P.T. Barnum and James Bailey for the Greatest Show on Earth in 1882.

Other aspects of *Dumbo* also align with a typical circus. For example, as a consequence of his mistake in the elephant-balancing stunt, which ultimately brought down the entire big top and injured all the elephants, Dumbo is sent to be a clown, which is seen by the other elephants as a shameful outcome. The matriarch of the elephants even goes so far as to place shame on Dumbo for being forced to become a clown, disowning the baby as "no longer ... [being] an elephant."

While clowns were a very important part of the circus, entertaining audiences between different acts, they were considered second-class members of the troupe. Many clowns were actually talented performers and acrobats, and eventually those successful in clowning developed a clown school where aspiring comics could go to learn how to make people laugh. Many of the clowns in *Dumbo* are accurate depictions of clowns in the early days of the circus: they often do not talk during their performances. Clowns during the years of multiple circus rings did not talk, but rather mimed, because so many clowns were needed to entertain the large crowds that their voices would not easily be heard above each other. As a result, clowns developed methods for making people laugh through slapstick humor and miming.

While *Dumbo* is not the most popular Disney animated film today, Dumbo the Flying Elephant has been delighting guests young and old at many of Disney's theme parks. A ring of Dumbo-shaped ride vehicles, each wearing a different colored hat, is attached to boom arms stretching out of a center hub. Once the ride begins, the arms lift into the air and begin to spin around the central hub, re-creating the scene from *Dumbo* when the young elephant flies through the sky.

Once a part of the original Fantasyland in Walt Disney World's Magic Kingdom when it opened in 1971, Dumbo the Flying Elephant was moved to Storybook Circus when New Fantasyland opened in 2012. Due to the immense popularity of the attraction, a second spinner was added, and Disney World fans across America dubbed the refurbished attraction the Dueling Dumbos.

"STORYBOOK CIRCUS: A WORLD OF CIRCUS FUN!"

When Storybook Circus opened in 2012 after a lengthy refurbishment, which eliminated the previous mini-land, Mickey's Toontown Fair, it featured a vastly different theme. Gone were Mickey and Minnie's houses, Goofy's Wiseacre Farm had…well…bought the farm, and Donald's Boat had sailed for the high seas. Instead, when guests first step foot into Storybook Circus, they find themselves in the middle of a circus that seems to have sprung up outside the village of Fantasyland overnight. Numerous tents have been set up, some selling circus souvenirs, while others feature the big top-themed play area in the queue for Dumbo, the Flying Elephant. Pete's Silly Sideshow sits off to the side, beckoning guests in to witness "astonishing acts of curiosity," while Casey Junior sits in the middle of a clearing, waiting to have his animal cargo unloaded. In their impatience, the assorted monkeys, giraffes, and elephants spray passersby with water in the Casey Jr. Splash 'N' Soak Station. A pair of spinners features numerous Dumbos performing their flying stunts to the amazement of circus visitors, while the circus daredevil, the Great Goofini, performs barnstorming stunts nearby.

Storybook Circus is a great representation of the golden days of the early circus, featuring numerous details that connect the Greatest Show on Earth to the canon of Walt Disney animated features and shorts. Traditionally, circuses have three rings where performances occur, and Storybook Circus is no exception: the three rings for this circus-themed land are Dumbo the Flying Elephant, Big Top Souvenirs, and Pete's Silly Sideshow.

When my family and I travel to Walt Disney World's Magic Kingdom, we travel through the park in a clockwise direction, as most guests veer to the right into Tomorrowland after leaving Main Street, U.S.A. We find that this actually gets us on the Adventureland and Frontierland attractions quicker, as many guests rush to Space Mountain and the Fantasyland attractions upon arriving at the park. As a result, as we approach Storybook Circus, we arrive from the Enchanted Forest portion of Fantasyland, rather than from Tomorrowland. As guests walk toward Storybook Circus, grooves are cut into the mud of the path as though a cart carrying the circus has arrived in the nearby field and sprung up overnight. A series of signs stretch over the path, designed to appear temporary. Wooden posts, designed to look like those that suspend circus tents, hold the signs up. Two signs, on the left and right sides of the path, are pieces of canvas, painted with the message in blue and red letters, "Come one! Come all! Welcome to the Storybook Circus. Entrance." The center sign looks more permanent and appears gilded, with golden woodwork around the outside border and blue and red letters spelling out "Storybook Circus" in the middle. Electric light bulbs outline the sign while a series of four lamps hang out of the top to illuminate the wording at night. On either side of the entrance to the land are a series of three canvas signs. On both sides, the center sign reads the same: "Storybook Circus. A World of Circus Fun. Featuring Astonishing Acts, Countless Wonders, and Stupendous Feats for All Ages." This sign is flanked by signs featuring the various acts visitors to the circus land will see during their visit, such as Pete's Silly Sideshow, Dumbo the Famous Flying Elephant, Casey Jr., and the Barnstormer.

After passing beneath the entrance to Storybook Circus, guests find themselves immediately thrust into the world of the circus. A series of big-top tents fill the area as guests step over a faux muddy path imprinted with the paw prints of various forms of circus animals, including lions and elephants. To the right is the signature attraction of Storybook Circus, Dumbo the Flying Elephant.

As guests enter the queue for Dumbot, they pass a series of snack kiosks designed to look like small train cars, as though the train left the cars there and are now serving guests circus-themed snacks. Dumbo is a FastPass+ attraction, but also has some perks for those who decide to wait in the standby line. The standby entrance is shaped like a ticket booth, in front of which stands a cast member wearing a uniform akin to someone who would work at a circus, with a red and white top with gold trim and black pants or shorts, depending on the weather. To enter the queue for the attraction, guests pass under an archway holding a sign reading "Dumbo, the Flying Elephant." The sign features circus-esque decoration, including gilded wood and geometric shapes. Timothy Mouse, Dumbo's friend from the film, stands perched atop the sign on a small cylindrical platform, spinning in a circle and waving a feather in his hand.

Guests waiting in the standby line for Dumbo wind their way under a canopy and into the big top that holds the main queue for the attraction. Look closely at the "muddy" concrete path and you will notice peanuts embedded into the ground. Upon entering the circus tent, banners and canvas signs advertise "The Amazing Dumbo" and educate guests about the unique system that allows them to receive a pager and return later to ride the attraction when it is their turn. The building truly looks like a circus tent, with strips of canvas hanging off the walls and from the ceiling. Strings of electric light bulbs also hang from the ceiling, adding to the great theming for the queue.

The queue for Dumbo is different from any other attraction on Walt Disney World property. Because the attraction caters primarily to young guests who generally don't enjoy waiting in line, parents can take a pager and enter a circus-themed play space with their children until it is their turn to get on the ride. This play space is very well themed and is set up to appear like children are playing on circus props and stunts as the circus is going on. Parents can sit on a circular bench dressed up like the ring of the circus, while children can climb into the play structure on platforms that look like trampolines, climb up through a tube that looks like an exploding cannon, and even peek through the windows of the burning building from the film that leads to the baby elephant flying. Dumbo himself soars in the peak of the big top among the platforms and trapezes that appear high through the use of forced perspective.

When summoned by their pager, guests leave the play area and return to a short line, where they are ushered onto the ride. Guests can choose from sixteen different ride vehicles on each spinner; each of the vehicles are identical except for the color of Dumbo's hat, collar, and saddle. Once on the vehicle, guests sit two to an elephant, using a small joystick to move the arm holding the vehicle up and down in elevation based on their personal preference. As guests board the ride vehicles, they may notice the backside of the entrance sign to the attraction, which has a short phrase the sums up the message of the film: "Believe and Soar!" This inspiring quote adds another dimension to the attraction, making guests feel as though they are not riding on Dumbo, but are the baby elephant themselves, believing in themselves to do something that has never been done before. The voice of Timothy Mouse comes over the intercom, giving the safety spiel, and then circus music begins as the elephant-shaped vehicles are lifted into the air and begin to fly. The ride lasts approximately ninety seconds and resembles a carousel, similar to the Magic Carpets of Aladdin attraction in Adventureland.

The spinners themselves are extremely detailed and are also identical, save for the fact that one spins clockwise while the other counterclockwise. The spinner features three colors: gold, red, and blue, and uses many different images and symbols from the film to help tell the story of the baby elephant who could fly. At the top of the spinner are four golden storks, each carrying a bundle in his beak, representing the character Mr. Stork who brings a newborn Dumbo to his mother at the opening of the film. Below the storks are a series of busts of a grinning elephant wearing a frilly cap. This grinning elephant is Dumbo's mother, excited to have a baby of her own. The hydraulic mechanism used to elevate the booms holding the ride vehicles is located under the face of Dumbo's mother, and is capped by a series of alternating crests featuring the letter D for Dumbo and a peanut, Dumbo's favorite treat. Ornate gold scrolling featuring peanuts and stars decorate the round casing that holds the booms. The bottom of the spinner features a series of different panels featuring artwork from the film that tells the story of *Dumbo*, such as the baby elephant learning how to fly and when he hallucinated about pink elephants after becoming intoxicated. A series of fountains that look like firehouses spray out a calm stream of water into a moat below the ride vehicles, which are illuminated by different colors at night, making the ride experience even more enriched and beautiful.

After unloading from the vehicles, guests exit the attraction and find themselves back in the entrance courtyard of Storybook Circus. Across from Dumbo the Flying Elephant is Big Top Souvenirs, also housed inside a large blue circus tent. A large red sign with an ornate, gilded outline names the store for guests. The word "souvenirs" is made of hollowed-out letters filled with electric light bulbs which are illuminated during the evening hours, while metallic blue lights hang above the sign. Different wooden signs hanging above the store's entrance tell guests what they can find inside the store, such as "Exciting Toys," "Amusing Momentos," "Cotton Candy," and "Caramel Apples." A yellow wooden ticket booth stands outside the building, as though circus guests would have to pay admission to enter the tent. However, the booth's windows are curtained, as though the circus is not currently open for business, and so guests can enter the tent without having to pay.

Upon entering Big Top Souvenirs, guests once again find themselves in the world of the circus, similar to the playroom in the queue of Dumbo the Flying Elephant. The building is designed to look like a circus tent, with a thick wooden pole in the center of the room holding up the tent. The pole is surrounded by a series of snack counters, featuring different types of circus treats. Humphrey the Bear serves as the mascot for Big Top Treats, which is very interesting because the character was not a circus bear in his animated shorts, but rather a wild bear used to promote the National Park Service. In fact, Humphrey is also used as the unofficial mascot of Disney's Wilderness Lodge, where he is a more logical fit.

When designing Big Top Souvenirs, Imagineers wanted to immerse the guests in the circus, and so they incorporated different elements of the Greatest Show on Earth into the shopping experience. All of the store displays and shelves utilize aspects of the circus, rather than simply being a utilitarian shelf or hanger rack. For example, a series of t-shirt racks are built into a train car that would have transported bears from town to town, complete with ornate gilded scrolling and stationary wheels. Guests who are thirsty and want a bottled water or soda can go to a set of drink coolers that are set into a train car labeled "Penguins." Wooden barrels that may have been used to carry circus supplies are used to hold plush Disney characters, while powdered candy dispensers are themed to look like spigots atop a barrel labeled water and capped with fire hoses in case a fiery stunt went awry.

The designers of the shopping location also went above and beyond with theming the actual building itself. Guests who look below their feet will notice that the floor is decorated to look as though they are standing on a canvas tarp that is stitched together, which would have added springiness for the circus performers. The area above the heads of the shoppers is also well themed to the circus: the ceiling looks to be made of canvas tenting, while strings of electric bulbs hang suspended, illuminating the

room. Thick poles stand to hold up the tent, from which platforms, trapezes, and rope ladders are made accessible to circus performers.

Upon exiting the back doors of Big Top Souvenirs, guests find themselves standing outside a third circus tent. According to the many signs
outside the red tent, the building houses Pete's Silly Sideshow. A large
wooden cutout of Pete himself, wearing a red-and-yellow striped jacket
and holding a cane in one hand and doffing his hat with the other, stands
approximately twelve feet tall and is leaning on a small booth outside the
tent's entrance which encases a calliope. The signs advertise the attractions
of the sideshow, enticing visitors to come in and see Minnie Magnifique,
Madame Daisy Fortuna, the Great Goofini, and the Astounding Donaldo.
The four characters featured in this meet-and-greet are representative of
some of the sideshow or circus acts one may have seen during the heyday
of the circus; Daisy Duck is dressed as a fortune teller, Minnie Mouse as
an animal trainer, Donald Duck as a hypnotist and snake charmer, and
Goofy as a daredevil. Pete's voice calls over the speakers, beckoning guests
inside to see the strange and mysterious; however, true to Pete's person-
ality, he speaks in a sneaky tone, leading one to believe that he is simply
trying to make a buck off the unsuspecting and gullible circus patrons.

The wooden cutout of Pete is leaning on a small wooden booth with a
large window showing a series of brass pipes inside. The booth is labeled
"Calliope—Toot Whistle Plunk Boom—Melody Time Brass Horn Band." A
small bronze plaque beneath the window reads "Manufactured by Melody
Time Brass Horns Co." This small calliope booth is full of historical
Disney references. The company that, according to the story being told,
manufactured the calliope is the Melody Time Brass Horns Company,
which references the 1948 Disney package film *Melody Time*. The tenth
animated feature produced by Disney, *Melody Time* featured seven animated featurettes set to music, including "Once Upon a Wintertime,"
"The Legend of Johnny Appleseed," and "Pecos Bill." The sign above the

window of the calliope booth explains that the instrument makes musical sounds including "Toot Whistle Plunk Boom." This is a reference to the 1953 animated short *Toot, Whistle, Plunk and Boom*, which traces the evolution of music, and won the Academy Award for Best Short Subject in 1954.

Upon reaching the entrance to Pete's Silly Sideshow, guests can choose to either enter on the left, where they can meet Minnie and Daisy, or right, where they can meet Goofy and Donald. After choosing their queue, guests pass into the entrance, where they can read a sign telling them about the circus characters they are about to meet. On either side of the sign are a series of props that represent the character. For example, Madame Daisy Fortuna is represented by a pedestal with a crystal ball, while Minnie Magnifique is represented by platforms, balls, and trampolines used by her trick poodles. In the opposite queue, tires represent the Great Goofini, while the Astounding Donaldo is represented by a large trunk with his name on it and clay jars and instruments for summoning snakes. The queue leads guests through the large, smiling mouth of Pete and into an open circus tent, similar in style to the queue for Dumbo and the interior of Big Top Souvenirs. Strings of lights are draped from the ceiling, which is peaked and made of tent canvas to resemble the big top of the circus.

Switchback queues made of ropes hanging between metal poles lead guests through the tent to a pair of meet-and-greet dioramas, in which the circus-themed characters pose for photographs. The first diorama is that of the Great Goofini. Goofy is dressed like a circus daredevil, wearing a white fireproof jump suit decked out in blue and red stripes and a large blue star on his chest. A helmet and goggles sit atop his head. A platform to the right side of his diorama features a large silver trophy, while the main background of Goofy's meet-and-greet is a large metal sphere through which a dirt bike has crashed. The assumption can be made that, true to his nature, Goofy has been unsuccessful at his stunt of driving a dirt bike inside the spherical cage, earning the displayed trophy, according to the banner above his head, by being the "broken bone record holder." To the left of Goofy's photo op is that of the Astounding Donaldo, who is dressed like a snake charmer with a striped cloak, red velvet cape, and blue and green turban. A curtained door, shaped like a Persian arch, is flanked on either side by large golden snakes with spirals in their eyes, leading guests to believe Donald has hypnotized the statues. Large urns on poles stand in woven baskets with fake flames burning in them, creating an almost dangerous feel to the Astounding Donaldo's feats.

In the opposite meet-and-greet queue, guests stand in line to meet Minnie Magnifique and Madame Daisy Fortuna. The first character in this queue that guests meet is Madame Daisy Fortuna, a circus fortune teller portrayed by Daisy Duck. Madame Daisy meets guests before the backside of a small gypsy cart, the door draped with colorful beads. The top of the cart is piled with suitcases, bags, blankets, and lanterns, leading visitors to believe that Madame Daisy travels long distances to perform in the circus and is only staying for a short while before continuing on her way. This assumption is confirmed by the sign above her stall, which explains that she is a "wandering mystic." Her cart helps to create the story of Madame Fortuna, explaining that she "forsees all … [including] fortune, health [and] fame." A wooden barrel stands to the left of her cart, atop which sits a small basket of daisies, of which the fortune teller is a namesake. Daisy herself is dressed in colorful silks cut in a medieval style and wears a headscarf, further establishing the story that Daisy has traveled far and wide, developing her exotic skills that may have been acquired in Eastern Europe or Asia. After leaving Madame Daisy Fortuna, guests proceed to the right to meet Minnie Magnifique, a circus performer who has trained her "Pirouetting Parisian Poodles." Minnie is dressed in a pink dress covered in silver polka dots, as well as pink feathers poking out of a tiara. Behind Minnie is a ladder with pillowed platforms, perched on which are Minnie's five trick poodles. Each of the poodles stands atop a name card: Genevieve, Lorraine, Brigitte, Sophie, and Lisette. Platforms and balls litter the floor, while trampolines emblazoned with "Minnie Magnifique" and "MM" stands in the background.

After meeting the circus-themed characters, guests are ushered toward the exit and into a hallway on which hang various posters advertising the "Storybook Circus All Animal Circus." Posters showing the different animal acts hang on either side of the poster. One example features "Lambert the Man Eater," showing a lion standing on a platform with a flower in his mouth. The character references the title character of the 1952 animated short *Lambert the Sheepish Lion*, a story about a lion left by the stork with a flock of sheep as an infant who must find himself to defend his family against a hungry wolf. Another banner hanging in this hallway shows "Humphrey the Unicycling Bear." This once again references Humphrey the Bear from the wilderness camping cartoons of the 1950s, in which Humphrey was actually a wild bear, not a unicycling bear. Instead, the character who *should* be shown in this poster as the unicycling bear is Bongo, the titular character of the animated segment "Bongo" from the 1947 film, *Fun and Fancy Free*. In the short, Bongo, a circus bear who unicycles, escapes from the circus and into the wild to attempt living amongst wild bears. The hallway empties into Big Top Souvenirs.

After exiting Big Top Souvenirs, guests find themselves in a courtyard with a food cart themed as a circus train car, which sells hotdogs, chips, and beverages. On the side of the cart is the number 55 in blue letters, which is a nod to the year that Disneyland opened, 1955. To the right of the food cart is a small seating area complete with round yellow tables with a large red star in the center. The seating area has the backdrop of banners also advertising the "only All Animal Circus" produced by Storybook Circus. The performers of the circus include "Strongman

Pete, the Lifter of All Things Heavy," "Pluto the Wonder Pup," "Clara Cluck the Pitch Perfect Prima Donna," "Salty the Seal and his Symphony of the Seas," and "Horace the Rubber Hose Horse."

A brick stairway runs between the food cart and the seating area, leading to the Casey Jr. Splash 'N' Soak Station, with a railroad crossing sign leading the way. Parked on a wooden turntable, Casey Jr., the circus train from the animated film *Dumbo*, sits attached to two boxcars, while two other boxcars have already been detached and are sitting on the brick walkway surrounding the turntable. A series of three tracks embedded in the concrete walkway branch out from the turntable toward the Storybook Circus restrooms, which are themed to look like a roundhouse, where trains might be parked when not in use. Sets of "rails" made of tiles continue into each restroom as though the restroom itself is the stall for the train. The roundhouse is a brick building with three large archways that serve as the entrances to the restrooms; two of the entrances are open, while the center entrance features two large wooden doors with windows. Three large lights hang from the front of the building, illuminating each of the entrances to the roundhouse, while a series of lampposts adjacent to the building stand against its front. A fourth track, separate from the others, runs away from the turntable, past the roundhouse, tracing the walkway to Tomorrowland and eventually dead-ending into the Walt Disney World Railroad. This setup of the Casey Jr. Splash 'N' Soak Station leads the keen eye to realize that Storybook Circus may be the home for the traveling circus, as the roundhouse may be the home location for Casey Jr. the Circus Train.

The Casey Jr. Splash 'N' Soak Station is made up of five different railroad cars that use water and steam features to cool guests young and old off during a long day in the Florida heat.

Casey, as well as the two cars attached to him, sits parked on the wooden turntable. Casey Jr. himself is located in the front and is surrounded by a wrought-iron fence to prevent guests from climbing him. The locomotive is painted red, blue, and yellow, and has anthropomorphic features; similar to the character in the film *Dumbo*, Casey has eyes that blink from behind lenses akin to glasses, a smile, a headlight shaped like a hat, and pistons that stretch from his side like arms. The train whistles and uses lines from *Dumbo*, such as "All aboard! Let's go!" as his bell rings and the sound of his engine chugs and steam bellows from his smokestack.

Behind Casey Jr. is a green car labeled "Giraffes" that has two of its residents stretching their necks out of the top of the car. Sitting atop one of the giraffe's heads is a monkey holding a fire hose. The two giraffes squirt water out of their mouths, while a stream of water sprays from the fire hose. On occasion, the necks of the giraffes spin, spraying passersby. The car itself is lime green in color with gold trim and a painting of giraffes on the side. On the backside of the car is the number 89, painted in red.

Attached to the giraffe car is a cream-and-blue colored car, similar in shape to the giraffe car, but instead labeled "Elephants" and with a painted 71 on the back. Each side of the car has a series of windows out of which smiling elephant faces peek above a basket of peanuts. A long elephant trunk stretches out of a hatch in the top of the car like a periscope. All three trunks spray water; the two elephants on each side of the car are stationary, while the periscope-like trunk out of the top of the car spins to spray guests on either side of the train.

Two other train cars sit off the turntable, on the outside of the courtyard, as though they have been detached from the train and are waiting to be unloaded. One car, which is located closest to Big Top Souvenirs, is red and labeled "Clowns." The side of the car features a painting of the clowns from *Dumbo* dressed as firemen and surrounding the words, "Storybook Circus—World Famous Clowns—Dumbo Shows." However, rather than clowns sitting atop the railroad car, five monkeys dressed in different clown clothing spray guests below. It appears that the monkeys have opened a suitcase full of clowning supplies and outfits strapped to the top of the car and have dressed themselves in various pieces of clothing. The monkey on the right side of the car wears a pink tutu and uses a seltzer bottle to spray guests, while the second monkey wears a battered gray top hat with a flower sticking out of the top, holding a handheld fire bellows that squirts water as he rotates left and right. Two monkeys explore the suitcase itself, with one poking its head out of the box wearing a green wig, while the other is sitting head-first in the storage container, using his tail to hold the fire hose for the monkey sitting atop the giraffe's head. The fifth monkey sits on a barrel atop a ball perched on a platform, with a squirting daisy attached to his chest. The red train car has a white painted 82 on the side.

The last train car, labeled "Camels," is a teal color and features a painting of a camel wandering the desert with an Egyptian pyramid in the distance. Two camel heads stick out of hatches in the top of the car, rotating back and forth as they spit water out of open lips at those playing below.

Casey Jr. Splash 'N' Soak Station features numerous references to Disney history. Casey Jr. is labeled as locomotive number 9, which is a reference to the number of one of the well-used locomotives for the Casey Jr. Circus Train attraction at Disneyland. Each of the railroad cars also feature different numbers that refer to important dates in the history of Walt Disney World. The green car that holds giraffes features the number 89, a reference to 1989, the year that Disney-MGM Studios, now Disney's Hollywood Studios, opened. The second car, holding the elephants, is painted with the number 71, referencing 1971, the year that the Magic Kingdom and the Walt Disney World Resort first began welcoming guests. The red railroad car that carried the clown supplies is numbered 82, for the year EPCOT Center opened in 1982, and the teal car holding the camels is labeled car number 98, for Disney's Animal Kingdom's opening in 1998.

The water playground also features numerous references to a key Disney animator and Imagineer, Ward Kimball. Kimball, one of Walt Disney's Nine Old Men, was the lead animator for the character of Casey Jr. in the film *Dumbo*. As a result, Imagineers who designed the Casey Jr. Splash 'N' Soak Station gave the locomotive thick circular black-rimmed glasses, giving the train an appearance similar to that of Kimball. The clown firefighters painted on the side of the red car also make a direct reference to Kimball; along with many other Disney animators in the 1950s, including Harper Goff and Frank Thomas, Ward Kimball performed in the Dixieland jazz band Firehouse Five Plus Two. The clowns are dressed as firefighters, and their fireman hats feature the number five, identical to the hats worn by the members of the Dixieland band. Kimball, like Walt Disney, was an avid fan of railroads and had his own full-size railroad at his home in San Gabriel. In fact, Kimball is credited with inspiring Walt to build his own miniature railroad at his home in Holmby Hills. As a result, in 2005, Kimball was posthumously given his own locomotive on the Disneyland Railroad, labeled Engine Number Five, once again referenced in the number on the firemen's caps worn by the clowns. The center clown also looks like Kimball, wearing round-rimmed glasses, and with a similar hairstyle and facial features.

As guests pass the teal camel car, they find themselves before a small, family roller coaster called the Barnstormer. As thrill seekers approach the attraction, they find a series of banners heralding the Great Goofini's different stunts, all of which show him failing in typical Goofy fashion. For example, one poster shows the Great Goofini participating in "Bear Wrasslin'," with a belted bear flexing his muscles while standing on top of a defeated Goofy. Another poster portrays Goofini as an "Aquamaniac," riding up a water ski jump, a small octopus wrapped around his face as he is entangled in seaweed. A third banner shows the stuntman as a tiger juggler, riding on a unicycle across a tightrope, the three tigers furious at being thrown into the air. Goofy seems clueless to this fact, his clothing in tatters from the bared fangs and claws of the wild cats. A small chimpanzee follows him across the tightrope, dressed as a doctor and carrying a small black bag labeled "M.D." Other banners show Goofy in similarly perilous situations, such as being blasted out of a cannon or strung up on the "Wheel of Peril" with thrown daggers.

Guests walk past these banners and beneath the entrance marquee of the attraction, which is made of wood and hanging between two circus tent poles. The sign is yellow and has wooden gilded flourishes, reading "The Barnstormer featuring Goofy as the Great Goofini" in painted letters. A stylized yellow G is featured in a red circle at the top of the sign with an airplane propeller projecting from the center of the letter. Flying from the poles on either side of the sign are a pair of blue-and-red striped knee-high socks and a pair of red pants, acting as windsocks for Goofy's upcoming flight. Separating the standby and FastPass + queues below the sign is a circus ticketbooth, similar to those found outside Dumbo the Flying Elephant and Big Top Souvenirs. The booth is red, with a yellow painted GG beneath the window, which is covered with a cloth patterned with red-and-yellow vertical stripes. A handwritten note hangs in the window, reading "OUT FLYING" and sits beneath a circular portrait of the Great Goofini wearing his flight gear, including a scarf, aviation coat and goggles strapped atop his head. Two signs shaped like flags hang below the sign: the standby entrance sign is fairly typical, telling guests how long they will be waiting in line. However, the FastPass+ sign is themed, with the phrase "TIME FOR FLYING!" written next to the clock used for guests to check their FastPass return times. Keen observers will note that the backside of the attraction marquee is yellow and painted with words that, when put together, spell out "Wise Acres Farms," a reference to the previous attraction at this location, the Barnstormer at Goofy's Wise Acres Farms.

After passing beneath the sign, guests learn more about the failed stunt attempts of the Great Goofini through various props located on either side of the queue. A series of trampolines cover the standby line, shading guests from the sun. One example is a crumpled rocket, wrapped in a brown saddle, which has crashed into the ground and partially buried itself in a flowerbed. Nearby, a sign shows the Great Goofini as the "Reckless Rocketeer," dressed as a cowboy and riding the rocket that would later crash nearby. Along the FastPass+ queue is a cannon, alongside which are a pile of cannonballs and bowling balls and a barrel of matches behind it. One of the matches is burned and the fuse of the cannon looks to have been freshly lit. Goofy appears to have modified the cannon, breaking the angle-controlling lever to pull past "High" and instead has written a new trajectory angle, "To the Moon!" Based on the direction this cannon is pointed, as well as its likely trajectory, Goofy was aiming for a trampoline on the left side of the standby queue, near the Fantasyland train station. This trampoline is similar to those shading guests, but stands on a pole and has a hole shaped like Goofy ripped in it, suggesting that it did not stop the dare-devil, but rather served as another example of a failed stunt.

After waiting in line, guests enter an airplane hangar, shaped like a barn, where they load onto the ride vehicles. The roller-coaster car pulls into the barn, complete with fake wings, seats that appear to be made of leather, and a spinning propeller on the front. The load area is complete with props that help tell the story of Goofy's failed daredevil feats. For example, two crates, one labeled "First Aid" and the other labeled "Second Aid" sit in the corner. A blue barrel labeled "X-1 Rocket Fuel" stands behind the crates, while a series of helmets, including one that is charred, sit atop the supplies. A black box with the warning "Cauti Explos" ironically appears to be damaged by an explosion. Three medicine bottles also sit amongst the crates and helmets. A white bottle sitting on top of the jet fuel is full of aspirin. A clear bottle featuring a biplane sits atop the Second Aid crate and is labeled "High Flyer Brand Altitude Discomfort Remedy," which is hailed as getting "Your Head Out of the Clouds." A final bottle, an opaque green with a maroon label, reads "'How to Fly' Brand Air Sickness Pills—Instant Relief for Beginner Pilots." This brand of air sickness reliever, which leads guests to believe this is Goofy's first time flying an airplane, references the animated series of shorts that Goofy is best known for, the "How-To" series. After the actor providing the voice of Goofy, Pinto Colvig, left the Disney studio in 1939, Disney decided to create a series where Goofy was not required to speak, putting him in different situations where he learned how to do things, such as play sports or acquire a skill. These shorts, narrated by John McLeish, showed Goofy attempting to master the skill that was the topic of the short, but doing so in true Goofy fashion. Interestingly, the Barnstormer attraction itself almost serves as a real-life "How-To" Goofy short.

The motor of the biplane roller-coaster cars whirs to life as it pulls out of the barn and onto the first lift hill toward a wooden observation tower covered in alternating red and white squares, topped with a red flag on each corner. However, Goofy's plane doesn't clear the observation tower and instead crashes through the tower, leaving a gaping hole complete with an outline of Goofy's head and hands. The biplane rushes toward the hangar before it quickly veers up and away before crashing through a billboard. The front side of the billboard advertises the Barnstormer, showing Goofy and his monkey assistant standing in front of the observation platform being circled by a biplane. A gaping hole in the shape of the biplane, again complete with an outline of Goofy's head and hands, is evidence of Goofy's recklessness behind the steering yoke of the plane. The plane curves around the edge of the billboard before coming in for a screeching landing outside the hangar. A yellow sign reads "Fly Again Soon!" in blue letters as the plane glides into the barn, coming to a stop to allow guests to disembark from the short coaster.

As guests exit the Barnstormer, they can choose to leave Storybook Circus three different ways: they can head to the left back into Fantasyland, turn right to take the path to Tomorrowland, or get on the train to Main Street, U.S.A. This method of leaving Storybook Circus actually makes the most sense, as a train is what brought the circus to New Fantasyland, and it is also the main form of transportation used during the era in which Storybook Circus is set. As guests leave Storybook Circus, past Tomorrowland, and into Main Street, U.S.A., a continuity exists, placing them in the story of the two lands of the Magic Kingdom: the train brings guests from the countryside, where the circus is set up, back into the bustling town of Main Street, U.S.A., where they can return "home," whether to their temporary domicile of a Disney or off-property resort hotel or back to their permanent home, wherever it may be.

CHAPTER ELEVEN

SPACESHIP EARTH

*L*eaving the Storybook Circus of the past behind, guests can cross property and jump years into the future for a very different experience at Epcot. "Like a grand and miraculous spaceship," Epcot's icon, a 180-foot geodesic sphere, stands greeting guests not far from the turnstiles of Walt Disney World's second theme park. While many call it "the big ball," Spaceship Earth actually serves as both the main symbol for the park and as a home for a fifteen-minute attraction by the same name. Originating from a concept imagined by science-fiction author Ray Bradbury, Spaceship Earth has gone through numerous refurbishments and incarnations, which have featured updated scripts and narrators, scenes, audio-animatronics, and even storylines. While many Disney fans have their own favorite narrator (mine was the last incarnation, hosted by Jeremy Irons, which closed in 2007), the most recent version of the beloved Epcot attraction is hosted by Dame Judi Dench, and traces the advances in technology from pre-history through the modern day. The attraction's sponsor, Siemens, uses the attraction as an opportunity to showcase some of its recent advances in technology.

While controversial for its elimination of the "descent scenes," which were replaced with LED triangles and a touch-screen film, the current version of Spaceship Earth is fairly historically accurate. The story, however, of the current version of the attraction can seem rather disjointed without historical context regarding who is being represented or what is going on in the many scenes. Americans, with an Anglo-centric understanding of history, often don't realize how important Arabic, Asian, and African societies have been to the development of Western European and American culture and society. Some of the scenes of Spaceship Earth scratch the surface in an effort to explain the influence that some of the under-represented cultures in world history have had on historical and technological advances that affect the lives of Americans on a daily basis.

Many may roll their eyes at the mention of riding a "historical" attraction while on vacation, but the concepts presented in Spaceship Earth are fascinating, as they align with an aspect of what it means to be American: constantly moving forward and making improvements to make life easier and better for all those that use technology.

QUEUE AND LOADING

Disney Imagineers set the story for their shows, lands, and attractions before guests enter show theaters or load onto a ride vehicle. Many guests may believe that Spaceship Earth does not follow this pattern when they approach the geodesic sphere, because the queue of the attraction is made up of simple switchbacks that do not contain any overt storytelling. However, whether guests realize it or not, the story of Spaceship Earth *does* begin before guests enter the building that houses the loading section of the attraction. The name of the attraction does not represent an actual spaceship, but rather is a metaphor that was first coined in print by American author and economic politician Henry George in his work, *Progress and Poverty*, which was published in 1879. In it, George explained that the entire planet had access to natural resources. In 1965, Adlai Stevenson, U.S. Ambassador to the United Nations, made a speech encouraging the UN to pass resolutions that would enact reform to preserve natural resources and well-being for humanity. However, one theme remained prominent in both George and Stevenson's metaphors, and that was that of the Earth as a spaceship, sailing through the universe, dependent on the "spaceship's crew" working together to ensure the survival of the Earth.

While the Disney attraction does not focus on the relationship between man and nature, it does focus on the theme of humanity making up the "many passengers" on the Earth, which has been a "spaceship sailing through the universe of time." According to the story of Spaceship Earth, throughout our journey humanity has had an interconnectedness and interdependence upon one another in terms of technological advances, which is where the narrative of the story continues.

As guests wind through the switchbacks beneath the enormous geodesic sphere, they realize how large the show building is, and as a result, how small and insignificant they are. To me, this puts into perspective how minute I am in the grand scheme of the world as a whole, and how many people are truly on this planet, how interconnected and interdependent we are upon one another as the human race. The queue finally winds up a ramp toward the entrance to the attraction. Prior to entering the building, a large mural to the right of the entrance depicts some of the scenes guests will experience on the ride, prominently displaying a caveman and an astronaut with a space satellite, and showing how modern technological advances harken back to the Paleolithic Era of man living in caves and painting on walls.

Upon entering the building, guests step onto a platform that moves at the same speed as the ride vehicles, which form a continuous chain. Interestingly enough, this fits into the metaphor of the attraction's story: the interconnected ride vehicles may possibly represent the interconnectedness of humanity on earth with man from the past. Each vehicle itself holds four passengers and rotates on its X-axis. Each seat has a touch screen in front of it, allowing riders to make selections such as their native language for the ride's narration, as well as to make selections for the final interactive video at the conclusion of the ride.

Upon boarding the ride vehicle, guests begin their ascent into the geodesic sphere via a ramp. The ride vehicles pass a mounted television screen, which encourages guests to smile as their pictures are taken to be used later in the descent film. Guests suddenly find themselves enveloped in darkness as British actress Dame Judi Dench begins narrating the story of the attraction. She identifies its thesis, asking "Where are we [humanity] going? And what kind of future will we discover there?" She continues by explaining that as a whole, our ancestors from across the world and throughout history have been "inventing the future, one step at a time." She then invites us to travel back into history with her and see how modern technology and advancements have had their roots in our past.

THE PALEOLITHIC AND NEOLITHIC ERAS

As the ride vehicles crest the top of the ramp, a star field and a bolt of lightning surrounds them, and a large screen shows a number of men standing before two towering woolly mammoths, hurling spears at the creatures in a blinding snow storm. This scene likely takes place in modern-day Europe, Russia, Alaska, Canada, or the Great Lakes region of North America, as that is where the woolly mammoths generally lived. Dench explains that man has difficulty surviving in a "hostile world" until communication is developed between individuals and groups of humanity. She explains that by learning to communicate, man is no longer dependent solely on himself, but rather humanity becomes interdependent on each other for survival. The ride vehicle turns right and passes the screen to show the interior of a cave, where a number of people are listening to a tribal chieftain speaking in an ancient Paleolithic language. It is obvious that he is a man of importance to the tribe, as he is outfitted with animal skins and a headdress with antlers, demonstrating his prowess as a hunter and the wealth associated with furs and animal resources. Other individuals sit on the ground of the cave around a fire or paint on the walls, including a small boy painting his handprint on one of the cave walls. Dench explains that during this time, man is recording his knowledge on cave walls, but the problem is that when man would migrate to a new area, his recorded knowledge stayed behind.

This scene represents what is known as the Paleolithic Era, or more commonly the Old Stone Age. During this era of history, which began when man originated approximately 200,000 years ago and lasted until the foundation of settled agricultural societies around 4,000 BC, humanity existed as a nomadic society, migrating from one place to another, searching for food. Often, tribes existed as a unit, usually practicing hunting and gathering. Men would often go off and hunt game, as represented by the opening scene where the men were fighting the mammoth, while women gathered wild produce, such as nuts and berries. These societies were often egalitarian, meaning that there was generally an equal and interdependent relationship between men and women; women depended on men for meat, while men depended on women for fruits and nuts.

Popular culture often portrays prehistoric man living in caves, and while this certainly happened in some places, it was not true for all groups. However, many caves, especially in places like Europe, show evidence of Paleolithic man. These caves often have tools and implements that were used many thousands of years ago, as well as cave paintings, which usually depicted animals and people with hunting tools, such as spears or bows and arrows. Historians are not clear on the purpose of these cave paintings, whether they were used to record the histories of the tribes, were religious in nature, or were meant to tell other groups who migrated to the area what animals they could find nearby. One of the most famous of these prehistoric caves is Lascaux Cave, located in southwestern France. Discovered in 1940, Lascaux Cave prominently features over ninety different paintings, including a seventeen-foot long bull. Most of the paintings feature animals that were previously found in the region. The cave paintings are estimated to be approximately 17,000 years old, and show that the inhabitants of the region were likely nomads that followed their food source (stags, reindeer, and cattle) as it migrated from place to place each year. However, these groups often were required to migrate throughout the year due to the seasons or to the movement of their food source, as with the group that painted the Lascaux Cave. As a result, all of the information that was recorded on cave, canyon, and rock walls was left behind, requiring people to start over their recording when they settled in a new location.

Limited agricultural production began in multiple places throughout the world around 8000 BC, as global temperatures began to rise and new crops began to appear approximately 4,000 years after the end of the last great Ice Age. Large game animals, such as the woolly mammoth and mastodon, became extinct as a result of the change in global climate. According to some historians' theories, women returning to their village after gathering nuts and seeds dropped some on the ground. When they returned to the area the following year to gather the wild harvests, they discovered more abundant produce than the year before. Animals, such as cows, sheep, and pigs, became domesticated, as well. As a result, there was no longer a need for groups to migrate from place to place to hunt animals, as animals were now raised for food purposes.

In order to support a more agricultural way of life, many of these groups settled around rivers and in river valleys, such as the Tigris/ Euphrates and Nile river valleys. This new system of food production allowed for individuals to amass large tracts of land and produce crops in large quantities to sustain local populations throughout the year. Social hierarchy and gender inequalities developed as men became wealthier than women. The need for a governmental system soon arose, with legal instruments such as law codes and a written language emerging to manage the collection of tax revenue based on the production of agricultural goods.

WRITTEN LANGUAGE IN EGYPT

The development of written language is shown in the next scene, with the introduction of papyrus in ancient Egypt. While papyrus was not the first writing system in world history, it was the first "paper" developed for writing, invented sometime around 3000 BC. The scene shows an "unknown Egyptian" sitting on a rock using a wooden mallet "pounding reeds flat." However, this is not how papyrus was manufactured. Instead, papyrus was cut from the marshes of the Nile River and then sliced into strips that were laid parallel to each other. Once they had been laid to the desired length, they were covered with strips that were laid on top perpendicularly. They were then covered with a large stone that would exert pressure, and once dried would form a sort of paper that could be glued or stitched to other pieces of papyrus. While Dame Dench explains that the "unknown Egyptian" is "pounding reeds flat," it is likely more accurate that he is using the hardwood mallet to polish the papyrus, which would make the paper easier to write upon. Egyptians did not have a written alphabet, but instead made use of a pictographic writing system—hieroglyphics—that represented ideas and letters.

The development of papyrus and the writing of governmental dictates on scrolls made it easier for empires to be ruled, leading to an all-powerful ruler—the Egyptian pharaoh—who is seen sitting on his throne in the Egyptian scene alongside his queen and an advisor. A curly-haired man sits cross-legged on the ground before the three writing on a papyrus scroll. This scribe, or someone who was educated in written language, was a valued commodity at this point in world history and was often employed by pharaohs and emperors for their skill in reading and writing. He is likely taking down the proclamation or law being dictated by the pharaoh in the scene.

Clues are present that suggest the identity of the pharoah and where the scene occurs. The crown atop the pharoah's head places him after the unification of Upper and Lower Egypt. Contrary to typical understanding, Upper and Lower Egypt actually referred to elevation of the Nile, rather than a north/south orientation. Therefore, the crown worn by the pharaoh in the scene includes both the white crown of Upper Egypt (in the south) and the red crown of Lower Egypt (in the north) combined, symbolizing their merger into a unified empire. This unification occurred during the reign of Menes, who established Egypt's first dynasty around 3000 BC, which places this scene after that date.

Hieroglyphics are also carved on the walls across from the "unknown Egyptian" and painted onto the stucco wall behind the pharaoh. To the right of and behind the pharaoh is a set of hieroglyphs inside an oval, which is called a "cartouche." A cartouche is a set of hieroglyphics that spell out the name of an individual, usually the pharaoh or subject of an Egyptian painting. Above the oval is a bird next to a black circle, while the symbols inside the cartouche identify the pharaoh as being Seti I, as identified on the Abydos King List. Seti I, the father of Ramesses II (the likely pharaoh of the Jewish Exodus), ruled during the nineteenth dynasty of Egypt, from approximately 1294–1279 BC.

Unfortunately, we find historical disconnect in this scene. Dench explains that papyrus is being invented, which according to the cartouche behind the pharaoh takes place sometime in the late 1200s BC. However, papyrus was developed as early as the 3000s BC. As a result, guests with an understanding of Egyptian history would find this scene to be historically inaccurate if given a longer period of time to analyze it. These historical details will not cause a break from the scene for most guests, though; many people don't realize that the Egyptian civilization was long lasting. For example, the pharaoh Tutankhamen, better known as King Tut, ruled 1200 years after the construction of the Great Pyramid of Giza. As a result, most guests will just assume that these historical details fit together and make a more immersive story, regardless of whether the scene is an accurate portrayal of Egypt during its golden age.

A CONTROVERSIAL "ALEPHBETH"

The ride vehicles continue their ascent and pass a pair of ships located to the right of the track where two men are trading. One man has his back to the guests and is holding a closed scroll, while the man facing guests is holding an open scroll. A third gentleman is holding a rope that allows the two ships to be drawn together so trade could take place. Dame Dench explains that the man facing the guests, wearing a striped red and blue tunic and a red fez, is a Phoenician merchant who uses a common alphabet that could be adapted to various written languages in their region. She concludes by encouraging passengers to "thank the Phoenicians" because "they invented" and made it "easy … to learn your ABCs."

The Phoenicians were a seafaring merchant society located on the east coast of the Mediterranean, in what is modern-day Lebanon, from 1550 BC until 300 BC. Establishing various cities on the coastline of the Mediterranean, the Phoenicians were famed traders of purple dye and purple cloth to various civilizations in their part of the world. Purple dye and purple clothing were a sign of royalty and extreme wealth, as it was obtained from the Murex snail, found in the shallows of the Mediterranean. When crushed, the Murex snail emits a few small drops of purple fluid, which, when combined with over 12,000 other snails, could dye a portion of a garment. Many surrounding societies, including ancient Greece, Rome, North Africa, and Egypt, traded with the Phoenicians. In order to reach the various trading ports, the seafaring peoples used galley ships, which were powered by a single large sail and by men below deck (usually slaves) who pulled oars to drive the ship forward.

The Phoenicians not only imported goods from other societies to their own and exported their goods to civilizations with whom they traded, they also acted as a shipping system, similar to modern-day semi-truck lines that transport goods from one place to another for a third party. This was mainly due to their advanced shipping and navigational techniques. For example, it was the Phoenicians who first began to navigate the seas through the use of Polaris, better known as the North Star. They participated in the trade of many different goods: they often exported products including cedar wood, fine linens, Murex-dyed cloth, wine, salt, and glass. In return, they often traded for imports, such as papyrus, ivory, spices, and various metals.

Phoenician merchant ships were often shaped like a tub and had a single mast. Their ships often used a single square-shaped sail, which only allowed them to move when the wind was directly behind them, rather than a triangular sail that would have allowed them to catch any wind moving in the same direction as the ship. The ship in the scene, while obviously smaller due to the limited space within the geodesic sphere of the show building, is an accurate representation. Merchants, especially in a society that gained notoriety as the shipping line of classical history, often had large ships with deep holds to accommodate the products being traded. They also traveled with multiple ships and retainers, slaves, and servants, because they were very wealthy and transported such large amounts of goods—though none are evident in the scene, save for the man holding the two ships together with the rope.

The scene on Spaceship Earth substantiates many of these historical implications. While the ship is obviously not a galley ship, one theory may be that the boat shown represents the type of smaller boat that was often hoisted or towed by larger merchant vessels. Because merchant vessels were generally large, smaller boats were used to float the merchants closer to each other with only the products they were trading, facilitating an easier method of exchange. Also, many of the goods the Phoenician is trading to the other merchant (possibly a Greek, based on his toga) are historically accurate. Large earthen jars are in the bow of the boat, which often held wine or other liquids. A basket of ivory elephant tusks stand behind the mast of the ship. It is likely that the Greek is receiving the ivory from the Phoenician, as there are also tusks in his boat, rather than the other way around; elephants are not native to Greece. The ivory would have originated in Africa, which means that the Phoenician would have gotten them from Egypt or Carthage, another large civilization on Africa's north coast.

Because the Phoenicians interacted with many different societies, each of which had their own complex writing system, it made it difficult for the Phoenicians to issue written documents and collect taxes from these societies. As a result, the Phoenicians developed their own alphabet based on Egyptian hieroglyphics. Whereas hieroglyphics are a form of pictogram and represent ideas or objects, the Phoenician writing system is more alphabetic, corresponding to specific sounds. In fact, the first two letters of the Phoenician alphabet, *alep* and *bet*, is where the term "alphabet" originates.

Through extensive interaction with the Greeks and Egyptians, the Phoenician alphabet spread and was adapted to the various groups with whom they interacted. For example, the Paleo-Hebrew alphabet, used to write early Hebrew, was almost identical to the Phoenician alphabet. The later Aramaic alphabet, which was used in modern-day Iraq and Turkey, eventually gave way to the modern Arabic written script. The Arabic script gave way to the Coptic script of Egypt, which is a combination of Greek and Egyptian symbols. The Greeks used the Phoenician alphabet to develop their own alphabet, which, in turn, led to more modern written languages, such as Latin.

Unfortunately, this scene has stirred debate and controversy since the 2008 refurbishment: Dench explains that the ease with which Americans have learned their ABCs is due to the Phoenicians. While the modern English alphabet has its origins in Phoenician script, it is many thousands of years removed from those of the seafarers, and has only three letters that even resemble the English alphabet:

𐤀: alep, the first letter in the Phoenician alphabet: the "A" sound

W: sin, the 21st letter in the Phoenician alphabet: the "S" sound

X: taw, the 22nd letter of the Phoenician alphabet: the "T" sound

English speakers who see texts written in Phoenician would not be able to read or speak it even if the script of the Phoenicians were translated into English characters. This would be similar to someone who is monolingual in English trying to understand a foreign language, such as Spanish or French, without ever having taken a course in school. Also, the Phoenicians did not invent the ABCs, but simply created their own standardized written language, something that was not new; written script originated as early as the 2600s BC (over 1,000 years prior to the Phoenician civilization) with the Egyptian hieroglyphic system and the Sumerian cuneiform lettering system.

CLASSICAL CIVILIZATION

The time travel vehicles continue on to the next scene, which encompasses the classical age of western history: the Greeks and Romans. On the right side of the ride vehicle is a small scene of a group of men sitting while an orator dressed in a red cloak speaks from an elevated platform. There are five individuals in the scene: three men seated, the speaker, and a fifth man standing off to the side. It appears that the men are outside, as the light cast onto the face of the speaker looks as though it is moonlight filtering through the leaves of a tree, while the other men are situated between tall Greek columns. The columns themselves could identify the period of Greek history in which this scene takes place; they are columns in the Doric order, which are very plain columns topped with a flat, horizontal slab of marble, and are fairly undecorative. As a result, we know that the scene takes place after 750 BC.

The clothing the five men are wearing is also representative of the period in which they live, as well as their social status. A few of the men, most notably the speaker, are wearing beards, which were more popular during early Greek history. Men generally became clean-shaven during the Hellenistic period (323–31 BC), which began as a result of the invasion and conquering of Greece by Alexander the Great of Macedonia. The speaker wears a *chiton*, a tunic made from a rectangular piece of linen that is stitched up the side and tied around the waist with some sort of rope or leather tie. His chiton reaches down to the ground and puddles around his feet, which signifies his wealth and/or his importance; in ancient societies, the more cloth one wore, the wealthier they were and the higher their status. He also wears a red *chlamys*, which was a piece of cloth, usually made of wool, that was dyed bright colors and usually had a decorative trim, especially if one was wealthy. The trim of the speaker's chlamys features a wave pattern, known as the Vitruvian Scroll or Vitruvian Wave, which was prevalent in architecture and developed by Marcus Vitruvius Pollio, who lived in Italy from 80–15 BC.

While the speaker's chlamys is elaborate, it is obvious that the students are of a higher status than he. The three seated men and the man standing in the back are all dressed in a more intricate manner than the lecturer; each of them wears long chitons with intricate patterns and folds, showing their wealth by the amount of cloth. The three seated wear *himations*, rectangular pieces of clothing that could be draped or worn in different ways, including wrapped around the shoulder or pinned as a shawl or cloak. These could sometimes be worn alone, instead of a chiton, but when worn over a chiton, signified the wealth of an individual. All three of the men are wearing himations draped over their chitons, and two of them have purple trim on their chitons' sleeves and collars, signifying extreme wealth or even royalty, as this required the Murex snail, as discussed in the interpretation of the Phoenician scene. The man standing in the back of the scene, however, may be the wealthiest of all, as he is wearing a long chiton trimmed in purple stripes, along with a himation trimmed with gold tassels. Extensive amounts of cloth and the use of tasseled trim show the extreme wealth of this individual, who can afford to bedeck himself in the outfit. A theory is that he is a father who is employing the lecturer to teach his three sons.

While we don't have any way to tell for sure, the orator *could be* one of two men: Hipparchus or Ptolemy. While it would be difficult to judge who the speaker is by looks alone, as many men in Greece likely had white hair and beards, it is what the lecturer holds in his right hand that is most interesting: a metal sphere made up of two bisecting rings with a solid sphere in the middle and bisected by an arrow. This object, called an armillary sphere, was used by Greek mathematicians and astronomers to make measurements of and observe the sky; it was an early form of the astrolabe.

Early astronomy was closely related to mathematics, which is why Dench explains the importance of Greek mathematics. While guests are unable to judge exactly who the speaker is, it is more likely to be Hipparchus than Ptolemy, who died in 168 AD, as the armillary sphere used by Ptolemy had nine rings, representing imaginary lines such as the horizon, tracks of the sun and moon, equinox lines, tropics lines, and more, whereas the sphere of Hipparchus, who lived prior to 127 BC, was much less intricate. As a result, we can assume that this scene takes place earlier in Greek history rather than later. The speaker may also be Aristotle, who helped develop the geocentric theory of astronomy during the mid-300s BC. However, Dench explains that Greeks helped to develop mathematics, and Aristotle himself did not make any advances in math, but rather dealt mainly in logic and astronomy.

Some of these details don't quite match up: a few of the men in the scene, including the speaker, have beards. While having a beard during the Hellenistic period of Greece from 323–31 BC was uncommon, it was not unlikely for men to wear one in public. However, the lecturer and some of his students wear beards. Based on ancient Greek artwork, we know that both Hipparchus, who lived during the mid-100s BC, and Ptolemy, who lived during the mid-100s AD, had beards. But the likelihood of three of the five men in the scene having beards was rare during and after the Hellenistic period, and as a result, this scene may not be historically accurate in terms of placement of the speaker in this time period, as Hipparchus lived during the Hellenistic period, while Ptolemy lived during the Roman rule of Greece.

Education in ancient Greece was especially important in the city of Athens. Similar to modern America, there were many different levels of education in Athens, including elementary education for young children under the direction of a tutor; gymnastic education, which helped boys to become physically fit and trained for war; secondary education, where adolescent boys learned philosophy and more advanced subjects; and post-secondary education, where young men could become specialized in a subject or in military studies. Boys and young men of higher class families were encouraged to be educated; girls were not permitted, but

instead were taught by their mothers how to be good wives and mothers and how to breed good Greek children. Also, poor families could not
afford to send their sons to school; they could not pay the fee to secure
the teacher, called a Sophist, nor could they afford to excuse their sons
from helping them work, thus improving the family economy.

Young Greeks learned many different subjects. It was important
in Greek society for young men to be physically fit and able to participate in military battles, as Greece was not a unified empire, but rather
a collection of independent city-states who were often at war with one
another. In Athens, the birthplace of democracy, public speaking and
rhetoric were highly valued, and so it was essential that educated young
men acquire these skills through the employment of a Sophist, who "sold
wisdom" to his patrons. Other subjects included music and basic mathematics. Greek academicians like Euclid and Pythagoras helped to develop
modern mathematics and geometry. These mathematical theories led to
the development of a new scientific focus, the discipline of astronomy.

With a pre-existing interest in astronomy as evidenced in
Greek mythology, this study quickly became ripe for exploration by
Greek mathematicians, theorists, philosophers, and academicians. One
of the most influential astronomers, Ptolemy, as well as the popular philosopher Aristotle, developed the geocentric theory, which stated that the
Earth, not the sun, was the center of the universe. Ironically, this theory
displaced a previous theory that the Earth rotated around the sun; however, due to limited technology, it could not be proven. As a result, geocentric theory stemmed from the observation that the stars, planets, sun,
and moon move, while the Earth is not felt to be moving. This would later
be disproven through the development of a more advanced telescope by
the European scientists Nicolaus Copernicus and Galileo Galilei. Because
the armillary sphere in the lecturer's hand has a globe at the center with
rings circling it, we might assume that the speaker is more likely Ptolemy

than Hipparchus, as the latter was a believer in the early heliocentric theory before the development of the geocentric theory. However, based on other details of the scene, this judgment does not necessarily fit.

All of these details may lead us to the realization that this scene may not represent a specific date or era of ancient Greece, but rather serves as a generalization of ancient Greece as a whole, due to the many different eras of Greek society and culture that are represented. The columns are of the Doric order, which were developed after 750 BC. The second form of columns, those in the Ionic order, were developed around 550 BC, and are best known for the scroll across the top of the column. Therefore, we know that the area the five men are located in was built after 750 BC. Three of the five men are wearing beards, which means that since beards were rare during the Hellenistic period of Alexander the Great, the scene likely takes place sometime before the 300s BC. The speaker is holding a geocentric armillary sphere, which would place the scene sometime in the mid-300–120s BC. However, the speaker's garment is what doesn't fit: the red cloak that the Sophist is wearing is trimmed in a Vitruvian wave, which Vitruvius developed in the mid-first century BC, about one hundred years from the end of the geocentric model's popularity. If not for the use of the Vitruvian wave on the teacher's clothing, the scene could have been pinpointed to be sometime between 360–120 BC, but the use of this pattern simply does not fit. As a result, the scene may represent the glories of what Westerners collectively remember from ancient Greece, not a specific period of Greek history.

Our time travel vehicle continues forward with the next scene on the left side of the track. Dench explains that the Roman Empire learned from the Greeks and developed a vast system of roads, allowing them to move their armies across the world, and likening the road network to the World Wide Web. As the vehicle approaches the scene, a tall marble statue of a man holding a scroll in his left hand stands in an alcove, while

his right hand is outstretched. The statue looks regal, the eyes of the figure staring off into the distance. A long, thick cloth is draped around his
shoulders and hanging down his body. Shortly after the statue, the vehicles pass two men talking to one another. One is dressed in a long white
gown lined with a magenta stripe, while the other wears a Roman soldier's uniform. A third character is standing behind the Roman soldier
holding the reins of a team of two horses attached to a chariot. The man
holding the reins is wearing a loose-fitting, plain brown garment that
looks to be of poor quality. The soldier and cloaked man are each holding scrolls in their hands, discussing what is written on them. A Roman
city stretches out into the distance behind the soldier, showing the vast
expanse of the Roman road system.

The first image places the Roman scene into historical context: the
statue in the alcove is a reproduction of a statue of Caesar Augustus,
nephew of the first leader of the Roman Empire, Julius Caesar. Augustus
ruled as the member of a triumvirate, sharing power after the assassination of Julius Caesar in 44 BC. The trio of rulers—Mark Antony, Marcus
Lepidus, and Augustus (known as Gaius Octavius at the time)—waged
war against the assassins of Julius shortly after his assassination. After
their victory, the three leaders split Caesar's Roman empire into three
parts. Not content with the land they had gained peacefully, the three
new dictators began to wage war against each other to try to expand their
own land holdings. Defeating Lepidus and Antony, Octavius became the
new ruler of the Roman Empire, renaming himself Augustus and taking
his uncle's last name, Caesar, as his title, thus securing his spot in history
as Augustus Caesar.

Augustus ruled Rome from 27 BC until his death in 14 AD. The statue,
which is currently housed in the Louvre art museum in Paris, France, is
not historically accurate to the Roman Empire. The head of the statue was
done as a portrait of Augustus, and was carved sometime around 20 BC,

approximately seven years after Augustus became Caesar and around the
time he was forty years old. However, the head was originally attached
to a torso wearing a cuirass, a sort of body armor for the chest worn by
Roman soldiers. The body of the statue shown in the scene wearing the
flowing robe was carved sometime during the second century AD, about
one hundred and forty years after the carving of the head. The statue that
is housed in the Louvre, which is represented in the scene, was constructed (head of Augustus and body with the flowing toga) sometime in
the 1700s. So, while the statue itself exists and is made up of historical
pieces carved during the Roman Empire, it was not a statue that would
have been on display during the rule of the Roman Empire.

The three figures in the scene each represent specific roles in
Roman society. The individual with his back to the guests is the most
important; he is a senator of the Roman Empire. We can judge his role
in Roman society based solely on what he is wearing. Roman senators
wore white gowns with a purple stripe, signifying their importance and
wealth; purple dye during this time was still extremely rare, and thus
could only be afforded by the wealthy and those of high status or rank.
Under the Roman Republic, which lasted from 509–27 BC, senators
served as the authority figures and lawmakers of the land under Roman
rule. However, once Augustus became Caesar in 27 BC, the power of the
Roman Senate began to dwindle. Rather than making the legal deci-
sions of the land, senators instead became a bureaucratic authority,
ruling on behalf of the Caesar. Because the landmass of the Roman
Empire was so large, the emperor could not effectively rule and control the people, relying instead on the compliance and enforcement of
his decrees and proclamations by the senators who lived in the various
provinces of the empire.

The second figure, standing on the steps and speaking to the senator, is facing guests as their time travel vehicles continue forward. He is

dressed in the uniform and armor of a Roman soldier; he wears a golden metal helmet on his head, as well as leather armor, a red toga, sandals with straps up his calves, and a red tunic, which was worn to symbolize his loyalty to the emperor. At his feet are a staff and shoulder bag, as well as a cloak, which the soldier likely threw to the ground before the senator, showing respect and deference toward his political and social superior. The rank of the soldier is not easily identified, but he is likely a member of the Praetorian Guard, based solely on his helmet. The helmet of the soldier does not feature the stereotypical red plume of a Roman soldier, but rather a solid metal crest with four circles of ornamentation, signifying a high rank in the Praetorians. The helmet features inscribed, gilded decoration, as well as a shield for the eyes. Protective flaps cover the ears and jawline of the soldier's head. The Praetorian Guard was a branch of the Roman military established during the reign of Augustus as a result of the rampant civil wars that plagued the empire. The guards provided personal protection for the caesar, and were extremely loyal to him. In fact, they only received their orders from the emperor himself. As such, the Praetorian Guard often assassinated political opponents or others who threatened the power of the caesar.

The third individual in the scene stands near the back right, holding the reins of the team of horses. The young man is clothed in a rough-looking piece of garment that is not tailored and has rough edges, similar to burlap. The cloth is dyed in an earthen brown or orange-red color. He is likely a slave for the senator, holding the reins of the horse for the senator's visitor. Other than the cloth he is wearing, two other things can visually classify that this individual is a slave: the length of his hair and the tone of his skin. Because slaves were considered property and not seen as human, they often were not treated in a dignified manner. As such, those who owned slaves often did not bother to cut the hair of their slaves. Also, because slaves often did manual labor outside (agriculture, tend to horses, transport supplies, deliver messages, etc.), their skin tanned; thus, many in the ancient world were identifiable by their skin tones: the richer you were, the paler your skin, while the poorer you were, or if you were enslaved, your skin was more tan. However, the Roman system of slavery was not based on skin color or race, as more modern examples of slavery have been. Many slaves in the Roman Empire were from surrounding regions conquered by the imperial powers.

The background mural that is painted behind the horses and three figures can be pinpointed to an exact place in the Roman Empire, which provides the viewer with some historical context of when and where the scene occurs. The mural depicts a large Roman city stretching off into the distance, while a series of buildings and statues are identifiable nearby. To the left of the scene, behind the horse-drawn chariot, are a series of statues capping Roman pillars, stretching on the left side of an avenue. Behind the tall statues is a building with columns holding up the roof with a triangular-shaped pediment. On the opposite side of the scene, behind the slave holding the reins of the horse, is another series of statues atop pillars, while statues of mounted horsemen are rearing on a platform alongside steps leading up to the scene. Behind the horsemen is a series of buildings with columned facades, one with a triangular pediment and the other capped with a dome. The avenue surrounded by the pillared statues identifies the location as being in the Roman Forum, the headquarters for government and mercantile activity in Rome, the capital of the Roman Empire. However, it is the location of the pedimented and domed buildings and the presence of the rearing horsemen that identify where the three men are congregated: the Temple of Castor and Pollux. The temple was built in 495 BC and dedicated in 484 BC as a tribute to the twin sons of the Roman god Jupiter for assisting the Romans in victorious battle. Interestingly enough, the statues of Castor and Pollux that are depicted standing at the bottom of the stairs in the scene's background mural are not historically accurate. While the scene shows the men riding on the backs of rearing horses, the real statuary figures of the Roman gods hold the reins of the rearing horses instead.

The location of this scene can also help to fix the date or period in which the scene is taking place. However, there is some discrepancy: one possibility would lead to historical inaccuracy, while the other is more plausible. During the time of the Roman Republic, from the temple's dedication in 484 BC until 27 BC when Augustus established the Roman Empire, the Temple of Castor and Pollux served as the meeting place for the Senate. However, the placement of this scene during this era of Roman history does not fit, as the statue of Augustus holding the scroll that precedes this scene was not constructed until 20 BC. Thus, the statue makes this theory, that of the temple being used as a meeting place for the Senate, unlikely. More likely is the second theory: from 37–41 AD, the Temple of Castor and Pollux was used as the palace of Caligula, who served as caesar for a short three years and ten months. The reason he chose the temple to be his palace was partially because Caligula would, on occasion, present himself at the top of the steps, making speeches, and attempt to personify himself as a god to be worshipped, in addition to his role as Roman emperor. This storyline for the scene would likely be more accurate, as the reign of Caligula took place twenty-three years after that of Augustus, which would maintain the historical integrity of the Temple of Castor and Pollux being the setting of the scene after the vehicles pass the statue of Augustus. While the important man handing the message off to the Praetorian is not Caligula, as evidenced by the senatorial robe he is wearing, senators and the emperors worked closely together, and it can be theorized that he is delivering a message on behalf of Caesar Caligula.

The presence of these three men standing on the steps of the Temple of Castor and Pollux identify what may be going on in this scene, which, whether intentional by the Imagineers or not, represents a dark event in the history of the Roman Empire. During the reign of Caligula, the Praetorian Guard began to amass political power. At the same time, Caligula increasingly began to mistreat the Senate and other high-powered individuals in the government of the Roman Empire, causing many to begin conspiring against him. In 40 AD, Caligula announced that he would be moving to Alexandria, the center of Roman power, on the Nile River in Egypt. His goal in moving to Egypt was to gain more power and followers, as Egyptians worshipped their leaders as gods. As a result, Caligula planned on moving the center of Roman government from Rome, the traditional location for Roman government and admin-istration, to Alexandria, which was located in a province (Egypt) looked down upon by the Roman government because the people there were not "true Romans," having been born outside the capital.

Because of this radical transition, the Roman Senate began to con-spire with the Praetorian Guard to assassinate Caligula, which ultimately occurred in 41 AD; he was stabbed thirty times while addressing a group at an athletic event. The senators, realizing how much the government had strayed from what they perceived as the glories of Rome's "golden age," planned to re-establish the Roman Republic after Caligula's death, thus restoring their political power. However, after being driven from the city, Caligula's uncle, Claudius, exacted revenge on those who con-spired and committed the assassination by naming himself the next caesar of the Roman Empire. With these details in mind, this scene may actually be a senator and a Praetorian guard passing messages between those conspiring to assassinate the emperor.

Dench explains the importance of the system of roads that allowed the Roman Empire to be efficient, using the metaphor that the network is "the first worldwide web," evidenced in the scene by the grid-style pattern of roads seen in the distance. The Roman Empire stretched across three continents. At its height, the road network totaled nearly 51,000 miles, connecting the different regions of the empire, including Gaul (France), the northern coast of Africa, and Constantinople, which is in modern-day Turkey. While roads existed to connect the expanses of the Roman Republic as early as the 400s BC, they were of poor quality. However, as different civilizations arose around Rome, and the land holdings of the empire continued to expand, greater expanses of roads and better quality roads were needed. Various nomadic groups lived in western Europe and traded extensively with the Roman government, while far-off civilizations in the east, like China and India, had exotic goods, including spices, silk, and other luxury products in which Rome was interested. Also, because the Roman Republic, and later, the Roman Empire, was so large, a system of transporting messages to the various senators serving as the Caesar's bureaucrats was essential in order to effectively govern ancient Rome.

As a result, around 450 BC, standardized expectations for the measurements and building procedures of roads were published in the Twelve Tables, the legal code of the Roman Republic. These laws set the width of roads at eight feet across, but later roads would be as wide as forty feet across to allow for chariots and travelers to pass each other and travel in both directions.

Road building in the Roman Empire reached its height during the second century AD, at which point roads were a marvel of ancient engineering: a trench would be dug, filled with sand, and topped with crushed rock or gravel. Also, ditches would be dug on either side of these roads to facilitate the draining of rain water to prevent flooding.

Roads were also used for military purposes. Beginning during the reign of Augustus, the era of Pax Romana, or the Roman peace, lasted from 27 BC until 180 AD and was a time of relative calm within the empire and surrounding societies. However, just because it was a time of peace did not mean that the empire did not continue to expand; because of the vast network of roads Rome had built, it became easier for troops to move from one area to another, making it easier for Roman authority to spread.

The road network fits with our theory of the events transpiring in the attraction's scene: when preparing to assassinate Caligula, the Praetorian guard needed to move large contingents of troops into Rome from all over the empire to establish their rule over the city. As a result, the conversation between the senator and the soldier on the steps of the Temple of Castor and Pollux may be regarding the movement of troops into the city to establish military rule after the Caligula's assassination.

THE FALL OF A GREAT EMPIRE

After displaying the glories and strength of ancient Rome, the following scene shows its decline. Interestingly enough, the scene representing the fall of Rome did not actually take place in Rome itself, but, rather, in the city of Alexandria, in Egypt. Amidst one of the favorite smells of many Disney fans, simply known as "Rome Burning," Dench explains that the Roman Empire fell and that much of the learning that was discovered during the time of the ancient Greeks and Romans was destroyed when the Library of Alexandria is burned. Originally built to house the wealth of Egypt when Alexander the Great established the capital city of his Hellenistic Empire at the mouth of the Nile River after conquering Greece and Egypt in 331 BC, the library had varying amounts of papyrus scrolls (books as we know them had not yet been invented), with some estimates as high as 400,000 scrolls in the library's collection at any given time.

While the attraction portrays the burning of the great library as being a result of the fall of the Roman Empire, or even leading to the empire's fall, neither is the case. In fact, the attraction doesn't even specify *which* burning of the Library of Alexandria is being portrayed. There were actually three different instances in which the library was destroyed.

The first burning occurred in 48 BC when, in an attempt to conquer Alexandria, Julius Caesar burned the Egyptian ships anchored in the harbor. The fire spread unintentionally from the ships to the library, causing all documents in the collection to be destroyed. However, this is not likely to be the fire depicted in the attraction, as Caesar's accidental destruction of Alexandria occurred eighty years prior to Caligula's rule over Rome depicted in the prior scene.

The second burning of the Library of Alexandria took place in 391 AD and was brought about by Theophilus, the patriarch of the Coptic Christian Church of Alexandria. Attempting to establish the power of the church in Egypt, Theophilus decided to destroy all examples of pagan religion, including the various shrines and temples to Egyptian and Roman gods that littered the city. One of these temples, the Temple of Serapis, held ten percent of the scrolls that made up the library's collection. In order to eradicate the city of all un-Christian influence, he burned the interior of the temple, destroying many of the texts in the process. He then established a Christian church in place of the Temple of Serapis, using the burned-out building as the shell for the new church. While this may be the historical event described by Dench, it is unlikely, due to the fact that she groups the library's destruction with the fall of the Roman Empire, which occurs approximately eighty-five years after Theophilus' destruction of the Temple of Serapis. Also, his destruction of the pagan temple did not destroy all of the records; ninety percent of them remained unscathed in the main building of the library nearby.

The most likely event as described by Dench occurred in 640 AD, one hundred sixty-four years after the fall of the Roman Empire in 476 AD. The two events are not actually linked; the power of the Roman Empire was no longer a threat, and as a result, it made the burning of the Library of Alexandria possible without opposition. In 640 AD, Muslim armies from the Arabian Peninsula invaded and conquered Egypt, taking it from the fairly weak Byzantine Empire. The conquering officer of the Muslim armies, Amr ibn al-As, wrote to the caliph of the Islamic Empire, Umar Ibn Al Khattab, requesting instruction on what to do with all of the texts stored in the Library of Alexandria. Umar responded famously that the texts "will either contradict the Koran, in which case they are heresy, or they will agree with it, so they are superfluous." As a result, he ordered the library to be destroyed and the texts burned. Arabic legend says that there were so many scrolls that it took six months to burn all of them, and that the burning paper was used to heat the baths of Alexandria for the invading armies.

This is likely the historical event that the scene represents, especially within the context of the following scene. The burning of the library in 640 AD is not a result of Rome's fall, as it occurred centuries after the end of the Roman Empire. After being sacked by the nomadic Huns in 476, Rome ceases to exist, and Alexandria becomes a part of the Byzantine Empire, whose capital was located in Constantinople (modern-day Turkey). Although the burning of the library, which this scene likely depicts, occurred in 640, the Byzantine Empire would continue for another 800 years, ultimately coming to an end in 1453 with the Ottoman sacking of the capital city. As a result, the library's destruction did not affect the stability of any empire, but rather caused the loss of great knowledge.

THE ARAB EMPIRES: "THE FIRST BACK-UP SYSTEM"

While the leaning columns, flickering flames, and piles of stone rubble that represent the destruction of the Library of Alexandria sits on the left side of the track, another scene unfolds nearby. On the right, three individuals sit on the ground talking around a low table with a candle flickering on it. Below them is a Persian rug, and light from hanging lanterns filters down. Across from this scene is a room with many square-shaped holes holding books and scrolls; a bearded man sits on a platform, reading through a text. Overlooking both of these scenes is a balcony with a man holding a quadrant, looking up at the stars.

This scene is full of historical implications. However, before analyzing the scene historically, one needs to understand the context. In the ancient world, regardless of their culture, philosophers, scientists, and academicians often met to discuss theories and learning. Often, rulers of great empires employed philosophers from other civilizations in order to enrich their empire, adding new practices and theories to their society. For example, Kublai Khan, the great khan, or emperor, of the Mongolian Empire in China, surrounded himself with Arab, Christian, European, Russian, and Indian scholars and scientists in order to make China more technologically and scientifically advanced. Often, when cultures meet, ideas are shared, leading to an intermingling of philosophies and ideas. As a result, while people from Western culture often attribute modern astronomy, medicine, and navigational techniques to Europe, they often came from Ancient Greece and Rome via the Arabs, who saved a lot of the learning that was lost in the fires of Alexandria.

Great armies of the time often included philosophers, holy men, and scientists, who were brought along on campaigns in order to glean information that could benefit the conquering empire. As a result, when the Muslim armies invaded Egypt and destroyed the Library of Alexandria in 640 AD, many of the scrolls were saved by Arab scholars, who brought them back to their cities on the Arabian Peninsula. However, it wasn't until the eight century that translation of these texts from Greek, Latin, and Egyptian into Arabic began. Caliph al-Mansur moved the Abbasid Islamic capital from Damascus, north of the Arabian Peninsula, to Baghdad, where he established the House of Wisdom, a school that translated, studied, and preserved the ancient texts of the

Greeks and Romans. Wanting to expand his collection, al-Mansur sent emissaries to the nearby Byzantine Empire to collect texts from them as well.

While it may seem that the Arabs stole many important texts from the Europeans, this simply was not the case. After the fall of the Roman Empire in 476 AD, Germanic tribes invaded the western portion of the empire. Because these tribes were illiterate, many people grew up never learning how to read or write, and as a result, even if the texts had been available, no one would have been able to read them. The eastern portion of the old Roman Empire, the Byzantine Empire, split away from Rome in 293 AD during the rule of Diocletian in an attempt to better rule the enormous empire. The Byzantines fostered trade and diplomatic relationships with the Umayyad and Abbasid Caliphates of Arabia. This economic relationship soured, however, in the eleventh century, when Pope Urban II proclaimed the First Crusade to take the Christian holy city of Jerusalem from the Muslims. During the Crusades, which lasted from 1095–1291, European and Muslim scholars interacted, and many of the ancient Greek and Roman texts, which had been translated into Hebrew and Arabic, were shared with the Europeans.

The Abbasid Caliphate ruled the Arab Empire from 750–1517. Known as the "Islamic Golden Age," knowledge was seen as extremely valuable, and during this time many new discoveries and advances were made in the fields of astronomy, architecture, technology, and art and literature. After interacting with various societies, these new advances were shared with different societies, diffusing ideas throughout Europe. However, because western culture is Eurocentric, many often attribute these discoveries to white Europeans. In reality, they were shared through interactions with the Chinese, Indians, and Arabs. European, Jewish, Indian, and African scholars traveled long distances to the heart of the Abbasid Empire, hoping to glean new information to better their own societies.

In 1258, the Ilkhanate forces of the Mongol Empire attacked and destroyed Baghdad, the capital of the Abbasid Caliphate. As a result, the enslaved military forces of the fractured Abbasid empire, the Mamluks, retreated to Cairo, Egypt, and established that city as the new capital of the Abbasid Caliphate. Cairo would serve as the capital of the Abbasid Caliphate from 1261 until 1517, as not only the political but also the intellectual center of the Arab Empire, until it was conquered by the Ottomans in the second decade of the sixteenth century.

The three small scenes in Spaceship Earth that make up this period of Arab history actually tell a larger story that encompasses the quest for knowledge throughout the Eastern hemisphere during the late first and early second millennium. The first scene, on the right side of the ride track, is dimly lit, likely because it doesn't take place in any specific location. The walls have rectangular, clay tiles set in them, each with a ten-pointed star and other decorative carvings. This pattern has been found in Cairo, specifically in the mosque of the emir Sayf al-Din Qawsun, which was built during the early part of the fourteenth century. While this scene may or may not be taking place in a mosque, it is likely that it occurs somewhere of significance in the city of Cairo since common areas did not have intricate clay carvings as depicted here. We can also assume that the scene takes place sometime between 1325 and 1517, as the ten-pointed star pattern was common during this period of the Mamluk rule of the Abbasid Empire in Cairo.

Three individuals sit cross-legged on the ground of the scene on hand-woven carpets around a table with a lantern on it. The lantern is cylindrical, with a wide mouth at the top and a bulbous bottom, tapered around the middle. The foot-tall lantern is covered in Arabic lettering engraved on its exterior. This type of lantern was specifically created for a *madrasa*, or a place of learning in the Arab world. Therefore, with the presence of the lantern, it can be concluded that the trio is discussing academic matters in an educational institution in Cairo. A second small table stands behind the intellectuals, on which is a tall, narrow vessel with a thin handle and spout. This is likely a coffee or tea service, providing refreshment to the three men, as they have likely been talking for many hours in the hot, dry climate of northern Egypt.

Examining the three characters closely, one realizes that while Dench labels them as "Arab ... scholars," it is clear that the three are from very different places. The scholar sitting on the right of the scene has dark skin, making it obvious that, in context of the time period in which the scene is set, he originates from Africa. He also has long, black dreadlocks which hang out of his orange turban onto his tunic, which is covered with a cheetah skin. While cheetah fur could be traded throughout Africa to anyone with wealth, cheetahs live mainly in northern and eastern Africa, making it likely that the scholar is from those regions. However, since Islam was practiced primarily in northern Africa during the 1300s and 1400s, the African scholar may have come from the empire of Mali, in northwest Africa. Mansa Musa, the emperor of Mali from 1312–1337, was known for his pilgrimage from his home in west Africa to the holy city of Mecca on the Arabian Peninsula, a practice encouraged for all Muslim faithful. During this pilgrimage, or *hajj*, Mansa Musa wrote about all he experienced along the way, leading to an expansion of learning and development for the Islamic empire of Mali. As a result, it would not be unlikely that Mansa Musa would have sent a scholar to Cairo to meet with other scholars from throughout the Islamic Empire.

The figure in the middle of the scene wears a long, white beard and moustache and a large, onion-shaped turban on his head. This type of turban was not common and was actually attributed to the Ottoman Empire. Most popularly worn by Caliph Suleiman the Magnificent during the early 1500s, these large white turbans signified the wearer's high status. However, rulers as early as the first caliph of the Ottoman

Empire, Osman the First, who ruled Turkey from approximately 1299 through 1326, wore this style of turban as well. Therefore, it is possible that the man sitting in the middle of the scene, while likely not an Ottoman caliph, could be a close advisor to the caliph or even an intellectual charged with gleaning more knowledge for the Ottoman Empire.

The third man, sitting on the left, wears a short turban, appearing to be wrapped around a fez. This man is not easily seen by guests, as his back is to riders and he is sitting in shadows. However, we are able to make some assumptions about him based on the limited detail we can glean. One of the main trade partners for luxury goods and knowledge during the fourteenth century was India, but we can't assume he is from India simply because they were a powerhouse of knowledge. The individual's turban does not provide enough clues; however, the man's facial hair is the main clue as to his Indian origin. The man wears a bristly moustache, a style of facial hair that was extremely popular in India. Therefore, while there is no definitive evidence of the intellectual's origin, these few pieces of evidence point us to the Indian subcontinent. While Indians are not technically part of the Arab ethnic group, during the 1300s the Delhi Sultanate ruled India. The sultanate was an Islamic government which took power after 1200. From the 900s until the 1100s, Muslim armies slowly began to push through the Himalayan and Hindu Kush mountain ranges, plundering for booty and other important products. Muslim rulers finally established a hold over the land in 1206, retaining power in India until the Mughal Empire, another Islamic theocracy, rose to power in 1526.

Across the track is a solitary individual reading a book while sitting cross-legged on a platform. The man, old and wizened, wears a blue turban on his head and a blue tunic striped in a Hebrew pattern. He is holding a book in his hand, while a second book sits in a wooden bookstand to his right and a scroll lies at his feet on the left. A small wooden box with a squared bottom and a rounded top sits on his left side, leaning against the pillow supporting him. The room in which he sits features mosaics of geometric shapes in colors of red, blue, green, and gold. Numerous shelves hold multiple books along the walls and Persian rugs cover the tiled floor.

This man is a Jewish scholar, studying a text in the Baghdad House of Wisdom. We know that this is the House of Wisdom based on various paintings of that institution, such as the illustration of the House of Wisdom by Yahya al-Wasiti from the Islamic text *The Maqamat of al-Hariri*, written in 1237. The painting features a number of men sitting in a room with numerous square shelves filled with books and elaborate mosaics lining the walls, almost identical to the room in which the Jewish scholar is sitting.

There are also quite a few clues that identify the man as a Jewish scholar. The first piece of evidence is his clothing, a striped Hebrew tunic and a wrapped turban on his head. Jews often wore turbans on their heads as a sign of submission to God, especially during prayer or times of reading the Holy Scriptures. Because there are multiple texts in front of him (two scrolls on the floor, a book in a book stand, and another in his hands), we can assume that he is translating texts. However, the biggest clue that he is a Jewish scholar may be the small wooden box sitting behind him. This box is brown, about eight inches tall, and has a rounded top, a squared bottom, and decorative carving across the front. The box is a case that Jewish scholars and rabbis would use to carry around the Torah, a portion of the Jewish holy text. The Torah was often in scroll form and, as a result, a special box was needed to carry the scrolls safely when traveling. It is possible that the two scrolls sitting at the feet of the scholar are his Torah scrolls and that he is looking between the two open books and his scrolls.

The third part of this scene features a man standing on a balcony, using a quadrant to observe the night sky. This scene, while not necessarily representative of a specific time or place, represents an important historical implication of medieval Arabic culture and economics. Called by some the Golden Age of Islam, the period from the 800s until the 1500s saw the rise in power, economics, and even academic discoveries by the great Arab empires. One of the most important disciplines of study, which would affect the entire world and even have far-reaching implications into the modern day, was the further development of astronomy by Arab scientists and philosophers. While Arabs were certainly not the first to look at and study the night sky, they would help to develop important techniques in navigation and timekeeping through the study of the placement of stars and the sun.

Navigation was extremely important during the Abbasid Caliphate, as a new form of Islam, Sufism, emerged. While not in direct opposition to traditional sects of Islam, Sunni, and Shia Islam, which focus on man's relationship to and with Allah in *this* life, Sufi Islam is a much more internalized sect which focuses on mysticism and man's relationship with Allah in the *next* life. Because Sunni and Shia Islam were politicized and were often spread through the conquering of an empire, Muslim armies and governments were often hesitant to spread their religion, as it would require more resources and less plunder for themselves, as Muslims are called to take care of their own and to share everything.

As a result, for the first few centuries of the Muslim empires, Islamic rule stayed near and around the Arabian Peninsula. However, after the rise of Sufism, and the belief that without Allah and his tenets man would be damned to hell, Sufi mystics began to travel the Eastern hemisphere, spreading their beliefs to all who would listen. Because they often gave up worldly possessions to follow and spread the teachings of Allah and Muhammad, they were required to ride along with Arabic merchants in small boats called *dhows* as they traded up and down the east African coast, and toward India, Southeast Asia, and Indonesia, or by caravan down into Egypt and the Saharan desert.

In order for this travel to be possible, a system of navigation was required, and thus Arab scholars began turning to the skies, developing tools, and improving upon existing ones like the astrolabe, the quadrant, armillary spheres, and sundials. These implements allowed navigators and ship pilots to understand their physical relationship to the sun and stars, and helped them to navigate to the different parts of the African and Eurasian continents to trade, inadvertently helping to spread Islam worldwide.

Another reason that Arabs began to look to the skies was for religious reasons. Islam has five main practices, or pillars, that are expected to be followed by all faithful Muslims: the Shahada (the statement of faith that "There is no god but Allah, and Muhammad is the messenger of Allah"), the Salat (praying five times daily facing the holy city of Mecca), the Zakat (the giving of alms to the poor), the Sawm (fasting from food or drink during the daylight hours of the holy month of Ramadan), and the Hajj (pilgrimage to Mecca at least once in a lifetime). While it is important for a practicing Muslim understand his cardinal directions so he can pray facing Mecca regardless of where he is, during the late first millennium time-keeping was in its infancy. The second daily prayer, *dhuhr*, is to be prayed after noon, when the sun has passed its highest point in the sky.

So, without an understanding of solar astronomy and a standardization of time, many in the Muslim community would have been confused as to when they were to pray. As a result, Arab astronomers began to study the position of the sun in the sky, using such tools as the quadrant to understand the angle of the sun in relationship to the earth, and helping them to understand when the sun was at its peak so that the Muslim faithful could avoid Allah's anger by praying at the correct time.

RESTORATION OF THE CLASSICS AND A REBIRTH

Dame Judi Dench resumes her narration as the time travel vehicles continue upward and to the right as she explains that Christian monks have taken the texts translated by the Muslims and have begun to record them by hand, restoring the lost knowledge to Western Europe. The scene features a dimly lit, dank room lined with wooden desks. Two men sit at the desks; one is studiously writing with a feather quill, while the other has fallen asleep at his desk. Empty desks are scattered between the columns that support the celling of the room.

During the late Middle Ages, books were a rare commodity, as they had to be copied by hand. Very few people, even in Western Europe, were able to read or write. As a result, books were very expensive, and literacy rates throughout the "civilized world" were low. As the Catholic Church began to develop into a political force between the 900s and 1300s, more priests needed copies of the Bible to teach their parishioners. Orders of monks, or men who chose a life of asceticism to study the holy ways of God in a monastery, were charged by Catholic leadership to copy the Bible by hand. Some of these monasteries had rooms called scriptoriums, literally translated as "a place for writing." However, because of the length of the Bible, it often took months to hand copy the scriptures. Because priests and monks held a basic monopoly on literacy, the people of Western Europe were required to trust Christian and political tenets ordered by the theocratic politics expressed by the Pope and his cardinals.

The scene slowly transitions from the scriptorium into a German workshop with a large wooden press; two men are working the machine with a clothesline draped with freshly printed paper hanging behind them. An older man stands in front of the machine, richly dressed, using a magnifying glass to look at a printed paper, and surrounded by stacks of books. Dench explains that in 1450, Johannes Gutenberg invented the movable type printing press, allowing for books to be printed more quickly and leading to the ease of sharing information in vast quantities. This innovation sparked the Renaissance. While the scene is somewhat historically accurate, Dench's spiel is not.

Johannes Gutenberg did not invent the movable type printing press. Using a press for printing was introduced sometime during the first century AD by the Romans, who used a screw press. Printing presses allowed for texts to be made with multiple copies, an attempt at replacing the hand-copying of texts, saving human time and effort. Unfortunately, these presses were expensive and took up a lot of physical space. In the 200s AD, artisans in China developed woodblock printing. This required a skilled craftsman to carve a piece of wood in relief; the areas that were to remain white were recessed, whereas the parts that were to transfer ink from the block to paper or cloth would be elevated. The craftsman would then press the block against the paper or cloth. However, if used to create multiple copies of a scroll, many different carved wood blocks would be needed and eventually stored, which required both significant time and physical space. During the mid-1000s, Bi Sheng, a Chinese inventor, developed movable type, carving Chinese characters onto small ceramic and wooden blocks, which would be arranged to create text. These pieces would be inked and a piece of cloth or paper would be laid atop and rubbed to transfer the ink on the type to the scroll. This occurred about four hundred years prior to Gutenberg, making Dench's statement inaccurate.

Gutenberg's true claim to fame was his new version of the moveable type printing press in 1436, combining the concepts of the screw press and Chinese movable type. Metal type would be arranged in the order of the text and inked. The operator of the press would insert a wet piece of parchment, and then screw down the press, which would distribute even pressure across the parchment onto the type. While all Gutenberg did was improve upon existing technology, the development of this system allowed for more efficient printing and therefore a higher prevalence of the printed word, causing literacy rates to skyrocket and people to begin to challenge pre-existing religious and political ideas. While he did print other texts, both political and religious, Gutenberg is best known for his printing of the Holy Bible. Although hundreds of copies were printed by Gutenberg and his assistants, only forty-eight survive today. In fact, they are so rare that in the 1970s one copy of the fifteenth century book sold for $2.2 million; in 2007, a single page sold for over $70,000.

Dench explains that the invention of the printing press led to the Renaissance. This again is not accurate: Gutenberg "invented" the printing press in Germany in the 1430s, while the Renaissance began in earnest in the 1300s in Italy. Focusing on human-centered art-work and literature for art's sake rather than for religious reasons, the Renaissance gave rise to famous artists like Leonardo da Vinci and Michelangelo. This mainly occurred as a result of the trade occurring between Western Europe and the regions surrounding the eastern Mediterranean Sea; merchants often stopped at the Italian peninsula for supplies and trade, causing the cultures of many different regions to be diffused. Individuals with artistic predispositions learned from these different cultures and began to apply the new techniques to their disciplines, whether inventing, painting, or sculpting. The printing press did not cause the Renaissance, but rather led to a quicker spread of it to other parts of the European continent, including northern Europe, ultimately leading to the *Northern* Renaissance during the late 1400s until the 1600s.

A more significant movement that sprung from the invention of Gutenberg's printing press was the Reformation. While smaller move-ments which challenged the political and religious power of the Catholic

Church had begun earlier, in 1517 Martin Luther, a German monk, published his famous Ninety-Five Theses, a text that attacked Pope Leo X, as well as many of the core beliefs and practices of Catholicism. Luther argued that the Pope did not have the power to absolve the sins of Christians, but rather that this power was reserved only for God. Luther also argued against the selling of indulgences—a tax given to the church that reduced the time spent in Purgatory. Arguing that the Bible explains man is saved by God's grace through faith alone, rather than man's good deeds, Luther condemned the church's collection of indulgences as dishonest and criminal. He was later excommunicated by the Pope but eventually was acquitted under the Peace of Augsburg, allowing German kingdoms to choose between Catholicism and Lutheranism in 1555. Gutenberg's printing press was used heavily during this period to disseminate Luther's Ninety-Five Theses and writings against the Pope, as well as German translations of the Holy Bible that Luther wrote during his time in self-imposed exile while hiding from the Catholic Church. Part of Luther's argument against the Papacy and Catholic leadership involved his belief that people should be able to read and interpret the Bible themselves, rather than relying on the literate priest to interpret scriptures for the masses. This resulted in the Bible written in vernacular, or the common language of a region, which ultimately led to a boom in literacy. Thus, Gutenberg's "invention" helped to change major political and religious belief systems that would lead to later movements including the Scientific Revolution and the Enlightenment during the seventeenth and eighteenth centuries, respectively.

While Spaceship Earth does not portray the effects of Gutenberg's printing press on religion, the attraction does show some of the more popular advances of the Italian Renaissance on the right side of the track. The Italian Renaissance manifested itself in new ideas of humanism, or the focus on the achievements of man rather than God's role in the universe. This manifestation was evidenced through many differ-ent artistic disciplines, including literature, painting, inventions, and sculpture. The attraction features five individual scenes surrounding the track to represent the Italian Renaissance. The first scene features two men sitting on a balcony holding books in their hand; one reads from the book, while the other listens. Nearby, in a courtyard, a man and woman play stringed instruments. On the opposite side of the track, three artists work on physical art: one man stirs paint, another paints a still-life of fruit, and a third chisels a statue of a woman. This is quickly followed by a man lying on scaffolding, painting the ceiling of a cathedral. While some of these scenes are simply generalizations of Renaissance art, others are very specific representations of famous pieces.

In the first scene representing the Renaissance, two men sit on a bal-cony overlooking an Italian landscape reading books. One man sits on a stool and is wearing a cloak lined with fur over pants and a shirt, leather boots on his feet. He wears a red hat on his head, which was inspired by Mongolian styles of the fourteenth century, but more popularized in Europe during the fifteenth and sixteenth centuries. This would not be rare or uncommon, as the Chinese, who were ruled by the Mongols during the thirteenth and fourteenth centuries, interacted with Europe during this time through trade and diplomacy. As a result, these influ-ences would have been common in Europe during the Renaissance. The other man in the scene is sitting cross-legged on the ground and is wear-ing a long red tunic with paned sleeves.

The clothing of these individuals help guests realize the wealth they likely possess. Animal furs were hard to come by, as they often came from the European countryside or even the New World. Also, the presence of paned sleeves on the long-haired man sitting on the ground signifies his wealth; known by laymen as "puffy sleeves," the stereotypical clothing feature of people from the Renaissance served no purpose except that of having more cloth to wear. The bigger the sleeves or the longer the dress, the wealthier one was because cloth was expensive; thus, sleeves like those worn by the man wearing the red tunic signifies wealth. Also, the fact that the two are literate and have books in their possession signifies wealth due to the rarity of the printed word during the infancy of Gutenberg's printing press. If the two men can read, it means that their parents could afford to send them to school, meaning they were not needed to help support the family economy.

Nearby, on the same side of the track, two musicians serenade passersby. The man is playing a lute, a short-necked stringed instrument with a gourd-shaped body and strings that are plucked like a guitar. Other than the short neck and the deep body, another main difference between the lute and the modern guitar is that the head of the lute, where the pegs that tighten or loosen the strings are located, is bent at a ninety-degree angle toward the back of the instrument. The woman plays a viol, a short, Renaissance ancestor of the violin.

These individuals are also likely to be wealthy. While music during the Renaissance was initially composed for Catholic masses and Protestant church services, there was also a small minority of wealthy people who would become amateur musicians. It was an expectation in European society during the 1400s and 1500s that the wealthy and those involved in political court life would learn artistic and musical skills as a form of leisure-time activity, mainly as a status symbol indicating that they could spend their time on leisure rather than work. Instruments during this period were also very expensive, as they were created by hand and manufactured by a skilled artisan, rather than the industrial machinery used to manufacture instruments today. Women who learned the skill of music were often very wealthy or from wealthy families, because they were able to take up leisure activities, including music, literature, and art, hiring others to take care of their families. In fact, many wealthy women often hired wet nurses to care for their children so they could participate in leisure activities or court life.

The Renaissance refers to a "rebirth" in interest in the Greek and Roman classical texts, many of which found their way back into Europe after the Europeans, who acquired them from the Arabs after the burning of Alexandria's library, brought them to the scriptoriums to have them translated back into Latin and the vernacular languages. Prior to being exposed to these classical texts, European thought and perceptions was heavily influenced by the Catholic Church, which put forth the ideas that God caused everything and that everything existed to give Him glory. However, after studying Greek and Roman texts, Renaissance thinkers such as Petrarch began to stress the importance of what we now consider "the humanities": rhetoric, literature, history, grammar, and moral philosophy. These new ideas led to influences on not only thought and philosophy, but also had an influence on artwork, as well. Many artists began to create art for art's sake, rather than for God's glory, and sometimes included themes that focused on man as an individual. However, because of the political and social influence of the church in Europe during the fourteenth and fifteenth centuries, many of these pieces combined humanistic influences with Christian themes.

With a focus on art for art's sake, new techniques were used to create more realistic paintings and sculptures. For example, many Renaissance painters began to use linear perspective to portray depth and human bodies more realistically. Whereas many believed that the only one who should be able to create the image of life was God, artists painted such realistic paintings that viewers thought the subjects of paintings to be real people sitting on the other side of the window. In fact, one Renaissance painter, Giotto di Bondone, once painted a fly on a subject of a painting; the insect looked so realistic that viewers were said to have tried swatting the fly off the painting, only to realize that it was added to the artwork as a ruse. Also, many conservative religious leaders of the fifteenth century believed there could be no representation of a physically perfect person because only Christ was perfect. However, the goal of many artists during this period was to portray men and women in physical perfection using exact ratios and mathematics. For example, the perfect rectangle and a perfect spiral were used by Leonardo da Vinci when he painted the Mona Lisa, while Michelangelo used both linear perspective and perfect ratios when he carved his famous statue, the *David*, making the biblical hero into an almost superhuman figure.

The second set of scenes that depict the visual results of the Italian Renaissance are found on the left side of the track, opposite from the musicians and literary figures. Three men work in an artist's workshop, involved in two different types of Renaissance art: painting and sculpture. The first individual that we see has his back to the guests as the time travel vehicles pass. He is standing against a table, using a pestle and bowl to mix pigments for paint. This man is likely an apprentice, and would realistically be a boy, or at the oldest, an adolescent, learning the skill of painting from the master, who is sitting to the apprentice's right. The paint that the apprentice is mixing is a new form of paint for the Renaissance; during the medieval period, which preceded the Renaissance, tempera paints were used, which were the result of pigments mixed with egg yolk. Because of the thickness of the paint, artwork often had dull, heavy colors, which often did not mix to create shading or color tones very well. As a result, around the year 1500, oil-based paint, utilizing the byproduct of olives grown on the Italian peninsula, began to be used. The oily paint, which was much thinner than tempera paint, allowed for easier mixing of colors, creating new color tones and allowing for chiaroscuro, or complex shading which allowed for greater depth and light sourcing in Renaissance artwork. We know that the apprentice is mixing oil-based paints rather than tempera paint due to the bright colors on the swatches hanging on the wall over the table: many different tones of warm and cool colors are seen, rather than single tones of blue, red, or yellow.

Nearby, the master artist sits at an easel, painting a still life of fruit. Still-life paintings by themselves during the Renaissance were rare for multiple reasons. The first was that artists during the Renaissance did not have a steady income; unlike today, many artists did not paint and hope to sell their art to connoisseurs. Rather, wealthy or powerful individuals patronized, or commissioned, artists to create art on their behalf, hoping to be portrayed in a certain way. The second reason that still-life painting during the Renaissance was unlikely was because the main subjects of Renaissance art were Biblical or classical events or individuals, not fruit, as shown on the canvas in the scene. While it was possible that artists would sketch fruit as a form of experimentation, such as da Vinci did, they likely would not have spent time actually painting fruit or other inanimate objects unless they were a part of a larger work, such as da Vinci's *Last Supper*.

To the right of the painter, who likely represents no single individual, but rather the idea of a painter during the Renaissance, is a man standing behind the figure of a woman, carving the piece from white marble. The sculpture is unfinished, but it is obvious that the woman is wearing a cloak and a passive expression on her face. While this artist is not identifiable, nor is the sculpture, he may be harkening back to famous, well-known sculptors such as Michelangelo and Donatello.

While Michelangelo is well known for some of his marble statues, including the *David* and the *Pieta*, one of his best-known works are the paintings in the Sistine Chapel, which is located in the Vatican in Rome, and was built between 1477 and 1480. Pope Julius II commissioned Michelangelo in 1508 to paint the ceiling of the chapel alongside other famous Renaissance artists, including Sandro Botticelli and Raphael. The ceiling features forty-seven individual scenes from the Old

Testament of the Bible, including God's creation of the world, the fall of man through Adam and Eve, and the great flood of Noah, as well as pagan prophetesses, known as Sibyls, likely showing that Jesus Christ died for both Jews and Gentiles. Michelangelo also painted a large fresco on the wall of the Sistine Chapel from 1536–1541 called *The Last Judgment*, depicting the second coming of Christ. Although many consider Michelangelo to be a Renaissance artist, his work in the sixteenth century places him at the end of the Renaissance period; his death in 1564 at the age of eighty-nine occurred forty-five years after the death of da Vinci in 1519, who did most of his work at the height of the Renaissance, when Michelangelo was only twenty-five years old.

In the scene on Spaceship Earth, Michelangelo is shown laying on his back, almost seventy feet above the ground, painting one of the best-known paintings in the Sistine Chapel, *The Creation of Adam*. This famous painting depicts God surrounded by cherubs and wrapped in a swirling, red cloak, reaching out to a naked Adam who is lying on a mountainside. The two are reaching toward each other; God's arm completely outstretched, while Adam makes only minimal effort, perhaps symbolizing man's separation from God. The medium used by Michelangelo when painting the ceiling and walls of the chapel was known as fresco painting. This painting was done by applying damp plaster and then applying the paint to the plaster, which allowed the pigments to absorb into the wall, making the painting a part of the wall, rather than simply sitting on the surface of it. The new plaster would have to be applied each day, and painting was done quickly before it would dry. This form of painting was often done in buildings made of stone, where the paint would chip or peel off over time. The scene of the attraction does show guests the fresco process, as Michelangelo is working on the scene depicting God's creation of Adam, with exposed areas of the stone ceiling not yet covered with plaster in the upper-left and right-hand corners of the piece.

Interestingly, this scene, which takes place above the ride vehicles and to the left, does not depict the creation of the artwork in a historically accurate way. The scene shows Michelangelo lying on his back a few feet from the ceiling. However, in a series of autobiographical sonnets he later wrote, The artist explains that he actually stood up to paint above his head and often got a sore neck from having to look up for long periods of time. According to Italian art historian, Giorgio Vasari, in his text *Lives of the Artists* in 1568, Michelangelo had developed a new form of scaffolding that allowed him to paint seven feet from the ceiling of the great Chapel. Michelangelo lamented the backbreaking work in a sonnet he penned in 1509, explaining that:

> *My stomach's squashed under my chin, my beard's*
> *pointing at heaven, my brain's crushed in a casket,*
> *my breast twists like a harpy's. My brush,*
> *above me all the time, dribbles paint*
> *so my face makes a fine floor for droppings!*
>
> *My haunches are grinding into my guts …*
> *strains to work as a counterweight …*
> *my skin hangs loose below me, my spine's*
> *all knotted from folding over itself.*

Historians looking at Michelangelo's sonnet and the information regarding his scaffolding system explained in Vasari's work quickly realized that the artist stood, painting over his head, often bending backwards over his head to reach the ceiling. This was likely a messy task, as, according to Michelangelo himself, paint was constantly dripping down his brush and off the ceiling into his face, likely making it difficult to see what he was doing. This scene in the time traveling attraction does not depict the messiness of Michelangelo's work, but even this detail would likely be lost on guests, as the amount of time spent in the scene, passing beneath the inaccurately portrayed artist, is minimal.

A TECHNOLOGICAL REVOLUTION

As their time travel vehicles continue their journey in a spiral up and to the right inside the geodesic sphere, guests find themselves three hundred and fifty years in the future, at the end of the American Civil War, during the Second Industrial Revolution. Dench makes a generic statement, explaining that books were the beginning of information sharing, which led to further innovations that allowed knowledge to be spread across long distances and between individuals. While she does not reference any specific events or innovations, a series of scenes shows some of the most important technological advancements during the sixty years surrounding the beginning of the twentieth century.

The first scene on the left side of the tracks features a black man holding a newspaper that is fresh off a large, steam-powered printing press, while a paperboy hawks one of these newspapers on a nearby street corner. The cobblestone street on which the paperboy stands is lined with brick apartment buildings with curtained, lit windows; shadowed figures of men and women stand behind the curtains, talking on turn-of-the-century telephones. The telephone conversations are represented by green glowing telephone lines ending in a telephone operator's exchange, at which sits a number of women who switch lines for callers.

Across the track from the operator's exchange is a cluttered office with a desk; one man sits at the desk, listening to Morse, while another man, standing alongside the desk, writes the message onto a notepad. Guests' attention is drawn back to the left side of the track, where a man stands inside a recording studio, standing in front of a microphone and

emphatically gesturing as he records audio for a radio show, while a second man sits on the other side of the window at a mixing board. Back
across the track is a cinema marquee, beneath which is a ticket booth
occupied by a woman holding a newspaper, while different films and
newsreels play on the movie screen.

Imagineers group this era of technological advancements into one
scene, which can confuse guests into thinking that these innovations
of communication occurred at the same time. However, although the
steam-powered printing press, telegraph, telephone, radio, and film all
occurred within seventy years of each other, the new methods of communication were definitely *not* contemporaneous.

In the first scene of the attraction, a black man stands in a large room
where a steam-powered printing press puts out numerous copies of a
newspaper. The steam-powered printing press, known as the rotary
printing press, was invented by American inventor Richard March Hoe
in 1843 and perfected in 1846–47. Similar to modern newspaper presses,
letters were printed on newsprint on large rollers, and the presses produced millions of copies of multiple individual pages each day. These
presses were powered by steam, allowing for factories to be located in
new industrial, urban areas away from moving water as a power source.
Water heated by burning coal created steam, causing the pressure to
move the machine parts and put the printing mechanisms in motion.

To the keen observer, Imagineers have located this part of the scene
representing the Second Industrial Revolution in a very specific date in
time. While the print on the newspapers is too small to read from the
ride vehicles, the large, bold headline of the newspaper reads "Civil War
Over!" It is likely that this part of the scene represents the days after
the surrender of the Confederate States of America to Union forces at
Appomattox Court House in Virginia on April 9, 1865. However, because
the Civil War was not officially ended until May 9, 1865, this scene prob-

ably takes place on either May 10 or May 11, 1865, as a result of the time it took for news to travel across long distances.

There are also several clues making it likely that the scene takes place in the northern regions of the United States. First, the newspaper says "Civil War Over!" If this scene took place in the south, the newspaper headline may have instead explained the end of the War of Northern Aggression or the War Between the States, as the south saw itself as a confederacy, a separate nation, and believed itself to be seceded from the United States. The south did not believe the war was a civil war, as this type of war only occurs between two groups within a nation, not two separate nations. Second, the economic basis of the northern United States was industry and, as a result, the majority of American industry was located in the north, especially along the Atlantic seaboard. The southern states, on the other hand, focused primarily on agriculture and had fewer steam-powered machines than the north. The third reason this diorama likely takes place in the north is that the machine operator is a black man. If the scene took place in the south, the machine worker would likely not have been black, as these individuals were enslaved as agricultural workers and domestic servants, and not typically working in machine shops.

Near the machine shop stands a small boy on a street corner with his back to the track, calling out the headlines in an attempt to sell papers. These paperboys, known popularly as "newsies," were often homeless children who turned to street life during the height of the immigration boom from Europe and the explosion in the population of cities during the second half of the nineteenth century. Many immigrant families were unable to support their large families and so young men turned to the streets to become pickpockets or peddlers. One of the most common forms of peddling for immigrant youth during the late 1800s was selling newspapers; newsies would purchase papers directly from the newspaper companies and then sell them at a higher price, pocketing the profits to support themselves, their parents, and their younger siblings. The young man selling his paper in the scene yells the signature paperboy phrase, "Extra! Extra! Read all about it!" followed by the headlines regarding the end of the Civil War. During this era of newspapers, printers would often print what was known as extra editions to release breaking news to the public, announcing the headline by yelling the well-known phrase to catch the attention of passersby.

Across the track is an office with a cluttered desk and wall. A man wearing a brown visor sits behind the desk, listening to Morse code being received and translating it audibly for a man standing beside the desk and writing the message on a notepad in his hand. The man is wearing a blazer jacket and a bowler hat on his head. The message being received reads: "MAY—10—1869—OFFICIALS—OF—THE—TWO—RAILROADS—HAVE—GATHERED—AT—PROMONTORY—POINT..."

Samuel Morse developed the electric telegraph in 1837, allowing for textual messages to be transmitted across long distances. Morse and his assistant, Alfred Vail, developed a language specific to the new communications network featuring electric dots and dashes, popularly known as Morse Code. Initially, telegraph lines allowed for communication between large metropolitan centers in the northeast United States. Some major patrons of the telegraph networks included the U.S. stock markets and news services. As American political dominance spread westward after the acquisition of Texas in the 1830s and the discovery of gold in California in 1849, the reach of the telegraph stretched from coast to coast. The telegraph became important in transmitting messages across distances, especially during the 1860s, when Union and Confederate generals reported back to their respective leaders, as well as supplying orders for the movement of troops and supplies. The development of this almost instantaneous communication network was a huge improvement over existing networks, which relied on the physical delivery of messages and could take many days or even weeks to transmit news from one place to another.

After the discovery of gold in 1849 in California, large groups of men rushed west to strike it rich. Virtually overnight, outposts became megacities, as tens of thousands descended on the town, settling there to mine the precious metal. With the economies of the west booming, a better system of transportation between the west and the last major city on the frontier, St. Louis, Missouri, was required. After acquiring land in the southwest after defeating Mexico in the Mexican-American War during the 1830s, the United States began to build a railroad between Council Bluffs, Iowa, and San Francisco Bay in California. The Transcontinental Railroad, which connected the Central Pacific and Union Pacific railroads, was completed on May 10, 1869, when the last railroad spike, which was made of gold, was driven in at Promontory Point, Utah. A message was immediately sent to both the east and west coast via Morse's telegraph, simply stating, "DONE."

While neither individual in the attraction's diorama represents a specific person, guests can at least deduce the roles of the two. The seated individual wears a reddish-brown visor, a striped shirt, and red suspenders. He sits behind a wooden desk, translating the incoming message that is being tapped in Morse code, bringing news of the completion of the Transcontinental Railroad. The standing individual is wearing a brown suit and a bowler cap with a feather in the brim. In his left hand he holds a pad of paper and in his right a pen. Based on his dress, this man is obviously a news reporter, preparing to publish a story about the completion of the railroad in an East Coast newspaper. The office is littered with objects of the period including a gas lighting fixture hanging from the ceiling, a hurricane lantern on a desk, a pendulum clock on the wall, and numerous brass spittoons for chewing tobacco. There is a good possibility that this scene takes place somewhere in the Great Plains or out west, as a pair of cattle horns hang on the right side of the diorama over the door and a mountainous desert can be seen in the twilight through the windows of the room.

Back across the tracks on the left-hand side are three women at a telephone switchboard. On the other side of the switchboard are brick apartments with shaded windows, behind which are people talking on turn-of-the-century telephones. Telephone wires that are illuminated to represent the moving of conversations throughout cities stretch above the women. The women are dressed in Victorian-era clothing of the late nineteenth century, with collared dresses that stretch to their ankles and their long hair pinned behind their heads. Electric lights hang from the switchboard to illuminate their workspace as they quickly answer phone calls and manually plug in wires to connect conversations.

When Alexander Graham Bell's invention was first introduced and perfected in the mid-nineteenth century, individuals could rent two connected telephone devices between which they could only communicate exclusively with one another. After a few years, telephone switchboards were developed, allowing for communication between multiple devices. The Boston Telephone Dispatch, established in 1878, connected those wealthy enough to have telephones to each other. Because it was cheap to do so, the dispatch hired young boys to work the switchboards. However, the young boys were extremely impatient with callers and often played pranks and cursed at the callers and, as a result, were fired. The owners of the dispatch instead decided to hire young women to exchange the calls because of their kind and patient temperaments.

The switchboard in the small diorama on the attraction is known as a divided multiple switchboard, which allowed multiple "cordboards" (as the operators were known) to work together on a single exchange; one team of women worked on the A Board, receiving calls, while a separate team worked on the B Board, connecting the received calls to the corresponding lines. In the mid-twentieth century, telephone exchange operators were phased out in larger cities and replaced by automatic dialing systems and computerized systems in the late 1900s.

The next scene on the left features two individuals: one gentleman sits with his back to the time-traveling guests, wearing a vest and a long-sleeved white shirt, fiddling with a control panel on the desk in front of him. A glass window separates this technician from a man in a suit coat and fedora, seated at a desk and speaking into a microphone, which is labeled with WDI as the radio station (WDI being a subtle nod by Imagineers for Walt Disney Imagineering). The man in the studio explains that:

> Today we have received word that Amelia Earhart and her flight team have landed safe and sound in Wales. Today, June 19th, 1928, will forever be known as the day that she flew across the Atlantic and into the hearts of people around the world. Amelia Earhart has gone where no other woman has gone before! And the memory of her daring deed will assure her a spot in aviation's firmament of stars.

The invention of the radio is attributed to Guglielmo Marconi in 1894, although Marconi simply perfected previous theories and technology developed by other scientists. Marconi's radio was able to transmit and receive electronic messages via radio waves across long distances. Long-distance transmission of news and radio programming began to be developed during the first decade of the twentieth century, becoming more viable for consumers during the 1920s. In fact, it was the sinking of the *Titanic* in 1912 that encouraged amateur radio operators to begin to offer content, including news, to consumer listeners.

While radio broadcasting first occurred in the Netherlands in 1919, American programming started in Pittsburgh, Pennsylvania, in 1920 under the call letters KDKA. Throughout the first half of the twentieth century, radio served as a medium of entertainment for families, bringing multiple generations together on a daily basis to listen to music, the news, and even broadcast radio dramas featuring voice actors, orchestral background music, and sound effects to tell a story. In fact, some of these radio dramas were so realistic that on October 30, 1938, radio actor Orson Welles starred as a news reporter explaining an attack from Martian destroyers from H.G. Wells' novel, *The War of the Worlds*. The broadcast was so realistic, and radio was so respected as a news medium, that many listeners thought it to be a live news broadcast, leading to hysteria throughout the country. This panic from a radio drama may be a result of the tension building during the beginning of the totalitarian movements in Europe prior to the outbreak of World War II.

Whether modern day Americans realize it or not, the radio shows of the early twentieth century still influence our culture today: the term "soap opera" was first used to describe a genre of radio broadcasting. Dramatic radio shows featuring larger-than-life characters, aimed at the consumer housewife, were often sponsored by detergent or soap companies, thus creating the genre of show that many women still find entertaining today.

Radios in the early 1900s also provided Americans with news. This news was sometimes local, but national radio broadcasters brought Americans broader news on a regular basis. During later decades, radio broadcasts were used by presidents to communicate with the American people, such as Franklin Delano Roosevelt's famous speech addressing the Japanese bombing of Pearl Harbor.

During the latter years of the 1920s, Americans had a fascination with flight. After the development of flying machines by the Wright Brothers during the early years of the twentieth century and the perfection of these flying machines leading up to World War I, Americans developed a fascination for airplanes. This frenzy reached its peak during 1927 and 1928 when Charles Lindbergh and Amelia Earhart flew across the Atlantic Ocean, respectively. After Lindbergh's successful crossing in 1927, a woman pilot, Amy Phipps Guest, decided to gain the distinction of the first female aviator to cross the Atlantic Ocean. However, she realized the danger that the rough skies and water could pose in the northern Atlantic region, and instead offered to sponsor the flight of another female pilot, Amelia Earhart.

Earhart, who broke the record for the highest elevation flight for women at 14,000 feet and was the sixteenth woman to be issued a pilot's license by the Federation Aeronautique Internationale, was asked to be the first woman to make the journey by air across the Atlantic Ocean. On June 17, 1928, she crossed the Atlantic Ocean from Newfoundland, Canada, to Wales, in the United Kingdom. However, while many believe she flew across the Atlantic, this is not the case; due to her lack of knowledge of the type of airplane used, she merely served as a passenger (or as she referred to herself, as "baggage") while pilot Wilmer Stultz and copilot Louis Gordon flew the plane. But the mere fact of a woman crossing the Atlantic was revolutionary and Earhart received a hero's welcome in England, and one when she returned to New York. Earhart would go on to make several solo flights, including one across the Atlantic Ocean, as well as multiple attempts to circumnavigate the globe via plane. Unfortunately, it was during Earhart's second attempt to circle the earth that she disappeared, a mystery which has yet to be solved.

On the right side of the track, adjacent to the telegraph diorama, is a small scene representing the advent of the film industry as a method for communication. A woman sits in a ticket booth beneath a theater marquee, holding a newspaper in her hand. The newspaper identifies the location of the movie theater as New York City. Interestingly, though, the title of the newspaper is TDE NEV YDRC OAILY. This may be Disney's attempt to place the attraction into geographical context from a distance (as the letters used appear to say THE NEW YORK DAILY), while avoiding trademark or copyright issues. The bolded headline reads OWENS WINS GOLD. On the back wall to the left of the theater's screen is a sandwich board, which lists the film reels theater patrons would see in the theater:

MOVIE NEWS

1936

Berlin Olympics

NEWSREEL

CARTOON SHORT

Mickey Mouse

In

The Band Concert

MAIN

FEATURE

Fred   Ginger
   and
Astaire   Rogers

In

Follow the Fleet

Because of the three shows listed, we know that the year for the diorama is 1936: *The Band Concert* premiered in 1935, *Follow the Fleet* was released on February 20, 1936, and Jesse Owens won gold medals in the Berlin Olympics in August 1936. As a result, guests can assume that the theater diorama takes place in New York City, sometime in mid-August of 1936.

During the 1930s and 1940s, prior to the era of television, Americans would go to cinemas as an all-day affair. People would pay their nickel or dime to spend an afternoon at the theater, where they would receive their news, see the latest animated shorts, and watch a feature film or two. Between feature films, which could be war films, Westerns, big budget musicals, or the latest Disney film, animated shorts from the Disney or Fleischer studios would expose American youngsters to new cartoon characters that millions of people around the world are still familiar with today. Also, newsreels would run, showing the progress of American and European troops overseas, the culture of the time, or even focusing on America's heroes, such as Lindbergh, Earhart, or American Olympic runner Jesse Owens.

In 1936, the Olympic games were held in Berlin, Germany, which was run by elected chancellor Adolf Hitler. The summer games featured popular sports including diving, boxing, wrestling, and track-and-field events. Germany had the highest medal count with 89 medals, an accomplishment that may have increased German nationalism during a time of unprecedented German expansion throughout Europe during the years leading up to World War II. The United States came in second to Germany, with 56 medals, and third place went to Italy with 22 medals. Ironically, during a time when Germany promoted Aryan racial superiority, Jesse Owens, an black sprinter and long jumper, won four gold medals. Hitler was obviously bothered by this, and refused to shake Owens' hand for his winning of the gold medals, after setting a precedent himself of shaking hands with every previous gold medal winner.

THE ERA OF THE COMPUTER

The time travel vehicles continue forward and guests find themselves in an American living room of the late 1960s. Dench explains that at this point, humanity can communicate from anywhere on earth, and by 1969, from somewhere *other* than Earth. The room features a bright orange wall on two sides of the room and a red brick wall on the third. Brown shag carpet stretches across the floor, upon which sit a modern bookshelf lined with books and knick-knacks. A floor-to-ceiling lamp stands in the corner, and a small, square Philco television set sits on a television stand. A plastic globe terrarium stands to the right of the bookshelf. A family sits in front of the television watching scenes from the 1969 moon landing; the mother and father sit on an over-stuffed couch, while the son lays on his stomach and the daughter sits in a chair. Imagineers jokingly placed a copy of the board game *Mouse Trap* behind the couch, a sly reference to Mickey Mouse. The audio from Neil Armstrong's message to Mission Control and all of humanity can be heard over the vehicles' speakers: "That's one small step for a man, one giant leap for mankind."

In the 1950s and 1960s, America was locked in an arms and space race with its superpower rival, the Soviet Union. The arms race began around 1945, at the end of World War II, when the United States dropped the atomic bomb on the two Japanese cities of Hiroshima and Nagasaki. The Soviet Union, a communist nation, had a polar opposite political and economic philosophy from the United States, which adhered to capitalism. Because of these differing beliefs, the Soviet Union decided to challenge American economic dominance in Europe and military dominance in the world. Shortly after the atom bomb was dropped in the Pacific, the Soviet Union began to develop their own atomic weapon, which set off an intense arms race between the two global superpowers. In an effort to send an atomic weapon to the United States without it being shot down, the Soviet Union began to develop rocket propulsion for its atomic bombs. The culmination of this technology reached a peak for the Russians in 1957, when they launched the space satellite *Sputnik* into orbit around the Earth.

Terrified that the Soviets were spying on the United States, the American government charged the U.S. Air Force, and later NASA, with developing a space program to send men into space ahead of their Soviet rivals. While the United States lost this distinction when the Soviets launched cosmonaut Yuri Gagarin into orbit in 1961, they were able to be the first nation to put a man on the moon. As a result, President John F. Kennedy began his domestic program, the New Frontier, where he advocated for government funding for science and mathematics education, the creation of the National Aeronautics and Space Administration (NASA), and other programs that benefited the people of the United States. In 1969, American astronauts Neil Armstrong and Buzz Aldrin landed on the moon as part of the Apollo 11 mission. The success of this mission led to further space missions and a continued interest in space.

The living room scene of the attraction is fairly representative of the décor of the late 1960s. Because of America's close association with Western Europe in the fight against Communism in the postwar world, influences from India, Spain, and the Mediterranean region brought bold orange, yellow, and green colors to walls and furniture. This is noticeable in the colors of the scene on Spaceship Earth, especially in the colors of the walls and clothing of the family. Clothing styles were fairly modest in adults during the late 1960s and 1970s, as well as in children. While the teenaged and college generations of the 1960s and 1970s were not as modest due to the Countercultural movements, those in their thirties and forties were generally more modest, having been raised pre-World War II by parents who were born during the Victorian Era, which held high morality standards for individuals.

Guests continue past the living room scene and to the exterior of the family's home, where a nighttime cityscape can be seen in the distance, above which hovers the moon that Armstrong and Aldrin had just landed on. It appears that the city in the distance may be New York City, as two matching buildings, which appear to be the World Trade Center towers, reach into the sky. This would not be unlikely, as construction on the twin towers began in 1968 and 1969.

Dench goes on to explain that in order for America to send a man to the moon, a new language was required, which was spoken by computers. She goes on to explain that these computers were initially very large and very expensive. The vehicles move into a new room, which surrounds the track on both sides. The room is brightly lit, and features numerous computer consoles lining the walls complete with flashing red lights and spinning magnetic tape reels. On the left side of the track, a male technician wearing a white lab coat stands over a wire metal cart full of magnetic tape, comparing them to the notes on a folder in his hand. Behind him is a desk with a molded plastic chair. On the opposite side of the track are more desks and shelves of magnetic tape line the walls. A black woman wearing a large Afro and a plaid skirt with yellow tights and knee-high boots reads notes off a clipboard. Large mirrors above the flashing computer terminals create the illusion that the room is actually larger than it is.

The computer terminals in the scene appear to be the IBM System/360 mainframe computer. Developed during the years between 1965 and 1978, these computers were created specifically to run applications for governments and corporations. They were often large computers, and in order for the system to function at its highest capacity, many of the consoles were networked together. The IBM System/360 mainframe featured nine-track magnetic tape on which information could be stored and accessed by direct-access storage drives, which were visible and accessible from the outside of the machine. Running on binary code, these computers operated using a language based on a combination of zeroes and ones. Initially developed by German philosopher Gottfried Wilhelm Leibniz in 1679, binary code was created to simplify and standardize language for different cultures. While the use of binary was never adopted the way Leibniz had hoped, those that developed the computer found his language to be helpful in programming. Interestingly, the computers featured in the scene are similar to those originally used to operate audio-animatronics at Disneyland in 1969 and Walt Disney World in 1971.

The time travel vehicles exit the large room of computer banks to find themselves in the front yard of a house. The vehicles pass a mailbox and a parked car on the left and enter the open garage of the home with lights on in front to guide the way. Guests immediately notice a bearded young man sitting in a corner on the left, hunched over a boxy computer with a small screen. Dench explains that entrepreneurial young people across America utilized their pioneering spirit to shrink the room-sized computers down to fit in the consumer household, attributing these personal computers to "a garage in California." She brings the scene into the modern day by explaining that the personal computer has allowed for people around the world to interact with each other, positioning us for a "new Renaissance." The details in the garage abound; the room is extremely cluttered, showing that the young man is more concerned with the creation of his computer than with keeping house. A bucket full of suds and a garden hose sit abandoned on the ground. A greasy pizza box sits open atop a red cooler. Newspaper clippings and band posters are pinned to the drywall above the computer workstation.

While Disney has never addressed who the individual in the garage is, evidence points that the young man may be Apple co-founder Steve Wozniak. The young man wears a purple shirt with vertical stripes and has long, shaggy hair and an unshaven face. A photograph taken of the two co-founders of Apple, Steve Jobs and Steve Wozniak, in the 1970s shows Wozniak as a hefty, shaggy haired, unshaven young man wearing a shirt with vertical stripes, which looks similar to the animatronic in the scene. In the same photograph, Jobs is tall and lanky, the antithesis of the animatronic figure on the ride. Also, the poster hanging above the computer workstation is that of band Fleetwood Mac, a favorite band of Wozniak's, which he actually asked to headline a music festival that he financed in the early 1980s. The figure is tinkering with the computer, which looks similar to the Apple-1, released in 1976.

As the time travel vehicles exit through the back wall of the garage, they enter a tunnel featuring green numbers flashing past on the walls and ceiling, akin to a scene from the film *The Matrix*. Dench explains that after "30,000 years," humanity has created "a truly global community poised to shape the future of this, our Spaceship Earth." The vehicles exit the tunnel at the top of the geodesic show building, with a 360-degree view of a star field with the Earth in the distance. The vehicles rotate backwards, and Dench invites guests to create their own future through a questionnaire taken on a touch screen on the seats in front of them. Using the photograph taken of guests at the beginning of the ride, computers incorporate guests' faces onto a cartoon video of a possible future created by Siemens, the attraction's sponsor.

Whether guests realize it or not, they have experienced something of a history lesson during their fifteen-minute adventure traveling through time. To add to the historical immersion is a fantastic score by composer Bruce Broughton, who has composed music for films such as *Silverado* and *Harry and the Hendersons*, Disney scores including those for *The Rescuers* and *Honey, I Blew Up the Kid*, and even scores for Disney attractions like Ellen's Energy Adventure and the now defunct Timekeeper. Broughton's musical score changes from scene to scene, with musical stylings that evoke the time period, leading to a more immersive experience. For example, as the time travel vehicles pass beneath Michelangelo painting *The Creation of Adam* on the ceiling of the Sistine Chapel, Broughton's score features the sound of a hallelujah chorus echoing through the chapel.

As the vehicles pass into the scene depicting the Second Industrial Revolution at the turn of the twentieth century, the music transitions to a ragtime style, and as guests pass into the scene featuring the large banks of computers, the music sounds much more synthesized and digital, as though the archaic computer banks themselves are producing the music.

While some guests, especially younger ones, may find this attraction boring, it features a large amount of historical context that is actually quite fascinating. Even a cursory understanding of the events depicted in the ride can provide a much more enjoyable experience "aboard this ... *our Spaceship Earth*."

CHAPTER TWELVE

SUNSET RANCH MARKET

t was a cool Saturday evening in late November. My parents, my brother, my wife, and I had traveled to Walt Disney World for a long Thanksgiving weekend. While my parents and brother went off to ride Rock 'n' Roller Coaster, my wife and I wandered through the Once Upon a Time shop on Sunset Boulevard. We decided to sit on a park bench in the alley outside the store and wait until my brother texted us.

The air was crisp as I put my arm around my wife, and she pulled herself close to me. I closed my eyes, listening to the World War II–era Big Band swing music of the 1940s. I opened my eyes to really *see* the illusion created by the Imagineers: my sweetheart and I were sitting on a bench in the golden days of Hollywood during the late 1930s and early 1940s, surrounded by numerous theaters showing the hit films of the era. I glanced at my wife, and for a moment pictured her dressed with her hair pulled up beneath a veiled hat, rosy red lipstick, a pleated sky blue colored dress, and heels, while I sat alongside her in my gray suit and a fedora on my head. Unfortunately, the illusion was broken as my stomach rumbled so violently that my wife turned to look at me. I quickly realized that we were not in the 1940s, but rather in 2014, and rather than wearing the clothing of the era, we were bundled up in hoodies and blue jeans.

"Hungry?" she asked. I nodded back at her, smiling. Looking at my phone, I realized it was quite a bit past eight o'clock, and we had been so busy with the different shows, attractions, and the Osborne Family Spectacle of Dancing Lights that we still had not taken the chance to eat dinner. Suddenly, my phone buzzed, signifying that my parents and brother were headed back up Sunset Boulevard toward us. With the park nearing close, we all decided to grab a quick bite at the nearest counter-service restaurant, Sunset Ranch Market, a series of small kiosks, similar to an outdoor food court, each serving different food.

As we finished our meal and made our way through the dispersing crowds of Sunset Boulevard, I explored the Sunset Ranch Market to realize that not only was the eating area reminiscent of a real California farmer's market, but was also set in the early days of American involvement in World War II, during the early 1940s, an era when those who experienced the events of the decade defined for generations forward what it truly meant to be American: a hard-working, brave, and unified nation working together for the benefit of the citizens of their country and the world as a whole.

THE HOLLYWOOD FARMERS AND SUNSET RANCH MARKETS: THE ORIGINALS, THE IDEAS

Sunset Ranch Market has a real-life counterpart, as does many of the buildings and facades in Disney's Hollywood Studios: the Hollywood Farmer's Market, located at the corner of West Third Street and Fairfax Street in Los Angeles. Originally owned by A.F. Gilmore in the 1880s, the land at the corner of Third and Fairfax was a 256-acre dairy farm. When Gilmore decided to increase his head of cattle, he realized he needed more resources for the herd and began to drill for water. He was quite surprised when, instead of water, he struck oil. He sold off the cows to establish a lucrative oil-drilling business, the Gilmore Oil Company, even establishing his own line of gas stations. When the city of Los Angeles began to limit the amount of oil derricks allowed on Gilmore's property, Gilmore lost money, eventually leading to the land sitting vacant. In the early 1930s, two entrepreneurs, Roger Dahlhjelm and Fred Beck approached Gilmore's son, Earl Bell Gilmore, with the idea for creating a "village" on the vacant land to allow farmers to sell their crops.

When the village opened in July 1934, local farmers gathered on the street corner to sell produce out of the backs of their trucks. As tourists began to discover the numerous types of produce being sold, even during the winter months, the popularity and profitability of the informal market skyrocketed, leading to a more permanent series of structures from which the farmers could sell their harvest. The early days of the Hollywood Farmer's Market in the 1930s occurred during the height of the Great Depression, when unemployment was 21%, and the majority of farming occurred in California; because of an extreme drought in the states of the Great Plains, known as the Dust Bowl, the crops on thousands of farms there were destroyed, leading to large amounts of foreclosures on farms. As a result, and as famously depicted by John Steinbeck in his books *Of Mice and Men* and *The Grapes of Wrath*, upwards of two hundred thousand Americans flocked to California for opportunities as farm hands. This huge increase in farm workers led to an explosion in the amount of produce in California, ultimately leading to the establishment of the Hollywood Farmer's Market.

The buildings of the Sunset Ranch Market at Hollywood Studios evoke the feeling of that market by featuring some common structures. According to an aerial photograph of the Hollywood Farmer's Market taken in 1938, it featured a series of interconnected buildings separated by open-air courtyards. The buildings had a green shingled roofs and white siding. A metal windmill was erected above one of the buildings, allowing visitors to see where the farmers' market was from a distance, and passersby to know what was located in the shopping district. In 1948, a clock tower was added atop one of the buildings, reading "Farmers Market" and the phrase, "An idea," a nod to its original founders of the early 1930s.

While the counter-service food court at Disney's Hollywood Studios looks similar to the Hollywood Farmer's Market, Imagineers modified the architecture and style of their reproductions to create more of a "golden age of Hollywood" feeling. This still allowed the area to be more functional for a counter-service eatery rather than a place for local farmers to sell their produce. For example, many of the buildings have cream-colored siding with green trim, as well as red clay tile roofing, rather than the green shingling of the Hollywood Farmer's Market. Both the real and imaginary markets feature a metal windmill, but in Hollywood Studios it is situated behind the buildings, rather than perched atop them, and surrounded by overgrown foliage. Also, the Disney version of the market features a tower similar to the clock tower in its California counterpart, but without a clock. This is interesting, as the period the Sunset Ranch Market is portrayed takes place during the early years of America's involvement in World War II, sometime after 1942. However, the clock tower of the Hollywood Farmers Market was built in 1948, three years after World War II ended. As a result, because of the period that is being portrayed in the eatery, the clock tower should not be present, and so it is historically inaccurate. The food court's buildings are set more apart from each other, rather than interconnected like those at the farmers market, and located on Sunset Boulevard, which in reality is two miles away from the corner of Fairfax Avenue and Third Street.

There are a total of six restaurants that make up the Sunset Ranch Market. As guests walk from Hollywood Boulevard, the first dining location in the market is on the left, a small white building topped with a weathervane of a turkey, the Toluca Legs Turkey Company, serving

(Disney) World-famous turkey legs. The next choice for food is set on the curb of the street, Anaheim Produce, offering fruits, drinks, and other healthy choices. It is the most representative of the Hollywood Farmer's Market, which may be why it is seen by passers-by, rather than the other counter-service locations, evoking the idea of a farmer's market, rather than a food court. Behind Anaheim Produce is Rosie's All-American Café, serving American-style foods, like hamburgers and chicken nuggets. Adjacent to Rosie's is Catalina Eddie's, with its salads, pizza, and sandwiches. Closer to the end of Sunset Boulevard is Fairfax Fare, evoking the actual location of the Hollywood Farmer's Market, serving ribs, chicken, and turkey legs, while its neighbor, Hollywood Scoops, cools guests down from the summer heat with ice cream, sundaes, and other desserts.

Interestingly, though, it is not just the food that paints the picture of an all-American experience, but the decoration on the exterior, interior, and general vicinity of the different counter-service locations that make up the Sunset Ranch Market. The theming of the different eateries, as well as the area in general, suggests that the market is set during the days of America's involvement in World War II, sometime between 1941 and 1945.

AMERICA ON A GLOBAL STAGE

America did not immediately participate in the Second World War when it broke out in 1939. The war started for numerous reasons, but a common origin dates back to the Great War, also known as World War I, which took place between 1914 and 1918. At the end of that war, Germany was assigned 100% of the blame for the war, known as the War Guilt Clause. While the war was not completely Germany's fault, the proud nation lost the war, and as a result, was forced to concede to the victorious nations of Britain, France, America, and Italy. Some of Germany's land was stripped away and given to France and Belgium, and many of its overseas colonies were given to Japan, an ally to Britain, France, and the United States in the war. Germany was also required to pay war reparations to the four victors for all damages they incurred from the war. However, Germany was more physically and economically destroyed than Britain or France, and so it was difficult for it to pay back the 269 billion gold German marks (about $4 billion in modern-day American money) of reparations. In an effort to do so, the nation's provisional government, the Weimar Republic, started printing more marks. This led to massive hyperinflation in Germany. For example, prior to the inflation of the mark at the end of World War I in 1918, a loaf of bread cost less than one mark. By the end of 1923, that same loaf of bread cost 200 billion marks. German money became so worthless that many citizens took their life savings and bundled them into blocks for their kids to play with or even burned the paper currency to help keep them warm during frigid winters.

In the meantime, victorious nations that had allied with Britain, France, and the United States began to feel shorted out of the spoils of war. Italy did not get much land from Germany's partition, or much of the reparation payments. Japan, on the other hand, began to have a period of expansion; because they had received Germany's old colonies, they became land hungry and started encroaching upon the colonies of other European nations. When Japan decided to challenge French rule in Indochina (present day Vietnam) in 1941, the United States decided to aid its European ally by cutting Japan off from the oil it provided to the island nation. This angered the Japanese, who had seen themselves as an emerging world military power during the late nineteenth and early twentieth centuries.

Because of these frustrations, new leaders began to emerge in the nations of Germany, Italy, and Japan. In Japan, a military dictatorship formed, led by military general Hideki Tojo. In Italy, a newspaper

columnist named Benito Mussolini rose to power to create the Fascist
Party, inspiring loyalty to himself, his party, and the nation of Italy. In
1933, Adolf Hitler was elected as the chancellor, or prime minister, of
Germany. Both Mussolini and Hitler made promises to their citizens that
they would help their respective nations get out of the depression caused
by the effects of the Great War.

Adolf Hitler began putting his plan into execution by breaking the
Treaty of Versailles, the peace treaty ending World War I, and beginning territorial expansion to reclaim the land stripped from Germany
at the end of the war in 1918. Hitler first set his eyes on the Rhineland
in 1936, which had been given to France. In 1938, Hitler moved to
Austria, a nation that held many ethnic Germans and had been an ally
with Germany during the First World War. In an act known as *anschluss*,
or "connection," the two nations united, adding a sizeable chunk to
Germany, as famously depicted in the Rodgers and Hammerstein musical and film, *The Sound of Music*.

In late 1938 and 1939, Hitler ordered German forces into
Czechoslovakia, taking back the Sudetenland. Throughout Germany's
expansion, the leaders of Europe adopted the policy of appeasement, giving in to Hitler's demands for expansion in an effort to prevent another
global conflict. Many of the European nations had suffered massive
damage and financial losses in the Great War only twenty years earlier
and still had not fully recovered enough to fight another war. The world
was also plunged deep into a worldwide depression which had begun in
earnest in 1929 after the crash of the American stock market and had
quickly spread to affect most of the European nations shortly thereaf-
ter. America had officially adopted the policies of isolationism and non-
interventionism; in fact, President Franklin Delano Roosevelt even went
as far as calling the events in Europe a disease. He gave a speech calling
on America and her allied nations in Europe to quarantine themselves,

explaining that "War is a contagion, whether it be declared or unde-
clared... We are adopting such measures as will minimize our risk of
involvement..." As a result, Europe was on its own. In an attempt to end
Hitler's land grabbing, the leaders of other European nations pressed
him to end his expansion. They specifically begged him to spare Poland,
which had been reinstated as a nation after land had been stripped from
Germany at the end of World War I. In 1938, as part of the Munich Pact,
Hitler conceded that after his acquisition of the Sudetenland, he would
no longer acquire more land. However, in 1939, Hitler reneged on his
promise, invading Poland, which led to a declaration of war against
Germany by France and Britain.

Unfortunately for their economic allies, the United States decided to
maintain their policy of neutrality and non-intervention, while still selling weapons to both sides. The United States issued two policies during
the early years of World War II. The Lend-Lease Act allowed America to
provide its allies food, oil, and wartime materials throughout the war
without officially supporting them as an ally. However, in an effort to
prove to Germany that they weren't choosing a side, the United States also
issued the Cash and Carry policy, which allowed *any* nation, whether it be
Britain or her enemies, to purchase weapons and war supplies from the
United States as long as that nation paid in cash and carried the supplies
back to its nation on its own ships. This prevented the United States from
being proven as the supplier, as the materials were bought in cash rather
than credit, as well as preventing American ships from being attacked as
they transported war goods, an event that had caused American involvement in World War I. However, one nation that America refused to provide oil to was Japan, mainly as a result of its continuing expansionism
throughout the Pacific Ocean and east Asia, which threatened our own
island colonies there. This further angered the Japanese, who began
plotting against America, leading to the surprise attack on the naval base

at Pearl Harbor on the Hawaiian island of Oahu on December 7, 1941, thrusting America into involvement in the Second World War until its conclusion in 1945.

Because thousands of young men were drafted or enlisted in the war effort, America had an unprecedented period of extreme patriotism. Propaganda, a form of advertising meant to convince and persuade, was used heavily to encourage Americans to participate in specific activities that would help the United States and its allies to win the war. Rationing of specific items was encouraged, as well as the purchase of war bonds and the collection of scrap metal. Everyone in the country was affected in some way by the war, including women who were required to step up and work in factories that produced wartime materials in the absence of the men who were off fighting.

AMERICAN DINING: PATRIOTISM AT ITS BEST

Evidence of this wartime patriotism can be seen throughout the Sunset Ranch Market, with each of the dining locations highlighting specific aspects of wartime American pride. Anaheim Produce has very few references to World War II, possibly because it represents the type of stall that would have been found in the Hollywood Farmer's Market. However, to the keen eye, a few references are still evident. For example, the crate sitting behind an open crate full of soda has a rectangular sticker plastered across it, explaining that the contents of the wooden crate contain "flame Tokay" grapes from Herbert Buck's ranches in Acampo, California. The sticker, though, compares the flame Tokay grape to "flying colors," which references the American flag. The sticker even has a small image of the flag waving across a field of stars, inspiring patriotism. A nearby truck with its bed full of crates of fruits and vegetables sits behind the fruit stand. The truck is a 1930 Model A Huckster, yet its license plate states the year is 1941. The nearby Toluca Legs Turkey Company seems to have no reference to the war overseas, but rather serves as a nod to Toluca Lake, an affluent residential area in Los Angeles, as well as an actual lake that spilled into nearby Burbank, where the Walt Disney Studios opened in 1940, fitting into the timeline of the food court.

Behind Anaheim Produce is possibly the best themed kiosk of the Sunset Ranch Market in terms of the World War II storyline, Rosie's All-American Café. The sign for Rosie's looks to be made of corrugated metal and features a woman in blue denim overalls, wearing work gloves and a welding mask while holding a red hot skillet in one hand and a welding tool in the other. Three pins are attached to the top of her overalls, with one being orange with a large black letter V. The outside of the kiosk features different signs with phrases like "Keep 'Em Flying," "Stay True to the Red, White, and Blue," and "V for Victory."

While it may not be in the official backstory for the food court, the different details in and around Rosie's suggest that it may actually be a food stand catering specifically to Los Angeles' female workforce during World War II. First, the namesake of Rosie's All-American Café does not reference a real person, but rather a fictional character, Rosie the Riveter, which was a generic term referring to all American women working in the industrial workforce during World War II. Almost nineteen million women participated in wartime industries during the war, filling in for the men who had gone off to fight in Europe and the Pacific. One of the most common jobs for women was riveting, which consisted of punching holes through two sheets of metal and then attaching them with a rivet, or a permanent fastener that joined the sheets together. This was used mainly in the construction of airplanes and ships manufactured for war.

First created for American war propaganda to represent all female industrial workers in 1942, Rosie is best known in the propaganda cartoon where she wears a red bandana and blue coveralls, flexing her bare arm above the phrase, "We can do it!" Women were not only called upon to work in existing industry to replace the men off fighting the war, but also in new industries created to support the war effort. This often occurred through the conversion of peacetime industries, such as the conversion of Ford auto plants in Detroit to the manufacturing of tanks, airplanes, and battleships. Los Angeles had numerous wartime industries, including the steel and aircraft industries.

Another way we can tell that this restaurant may have catered to the working women in Los Angeles' wartime industries is due to the signage on the outside of the kiosk. "Keep 'Em Flying" is actually a reference to a piece of propaganda encouraging women to enlist as stenographers for the U.S. military, bearing the catchphrase, "Victory Waits on Your Fingers—Keep 'Em Flying, Miss U.S.A." The propaganda on the outside of the kiosk that would be seen by women waiting in line for their food during their lunch breaks alludes to the demographic that this counter would serve in the story of the Sunset Ranch Market.

Although the restaurant is just a food kiosk and guests don't enter the building of Rosie's to order or receive their food, the interior also features different signs, photographs, and World War II artifacts. As guests step up to the windows to order at Rosie's, they find glass cases on either side full of photographs, notes, postcards, and even drawings of World War II airplanes and servicemen. Because this restaurant would have served the women of nearby factories, it may be that these photographs and postcards are encouragement to the women that their sweethearts will be returning from the war soon. On the walls on either side of the kitchen, as well as the overhang above the kitchen, airplane propellers, propaganda posters, and even cartoon posters featuring Disney characters including Mickey Mouse, Goofy, and Donald Duck line the walls.

These wartime images of the beloved Disney characters are extremely interesting. One example features Donald Duck wearing aviation goggles and riding on a red airplane while saluting in front of a crescent moon.

Another features Goofy wearing a sailor's outfit in front of a blue anchor, while a third image features a brown cartoon bunny riding a red bomb. These images are war insignia, which were often painted for different units and squadrons, specifically in the navy. Originally unsanctioned, these images began to feature the popular Disney characters as some animators were either drafted or enlisted into military service. Some Disney animators that did not participate in the war effort voluntarily drew these insignia to boost the morale of the servicemen. While off fighting in Europe or the Pacific, the insignia, often painted on ships or airplanes, helped the soldiers to remember who and what they were fighting for back home, embodying American innocence and values. Ultimately, the Walt Disney Studios would illustrate approximately 1,200 insignia for different divisions of the military branches, doing their part to support the war effort in a small but meaningful way.

To the left of Rosie's All-American Café is the condiment bar, which seems an unlikely place for theming around World War II. However, between the mirrored sides of the condiments queue are a series of glass display cases containing small figurines participating in wartime activities. There are also patches, postcards, photographs, and toys depicting various World War II roles and events, further enriching the story of America at war in Europe and the Pacific, as well as how the war affected and was experienced by people left at home.

The next restaurant to the right of Rosie's is Catalina Eddie's. This nautical-themed restaurant fits into the general theming of coastal California. Decked out with nets, spears, and harpoons, it sells pizza, salads, and subs. The name of the restaurant is actually a play on words; Catalina Eddie does not refer to a person, but rather to the Catalina eddy, also known as the coastal eddy, which develops when there is an area of dead air due to wind coming off the Pacific that is blocked by the mountains, creating a vortex and leading to clouds and fog along the California coastline. Imagineers further fleshed out the theming of the nautical areas of the Pacific by adding a series of nautical flags strung above the restaurant's queue, spelling "C-A-T-E-D-D-I-E-S," or "Cat Eddies," a reference to the restaurant's name. Inside, on the wall above the kitchen, there are photographs, figurines, and small boats tying the restaurant to the life of coastal California.

To the right of Catalina Eddie's is a garden with interesting theming that requires some background information to truly understand and appreciate. While at first glance it looks like a normal garden, a large white sign with red and blue letters explains to guests that it is "Rosie's Victory Garden" and will bring "Victory with Vegetables." The garden, surrounded by a white picket fence, sits adjacent to Catalina Eddie's, with gardening implements hanging from pegs on the exterior wall of the restaurant. A scarecrow stands off to one side, but rather than being the typical straw-stuffed burlap scarecrow, this figure is instead decked out like a World War II fighter pilot, complete with khaki uniform, a life vest, aviation goggles, flight helmet, and oxygen mask. Wooden garden decorations of Uncle Sam, whose arms spin in the wind, and a battleship that moves back and forth on painted blue wooden waves when the breeze blows, are also present. The garden grows different types of plants, including peppers and the occasional pineapple. The name of the garden, Rosie's Victory Garden, obviously ties it to Rosie's All-American Café, but the name is not the only similarity between the garden and the restaurant.

The sign in the garden explains that it is a Victory Garden. During World War I, the United States government created different wartime commissions and committees whose tasks assisted the American military and soldiers win the war on the home front. Some of these commissions dealt with things like propaganda or even monitoring media to ensure that only positive messages about the war were being released to the American public. The United States Food Administration, headed by future president Herbert Hoover, was tasked with limiting the amount and types of foods consumed by Americans at home so soldiers had more to eat on the frontlines. This occurred through the designation of days as "Meatless Tuesdays" and "Wheatless Wednesdays," encouraging citizens to fast from meat or wheat on specific days so there was more to send the troops overseas. Partnering with the United States Food Administration, Charles Lathrop Pack created the U.S. National War Garden Commission, which encouraged Americans to create their own Victory Gardens in which they could grow their own produce, causing them to purchase less so more could be sent from the fields of farmers directly to support the war effort in Europe. With Americans consuming less vegetables produced on farms, this also helped to conserve gasoline and rubber, as farmers did not have to transport as many goods to market or grocery stores. Propaganda was created to encourage Americans to invest in a Victory Garden, including catchphrases like "Food will Win the War," which helped the average civilian to see that they played a large role in whether the Allies won or lost the war against Germany and the other nations of the Central Powers.

During World War II, rationing continued in a similar fashion as it did during the First World War, albeit more regulated. Rather than simply encouraging Americans to not consume meat or wheat on certain days, the U.S. government instead created a program to limit what citizens could purchase and consume. This was done through the distribution of ration books. These booklets were full of small stamps, which would be handed out to the seller of a product with the money in order for the patron to purchase the item. For example, if someone wanted to purchase sugar, they had to have a sugar stamp out of the ration book; once their sugar stamps were depleted, they were unable to purchase more sugar until the following week when they received a new ration book. Other stamps had specific dates on which consumers could purchase specific items, which would be listed in local newspapers. For example, if a housewife of the 1940s wanted to purchase meat or cheese, they would have to use the red-colored stamps in their book and might only have from July 24 through July 31 to purchase them; otherwise, they would have to wait until the following month. In order to offset the rationing books, Americans were once again encouraged to plant their own Victory Gardens. These became especially important in large cities, and were often planted on the flat roofs of buildings, in alleyways, vacant lots, and in the grassy areas along streets, eventually leading to the establishment of community gardens in large cities like Los Angeles, San Francisco, and New York City in later decades.

In front of Rosie's Victory Garden is another quick-service kiosk, Fairfax Fare, which references the location of the Hollywood Farmer's Market, on the corner of Third and Fairfax. The sign for the restaurant features a farm with rolling hills, complete with a farm house, perhaps referencing the original intention of the land that the Hollywood Farmer's Market would eventually sit on, A.F. Gilmore's dairy farm. Next door is Hollywood Scoops Ice Cream, complete with a sign highlighting the word "scoops" in neon. The sign features a small chef holding an ice cream scoop in one hand while saluting with the other, a popular gesture in wartime America.

While the theming of the Sunset Ranch Market through its architecture and World War II signage and props helps to immerse guests in the story of Los Angeles during the early 1940s, it may be the background music that helps to complete the illusion of the time and place. The musical background loop features period music including Big Band orchestral songs from Benny Goodman and the Glenn Miller Orchestra, jazz music from Duke Ellington, and the harmonic swing music of The Andrews Sisters, who sang popular wartime songs like "The Boogie-Woogie Bugle Boy" and "Don't Sit Under the Apple Tree."

AFTERWORD

*W*hat does it mean to be an "American"?

As a history teacher, I would tell you that there is no singular definition of American. In fact, the only real Americans are those who have descended from the Native American population who lived here prior to when European explorers first set foot on the soil of the New World. And even they aren't truly American, as they themselves migrated to the American continents thousands of years ago from Eurasia via a land bridge that spanned the Bering Strait between modern day Alaska and northeast Russia.

Now, this may not be the answer that hard-core "Mericans" like to hear, those who fly the Stars and Stripes from their front porches or tout how America is the "best nation on earth." Please don't get me wrong: I am very grateful for the freedoms and blessings that come with living in this nation. However, even those who have red, white, and blue running through their veins may have a difficult time defining what it means to be American, simply because there is no real definition.

Our great nation is a conglomeration of many different cultures that have meshed over time to create our current state, economy, and culture. Many Americans may argue that hotdogs are a true American dish, but they may not realize that hotdogs are a form of sausage that likely emerged when German immigrants settled in the United States. Baseball is considered an all-American pastime, but few realize that it actually

originated in Great Britain and has many similarities to the British game
of cricket. Country music may be the "most American" genre of music,
but its roots have ties to blues, which has some influence from the
African population of slaves who lived in the American South.

So, really, what does it mean to be American?

Whether he intended it or not, Walt Disney summed up what it meant
to be American when he described his company: "Around here, however, we don't look backwards for very long. We keep moving forward,
opening up new doors and doing new things ... " *This* is what it means to
be American.

Being American means that we turn our back on the past and we *keep
moving forward*.

* * *

I wasn't sure how I was going to conclude this book until I realized the
connection between this volume's introduction and the idea of American
progress as exemplified by Walt Disney.

You see, on September 1, 2015, while teaching my second period
world history class, I experienced the most terrifying moment of my life
as I had a cerebral hemorrhage. While I was lucky that the blood vessel
did not burst somewhere else in my brain, the injury left me in the hospital for four days and has left me with a visual disability causing my eyes
to not work in concert, leading to severe double vision, a symptom that
has since healed. As a result, I was unable to walk long distances, drive,
or even read or easily write due to my inability to accurately interact with
the world around me or focus on individual objects. Because I interact
with my world primarily through my sight, this has been a huge blow
to me.

As I lay at home recuperating, however, my wife, children, and family
continued to encourage me that I *would* make a comeback, that my vision

would return, and that I would be able to lead a normal life again soon. At that point, I made a decision that aligns with the American Dream and the mantra of Walt Disney and his company: *keep moving forward*. To not look back at the past. Yesterday may have been a day when I was hampered by my visual disability, but today will be a day that I will push the limits and do something despite my lingering symptoms that I didn't think I could do yesterday. And so, after eight days of laying around, telling myself that I couldn't write because my vision limited my ability to focus on my computer screen, I picked up my computer and decided to write this conclusion.

Because, ultimately, while this conclusion does have a personal connection, it also sums up the entire book.

Americans were not content with their sultry form of entertainment, so they cleaned it up and made it more wholesome for the entire family to enjoy. Walt and his Imagineers were not content with their limiting technology, so they created new forms of storytelling. Sports enthusiasts weren't content with the old style of athletics, so they created a new game. People weren't interested in what the body could do, so they pushed the limits and exposed the strange and uncommon. Technology and communication had limited the human experience, so mankind has improved and adapted. Americans were tired of letting international bullies throw their weight around, so they united and did something about it.

They kept moving forward.

SELECTED BIBLIOGRAPHY

In the process of researching this book, I have drawn upon numerous sources, both print and electronic. I generally started with a search engine, and then focused on more in-depth sources. Some sources were found through the use of academic databases, while others were found using footnotes on encyclopedic websites and online articles. I also relied heavily on images found on search engines, using key words to describe objects and comparing them to items and locations found on Disney attractions.

A selection of sources are listed below for readers who are more interested in some of the topics discussed:

A.F. Gilmore, Co.. "Farmers Market: History." http://www.farmersmarketla.com/index.php?/history/.

All-Things-Aviation.com. "The History of Barnstorming." https://all-things-aviation.com/flying/history-of-barnstorming/.

Auerbach, Jeffrey A. *The Great Exhibition of 1851: A Nation on Display*. New Haven, CT: Yale University Press, 1999.

Barrier, Michael. "The Mysterious Dumbo Roll-A-Book." http://www.michaelbarrier.com/Essays/DumboRollABook/DumboRollABook.html.

Bio. "PT Barnum Biography." http://www.biography.com/people/pt-barnum-9199751.

Brendon, Piers. *The Decline and Fall of the British Empire, 1781–1997*. N.p.: Vintage, 2010.

Briner, Lisa. "Walt Disney Goes to War." U.S. Army. http://www.army.mil/article/19340/Walt_Disney_Goes_to_War/.

Burns, Geoffrey C., and Ken Burns. *Baseball: An Illustrated History*. New York City: Alfred A. Knopf, 1994.

Cantrell, M A. "The True Stories Behind 11 Famous Sideshow Performers." Mental Floss. http://mentalfloss.com/article/50078/true-stories-behind-11-famous-sideshow-performers.

Conrad, Joseph. *Heart of Darkness*. London: Harper Collins, 1902.

Daly, John. "Disney Insignia from World War II." USNI News. http://news.usni.org/2013/07/31/disney-insignia-from-world-war-ii.

Davis, John R. "The Great Exhibition." *British Heritage* 22, no. 4 (June 2001): 15–19.

Di Lodovico Buonarroti Simoni, Michelangelo. "When the Author Was Painting the Vault of the Sistine Chapel." 1509.

Diner, Stephen J. *A Very Different Age: Americans of the Progressive Era*. N.p.: Hill and Wang, 1998.

Ernst, Dorothy J. "Daniel Wells, Jr.: Wisconsin Commissioner to the Crystal Palace Exhibition of 1851." *The Wisconsin Magazine of History* 42, no. 4 (1959): 243–56. JSTOR.

Eyewitness to History. "P.T. Barnum Discovers Tom Thumb." http://www.eyewitnesstohistory.com/tomthumbbarnum.htm.

Fenton, Edward. "The Palace Made of Windows." *The Metropolitan Museum of Art Bulletin* 10, no. 4 (December 1951): 113–22. JSTOR.

Francaviglia, Richard. "Walt Disney's Frontierland as an Allegorical Map of the American West." *The Western Historical Quarterly* 30, no. 2 (1999): 155–82.

Gabler, Neal. *Walt Disney: The Triumph of the American Imagination*. New York: Vintage Books, 2006.

Groner, Alex. In *The American Heritage History of American Business and Industry*, edited by Alvin M. Josephy Jr., New York: American Heritage Publishing Co. Inc., 1972.

Hadsel, Christine. Curtains without Borders. http://www.curtainswithoutborders.org/.

Hillsborough Historical Society. "Painted Theater Curtains." http://hillsboroughhistory.org/Painted_Theater_Curtains.html.

JuggleNow.com. "History of the Circus." http://www.jugglenow.com/history-of-the-circus.html.

Korkis, Jim. "World War I Walt." The Walt Disney Family Museum. http://www.waltdisney.org/blog/world-war-one-walt.

Monstrous.com. "History of Sideshows." http://freaks.monstrous.com/history_of_sideshows.htm.

Passport to Dreams Old and New. "The Music of Country Bear Jamboree Part One and Two." http://passport2dreams.blogspot.com/2013/05/the-music-of-country-bear-jamboree-part.html.

PBS. "History of the Circus." http://www.pbs.org/opb/circus/in-the-ring/history-circus/.

Polk, William R. *The Birth of America: From Before Columbus to the Revolution*. New York: Harper Collins, 2006.

Ringling Bros. and Barnum & Bailey. "Bailey and the Ringlings." http://www.ringling.com/ContentPage.aspx?id=45833§ion=45825.

Ringling Bros. and Barnum & Bailey. "P.T. Barnum." http://www.ringling.com/ContentPage.aspx?id=45831§ion=45825.

Roosevelt, Franklin D. "Quarantine Speech" (Chicago, IL, October 5, 1937), Miller Center, University of Virginia. http://millercenter.org/president/speeches/speech-3310.

Sampson, Wade. "The Original Story of Dumbo." Jim Hill Media. http://jimhillmedia.com/alumni1/b/wade_sampson/archive/2004/12/27/the-original-story-of-dumbo.aspx.

Schoenefeldt, Henrik. "The Crystal Palace, Environmentally Considered." ARQ 12, no. 3/4 (2008): 283–93.The Lost Museum Archive. "Barnum's American Museum." http://lostmuseum.cuny.edu/archive/barnums-american-museum.

Smith, Nicole. "Blueprint: The Crystal Palace." *Engineering & Technology* (January 2012): 112–13.

The Museum of Hoaxes. "The FeeJee Mermaid." http://hoaxes.org/archive/permalink/the_feejee_mermaid/.

Today I Found Out. "From 1860–1916 the Uniform Regulations for the British Army Required Every Soldier to Have a Moustache." http://www.todayifoundout.com/index.php/2012/08/from-1860-1916-the-uniform-regulations-for-the-british-army-required-every-soldier-to-have-a-moustache/.

University of North Carolina at Chapel Hill. "Goodbye, Girlie, and Remember Me: An Illustrated Song." http://www.docsouth.unc.edu/gtts/learn/IllustratedSong.html.

Vasari, Giorgio. *The Lives of the Artists*. 1568.

Westchester County Historical Society. "James A. Bailey." http://westchesterhistory.com/index.php/exhibits/people?display=bailey.

Wood, Sharon E. *The Freedom of the Streets: Work, Citizenship, and Sexuality in a Gilded Age City*. Chapel Hill, NC: University of North Carolina Press, 2005.

ACKNOWLEDGMENTS

First and foremost, I thank God for the opportunity to achieve my dream of becoming an author. He instilled in me a love for writing from a young age. He also blessed my family with the ability to travel on a regular basis, often to Walt Disney World. I am grateful for the spirit of curiosity He has given to me, and I look forward to the adventures He has in store for my wife and I in the future.

The first person that I would like to thank is my wife, Andrea. She puts up with my constant begging to go back to Walt Disney World, even though we visit approximately every two years; she often acts interested for my sake as I randomly begin conversing with her about my favorite ride, show, restaurant, resort, or even new tidbits of news coming from the Disney community. However, more importantly, I want to thank her for her constant support as I have written this book; I never believed that my dream of becoming an author would be realized, and she never gave up on my dream, encouraging me every step of the way.

I would also like to thank my parents, brother, and in-laws for all the support that they have provided to me as I wrote the book. Their belief in the fulfillment of my dream of becoming a published author has been inspiring and has kept me pushing toward its fulfillment.

I also appreciate my father, Stan, and my wife, Andrea, because they helped read the first version of this book, vetting it in terms of historical continuity and basic understanding of the connections between Disney's Magic Kingdom and historical context.

ABOUT THE AUTHOR

Andrew Kiste teaches high school history in Greensboro, North Carolina, and has loved both Disney World and writing for as long as he can remember. He was raised in Grand Rapids, Michigan, and made many family trips to Walt Disney World over the years. Always interested in American and world history, he found himself gravitating to the rides and attractions that centered around historical topics, such as the Hall of Presidents, Pirates of the Caribbean, Walt Disney's Carousel of Progress, Spaceship Earth, and The American Adventure.

After a lengthy trip to Walt Disney World while still in high school, Andrew began doing research online about the park and frequenting fan blogs, forums, and websites. Some time later, he published his first historical article about a Disney attraction. From there has not looked back.